Praise For *My View From the Back of the Bus*

"Merritt Long's tale belongs to all of us. This is not just personal memoir. This is a history of a country. It gripped me from the first word to the last. Engrossing. Poignant. And ultimately triumphant. When you wonder how people triumphed over adverse circumstances, look no further than Merritt Long's story. This book will educate, but it will also inspire. I hope everyone who is lucky enough to get their hands on a copy will read it."

— Dolen Perkins-Valdez, author of *Balm* and
The New York Times bestseller *Wench*

"*My View from the Back of the Bus* is an inspiring and eloquent chronicle of a courageous journey through discrimination and inequality to the pinnacle of power and influence in Washington State government. Merritt successfully navigated through biases, political adversity, and outright hostility to break barriers for successive generations of people of color. Mesmerizing and powerfully written, *My View* was hard to put down!"

— Gary Locke, former Washington State Governor, former
U.S. Secretary of Commerce, and former U.S. Ambassador to China

"There is no higher calling than public service. Merritt's journey from humble beginnings in the deep South during segregation and overt racism to leadership in Washington State government inspires us to do more, to do better. I am honored to recommend this book!"

— Chris Gregoire, former Washington State Governor,
and former Washington State Attorney General

"*My View from the Back of the Bus* tells one of the most significant stories of the last half century: how many African Americans successfully rose into the professional middle class (and beyond), overcoming many obstacles and challenges. It is a must read!"

— Congressman Denny Heck, Washington State 10th Congressional
District, author of *Challenges and Opportunities* (education),
The Enemy You Know (fiction), and *Lucky Bounce* (biographical)

"Long's book captures icons from the mid-20th century—Martin Luther King, Jr., Muhammed Ali, Rosa Parks, Julian Bond—who not only shaped American history but a young man from Alabama. His education at HBCU (Historically Black Colleges and Universities) Morehouse College set the rock-solid foundation for the rest of his life."

— Michael Lomax, Morehouse College classmate, President/CEO of the
United Negro College Fund, and former President of Dillard University

"Merritt, my Morehouse College classmate, Omega Psi Phi brother and good friend, has captured so vividly the powerful influences and motivations in his life which have propelled his outstanding and successful career. Chief among these influences were his days spent at Morehouse College during the turbulent 1960's, where he was imbued with the spirit and mystique of the "Morehouse Man," and made to believe the words of our late Morehouse College President Benjamin E. Mays, who implored us: 'Whatever you do, strive to do it so well that no man living and no man dead and no man yet to be born could do it any better.' Merritt's life work clearly met Dr. Mays' challenge, and his book shall serve as an inspiration to us all."

— Thomas Sampson, Morehouse College classmate, Managing
Partner of Thomas Kennedy Sampson & Tompkins LLP,
the oldest minority-owned law firm in Georgia

Hi AJ₃   1-6-21

MY VIEW
FROM THE
BACK OF
THE BUS

Hope fully, you will Enjoy This Book + Enjoy your Trip BACK in Time to The Pesent and see Through my eyes my view as my Life Unfolds befoe your very eyes. Some Time in An Unbelievable way.

An Inspirational Memoir by

MERRITT D. LONG

The EVENTS, EXPESiences, CiRCUMSTances Provide a Keen Insight into The Enviroment of RaCism and Discrimination.
Enjoy my view
MERR. D

Library of Congress Control Number: 2020923274

Paperback Edition ISBN: 978-1-7358711-0-3
Ebook ISBN: 978-1-7358711-1-0

Front and back cover photos by Nate Naismith
Author page photo by Cortney Kelley Photography
All photographs appear courtesy of the author and his family.
Photo restoration and retouching by Nate Naismith

Publisher: Merritt D. Long
120 State Avenue NE #1422
Olympia, WA 98501

Printed in the United States of America
By Gorham Printing, Centralia, WA

For my parents, Katie and Mack Long.
I am who I am today
because of their love and guidance.

For Marsha Tadano Long,
my best friend, girlfriend, and wife.
Always by my side, behind me,
and in front of me, when needed.

CONTENTS

Prologue... ix

Preface x

PART I. THE EARLY YEARS ON GLADSTONE ALLEY 1946-1951

1   Gladstone Alley, Just the Basics 1

2   Sweet Moment With Dad...................................... 5

3   Mom's a Cool Customer...................................... 7

4   My First Christmas Memory.................................. 10

5   Mom Cuts Me Loose 12

6   First Grade Trauma 14

7   The Back of the Bus 17

8   Survival Skills from Mom.................................... 20

9   Mean Strangers 23

PART II: MOVIN' ON UP TO EXETER AVENUE 1951-1960

10 Moving to Exeter and Grandma.............................. 27

11 Going North.. 32

12 Living in a Cocoon.. 34

13 Yankee Stadium, Bessemer Style.............................. 39

14 Aunt Bessie Teaches Me a Lesson 44

15 My Daredevil Brother 48

16 Bought Sense 52

17 The Many Sides of Mack Long/Will Long..................... 59

18 Lifelong Friends... 74

19 Paying a Price for Getting What You Want 84

20 Good Things Come to Those Who Wait 90

PART III: HIGH SCHOOL YEARS 1960-1964

21 Marilee's Flower Shop 95
22 My Mother's Smile 111
23 Guess Who Came After Dinner 113
24 A Teacher Makes a Difference 117
25 Rude Awakening 127
26 Business in the Black Community 129
27 A Field Trip to Remember 132
28 Clark College Homecoming Weekend 136

PART IV: MY COLLEGE YEARS 1964-1968

29 Morehouse College 151
30 Muhammad Ali 162
31 Graduation 170
32 Jail Time 173
33 Back-Breaking Work 178
34 Choice Words from Pop 181
35 Unlikely Teacher 183

PART V: MY PROFESSIONAL LIFE 1968-2006

36 Seattle and Corrections 189
37 Washington National Guard 198
38 Commission for Vocational Education 204
39 Two Role Models 211
40 Thank You, Governors 216
41 Learning Seed Foundation 233

Part VI: Mistaken Identity

42 Who Am I?. 243

Part VII: My Family

43 My Wife Marsha Tadano Long 255
44 Our Daughter Merisa 260
45 Our Family Grows 267

Final Thoughts. 272
Acknowledgments. 274
About the Author 277

I'm the One

I'M THE ONE you called nigger with relish and glee.

I'm the one you forced to use the "Colored" restroom in the land of the free and the home of the brave.

I'm the one who was so special that I had my own "Colored" water fountain.

I'm the one who sat in the back of the bus even when there were vacant seats available...but those seats, which were so close, were so far away, and were off limits to me and anyone who looked like me.

I'm the one you looked at with disdain and disgust for simply asking you why the White person, who just entered the store and came to the front of the line for service, automatically received immediate service, and the visible Black people in the store became invisible.

I'm the one you and two of your buddies pulled guns on when ten of us were swimming and playing in a lake in the woods that nobody owned, forcing us to leave in a hurry. We had no swimming pool—the city-owned swimming pools were for Whites, and Whites only—although we paid our fair share of local taxes.

I'm the one who occasionally watched you with much curiosity as you baked in the Alabama sun, trying, ironically, to look more like me and my beautiful God-given tan. Then, in five minutes, fifty minutes, or five days, with your skin almost as dark as mine, you labeled me or someone who looked like me a lazy, Black-ass nigger.

I'm the one who mowed your lawn to make some money, and you paid me as little as possible, because you could.

I'm the one who would duck and dive to avoid being hit by bottles of urine filled by you and your homeboys as you hurriedly drove through our neighborhood, hurling these bottles as if it was some kind of a game of how many niggers you could piss on in one evening.

I'm the one who was invisible, who didn't count. You thought I would never amount to anything.

I'm Merritt Douglas Long.

PREFACE

FROM ZERO TO sixty in a matter of seconds. After it happens, the burst of temper, anger, and outrage surprises even me some of the time. Why? My livid response is usually disproportionate to the slight or perceived insult. When did this first begin? Can I pinpoint the moment, the person, or the situation that started this seemingly never-ending conveyor belt feeling of slights and insults.

Maybe it's totally beyond my control. Is this historical baggage, just an inevitability born of the brutal captive, torture, rape, humiliation, shackling, castration, and other inhumane treatment of my African ancestors? Is it part of my DNA that, over time from living and working in this racist world, causes me to snap?

The eventual crescendo of emotions may begin with an activity as simple as checking into a downtown hotel. I arrive with a reservation confirmation in hand. After a quick scan of the hotel guest list by a front desk clerk, he looks up, face expressionless, and says almost like a recording, "We don't have a reservation for you and our hotel is completely booked. There's a convention in town for the next couple of days and rooms are difficult to come by."

Apparently, my previously issued hotel confirmation possesses no meaning. The hotel clerk makes no effort to explain why I have a confirmation receipt and no room. The idea of him checking with some other local hotel is beyond his thinking.

Earlier, if he had said something such as, "I'm sorry. I'm not sure how this happened, but I'm going to try to figure this out and get you and your wife a room tonight," that might have been easier to accept. Instead, it was more like, "Tough luck, you're on your own, fella. Next in line, please."

Now my gasket is about to blow. My wife, Marsha, starts to gently rub my arm, because she has been with me on several occasions where I have gone from zero to sixty in a matter of seconds. Her attention is aimed at calming me down, because she knows I've reached the tipping point. The "other me," the beast, is about to emerge. The beast is always present, sometimes closer to the surface than others. His proximity to the surface, and eventual emergence, is usually triggered by a perceived slight, lack of respect, being talked down to, or being dismissed without a fair hearing.

I'm usually mild mannered and easy to get along with, but I can quickly experience a metamorphosis. This isn't a good thing. Once the change occurs, someone is going to pay.

What happens is that I think someone has offended and disrespected me. Now it's my turn to let them know how it feels. I'm also thinking we didn't have to be here, but they started this and I'm going to finish it.

Growing up in Bessemer, Alabama, attending college in Atlanta, Georgia, working for the state of Washington, and traveling across the country and abroad, I've had experiences and encounters that place a negative premium on being a Black man. Sometimes, I see it coming or I feel a racial current just by how some folks talk or convey their body language. It's reflected in uneasy laughter, in trying too hard to be Mr. Regular, or being the White neighbor who hardly speaks to me in my own neighborhood. But when that neighbor is in a primarily Black setting or event, where there are more people of color than White, he's my best friend. He's rather pathetic because he wants everyone within the sound of his voice to know that the two of you are neighbors and good buddies, at least for the evening. But the next day, reality returns and my White neighbor barely knows or acknowledges me.

Over years of moving in and out of life's White scenes and having been serenaded by many different musical arrangements that layer one upon the other, I thought climbing up the hill from the bottom would finally end. It never does, really. This is fortunate because the battle-tested beginning, middle, and end of this drama provides me with the armor to endure and withstand the next incoming missile. Trust me, they keep coming. It becomes the manner in which you handle them that's key to one's sanity and success.

Let me begin by sharing with you stories and reflections (including growing up in the segregated South) I think helped shape and fashion who I am today. These experiences during different decades, cities, and states often had the same theme: how the color of my skin dominated and governed others' perceptions of me.

PART I

THE EARLY YEARS ON GLADSTONE ALLEY
1946-1951

1   GLADSTONE ALLEY, JUST THE BASICS

I GREW UP in Bessemer, Alabama, a town of about 25,000, located 18 miles southwest of Birmingham. My parents, Katie and Mack Long, my older brother Ken, and I lived in a shotgun house on Gladstone Alley.

My definition of a shotgun house is: if you stood at the front door of this house and pointed the shotgun directly in front of you and pulled the trigger, the buckshot would travel from the living room, through the bedroom, and exit the kitchen without hitting anything. Although, depending on where the outhouse was located, you might hit it.

Gladstone Alley, where we and other Black families lived, was on a dirt road. When it rained, especially a heavy downpour, the dirt road became a mud road. I remember my mom putting down newspaper to get the dirt and mud off our feet so the wooden floors wouldn't get dirty.

Right across the street where the White section of town began, the streets were paved and the alleys, too. This was the norm in Bessemer, not the exception.

Less than a block away from where we lived were large homes with upstairs and downstairs, and some with white columns that seemed to reach the sky. Some homes had white picket fences, while others had iron gates with statues of men in blackface holding up the address of the residence. Lawns appeared manicured and the flower gardens were meticulously kept, usually by a Black gardener.

To my surprise, there was one home on Gladstone Alley that didn't fit the shotgun model of our home. It had a front porch, living room, bedroom, kitchen, and small back porch. This stately home, with a wrap-around front porch, gated and fenced yard, and green grass even in the summer, was owned by the Koyton family. Mr. Koyton, a Black man, worked for the post office, which during those times in Bessemer, amounted to something of a miracle. This family was extremely well-regarded in the community, and the family was active in the First Baptist Church in South Bessemer.

My family lived for several years in our three-room house. It was always clean and comfortable. Considering how some of our neighbors lived with limited food and an absent or unemployed father, our situation was good. In fact, I didn't think of it as being bad or good, but simply the way it was.

Getting up at night and going to the kitchen took bravery. On a number of occasions, when the lights were turned on, I witnessed the roaches having their nightly party. The roaches liked to hang out in the dark. They would hurry and scurry over your feet on their way to a crevice or a hidey-hole. Eventually, I stopped going to the kitchen at night. I accepted the fact that it belonged to the roaches after dark.

There was no bathroom in our home on Gladstone Alley; we had an outhouse. Regardless of your need, a white bucket about two feet deep accommodated us at night. We called it the slop jar. Sitting on this bucket required good balance. I hated taking the slop jar and its contents to deposit in the outhouse.

No bathroom meant we didn't have a bathtub or a shower. My brother and I received our baths in a round tin tub with water that had been heated—sometimes more than needed, sometimes less than needed—on the kitchen stove. Our bath usually took place on Saturday night, and our father performed this task with brutal efficiency. Having worked in the coal mines, ore mines, and other jobs requiring strength and exposure to the elements, his hands reminded me of sandpaper, even though he used a washcloth. I always wondered why he was so rough with my brother and me.

My mother cooked using a stove made of iron heated by coal most of the time, but sometimes by wood. She had to regulate the heat by moving the coal around to certain sections of the stove, a real balancing act. Sometimes, the coal would be damp and wet and difficult to start, or the ventilation wouldn't quite work, and our small three-room house would momentarily be consumed by smoke. My mother would fan the immediate area by using whatever was close by. It wasn't a big deal for her. Before long, the smoke would be gone, and dinner or breakfast ready.

On Gladstone Alley, we had an icebox to prevent meats and other perishable items from going bad. Getting ice was an ongoing chore because it eventually melted.

· · ·

The icehouse was located on what was called Brickyard Hill, a 15-minute walk from our home. This grayish wood structure was old, with darker gray wooden planks encasing it.

When the doors were open, the frigid air slowly moved toward you in a fine, bone-chilling mist. The Black workers were dressed in at least three layers of clothing, thick gloves, hats that covered their ears, and steel-toed boots.

When I peeked inside, I saw huge chunks of ice stacked one upon another. I watched in amazement as large blocks of ice were slowly rolled out for customers like my father. The big porch was taller than my father, who was about six feet tall. My father, without skipping a beat, laid out a large, light brown gunny sack on the deck, and the workers opened the sack and rolled the block of ice inside. When this was completed, my father turned around with his back facing the porch and, in one smooth motion, slung the block of ice over his right shoulder and started the walk home without saying a word. He likely paid for the ice in advance.

I watched him with pride and awe, because of his ability to carry such a heavy load. He didn't stop, rest, or slow down as he steadily made his way home from the top of the Brickyard Hill. Although the ice truck also delivered to our home, my father periodically decided to make this laborious trip to the icehouse. Not once, not ever, did I hear him complain. Accustomed to carrying a heavy load, he did so amazingly well. Whether during the long dog days of summer or the frigid winter months, he didn't complain, although he did have a blank expression on his face. I often wondered what he thought about, but I never found the nerve to ask.

One time though, during one of our walks home from the icehouse, my father stated that he didn't want my brother and me working like him. He wanted us to go to college where we would be in a position to use our heads and not our hands to earn a living.

2 SWEET MOMENT WITH DAD

ONE UNIQUE AND cherished memory I have from Gladstone Alley as a very young child involves my father. Mack Long was a gruff, self-made man. His education extended through the fifth grade, which meant he could barely read and write aside from signing his name. My father, throughout his entire life, never spoke of his parents. Apparently, he never really knew them. It's still a mystery to me and other family members how he was raised, who raised him, and what his life was like.

As a child, teen, and young adult, the primary emotions I saw my father show involved anger, displeasure, remoteness, and physical and verbal abuse toward my mother, my brother, and me. He saw his role as the primary financial provider and disciplinarian. Fortunately, on one count and unfortunately on the other, he excelled well beyond expectations on both. These facts are why I share this lasting memory.

It was an extremely muggy summer day when my father was lying on this stomach on the living room floor with the front door open. The open screen door allowed for a gentle warm breeze to circulate as the cooling fan buzzed and turned slowly, bringing some relief to my hot and exhausted father as he rested with eyes closed. But he wasn't asleep.

As he laid on the floor, I picked up his comb and hairbrush and sat on his back, gently combing and brushing his hair. He didn't move or say a word. It soon started to rain. Before too long, we experienced a major rainstorm, complete with white flashes of lightning. This was followed by a momentary silence and then the ear-shattering boom of thunder. Still my father didn't move or, more importantly, didn't ask me to leave him alone. This, of course, meant I was doing a good job, and he liked having me comb his hair.

My father's hair was like a matinee idol's—jet black, straight, but with a few waves in the front speckled with strands that were white like snow. Combing his hair was easy, and it would go in any direction I wanted. My big move was to try to part his hair in the middle of his head. After multiple attempts, I finally gave up. When I made the part, his hair would immediately go back to its original position.

This moment in time with my father was just that—a singular moment. When it was over, it was over. It wasn't until I graduated from college and started working that my father and I developed a relationship in which we could talk and joke.

3 MOM'S A COOL CUSTOMER

ONE OF THE traits my mom passed along to me was that whenever she blew her stack—fortunately not very often—she was done. After she expressed her displeasure at whatever level of anger, she never revisited the issue or situation again.

I was amazed at how she would "light you up" like a Christmas tree, and that wasn't during the season to be jolly. Her message was clear and direct, with no need to read between the lines. In my case, if she thought I was only thinking about myself and not considering the feelings of others and how my actions affected them, she would quickly and not in hushed tones tell me about it in no uncertain terms.

The end of the blowup usually occurred when she would actually exhale and transition to a totally different topic, such as, "What do you want for dinner, little man?" I knew then the Mom I adored was back, and I was in her good graces once again.

Seldom, if ever, did I see my mom rattled. She was almost always a cool customer. I first experienced the icy coolness in her veins when I was very young. This memorable moment occurred one day when my mother was barbequing while at the same time holding me in her arms.

Several days before, I'd observed my father transforming a tin tub that he and my mother previously used for hand washing clothes. After years of wear, tear, and rub-a-dub-tub, it was almost worn out. The bottom of the tub was thin with small cracks around its edges. Although falling apart, the tin tub's bottom was strong enough to hold charcoal coals. My father used a screwdriver to make small holes along the sides of the tub for, I later learned, ventilation.

The crowning jewel to top off the barbecue grill was the mesh wire that my father had cut from the chicken coop fencing that enclosed the six chickens or so and one rooster in our backyard.

As my mom slowly started putting the ribs on the grill with her right hand, while holding me with her left arm, I noticed that her weight shifted as she leaned down. This shift caused me to feel as though I was on the upward end of a teeter-totter. The tub that had been used to wash clothes was not deep and was close to the ground. This distance caused her to reach down quite a ways while at the same time angling me skyward. As the last rib was placed on the grill and my mother came back to an upright position, I returned to earth still safe and sound in her arms.

Next to the barbecue grill was a small table where my mom had placed:

- A pan with barbecue sauce.

- A Coca-Cola bottle filled with water. The bottle cap was punctured with holes and was used to put out any flames that flared up.

- A long silver fork.

- A stick with white fabric securely wrapped around the top for swabbing the barbecue sauce on the ribs.

Suddenly out of nowhere a thunderstorm broke out, instantly covering the once blue sky scattered with white clouds. The raindrops felt like small marbles as they splattered one by one on my head. The raindrops that fell around us landed with such force, the dust started to puff up around us. The place where my mom was attempting to barbeque was between our house and our neighbor's house, the Koytons.

As the rain continued to come down with no end in sight, Mom paused for a moment, quickly turned around, and went into our house, still holding me. She found a black umbrella in the front room and went back outside to continue barbequing. My mother held me in the crook of her left arm and the umbrella in her left hand to keep the rain away. The barbeque sauce brush was in her right hand.

While leaning down to put some barbecue sauce on the ribs, the umbrella slipped forward and caught fire. No panic, fear, or hysteria on my mom's part. She quickly dropped the umbrella, grabbed the water-filled Coke bottle, and doused the flames. She continued to barbecue with me still in her arms as though nothing, nothing at all, had happened.

Later that evening as our family enjoyed the fruits of her labor, she never mentioned anything about the rain and the umbrella catching fire. I believe to her it wasn't a big deal. She was someone who was seldom, if ever, unnerved; always focused and determined. Our mother was a "no-excuses" person, and she would do anything for her family.

4 MY FIRST CHRISTMAS MEMORY

When I was about four years old, I remember one special Christmas Eve. This night before Christmas was almost as exciting as Christmas itself. Mama had tucked me in bed, gently moving the covers from my waist to under my chin to protect me from the evening chill.

She looked so happy and peaceful, which in turn made me happy and peaceful. That night I was completely wrapped up by her love and attention. My mother was totally focused on me and just me. It was a magical moment.

Ten minutes or so later, she returned to my bed, which I shared with her and my father, and told me that if I didn't go to sleep, Christmas wouldn't come. I felt I might delay Santa Claus and Christmas by not being able to go to sleep. My primary concern: Santa Claus wouldn't be bringing me presents.

The front room of our shotgun house was like a movie set. The Christmas tree was a real pine tree with aromatic smells scenting the entire house. The multi-colored Christmas lights and other adornments flashed off and on like stars twinkling in the sky. Also, the wood burning fireplace glowed with an occasional popping sound of the wood. The fireplace wasn't for looks, it was an important way of keeping our family warm during the winter months.

Finally, after tossing and turning for what seemed like an eternity, I eventually fell asleep and Christmas arrived in all its glory. After that almost sleepless night, we all enjoyed a memorable, fun-filled Christmas Day.

5　MOM CUTS ME LOOSE

KINDERGARTEN IS THE first time I remember spending much time away from home. I attended kindergarten for one year, and I started when I was almost five years old. It was a fun time, more social and play time than schoolwork, which suited me just fine. There was always lunch, and, of course, nap time where, although everyone had their heads on their desk, practically no one slept. We just looked at each other while playfully sticking out our tongues. But I liked recess the best, when we would all run around laughing for no apparent reason. I guess we were just a class of Happy Jacks.

Almost every day my mom would walk with me from our home on Gladstone Alley to kindergarten, which was about ten minutes away. This was a very special time for me, because I had my mother all to myself. She held my left hand in her right hand, and we would just take our time getting there. No hurry, no worry, just the two of us. Sometimes, out of nowhere, she would suddenly swing our arms up toward the sky. For me, it became a game of when she was going to do it. Sometimes, the thought of this happening drove me nuts, but in a fun way. I felt so safe, happy, and content during this time, because other than weekends, tomorrow would be another joyous day with my mom.

However, there was one major obstacle that I faced every day and that was walking across a narrow bridge about eight feet long and three feet wide. About five feet below this bridge was an ever-flowing, bubbling brook. For a kid like me who was terrified of heights, even crossing the bridge while holding my mom's hand proved to be a frightening experience. For the first three months or so of kindergarten, my mom dutifully held my hand to ease my fear and ensure my safe passage to the other side.

Once we crossed the bridge, she released my hand and allowed me to walk the short distance from the end of the bridge to the front door of our kindergarten class, which was just a few feet away. As I walked the remaining short distance by myself, I felt her watching every single step I took until I entered the front door.

But one day, I had a huge surprise. My mother decided it was time for me to cross the bridge by myself. No early warning telling me, "Tomorrow or the next day I won't be holding your hand," or better yet, "You'll walk across the bridge all by yourself."

I felt betrayed and scared to death. I thought she would hold my hand forever and continue to lead me safely across this bridge, and any other bridges I might need help crossing.

After endless whining and complaining about this possible death walk across the plank, I summoned the nerve and courage to slowly, and I mean slowly, walk across the bridge by myself. As I looked back at my mother, she'd already started walking home. I glimpsed a big smile on her face as she turned around, realizing this bridge had been crossed. She kept walking, not even staying long enough to make sure I entered the kindergarten door. This was the last time she walked me to kindergarten. After that, I was on my own.

6 FIRST GRADE TRAUMA

It was September 12, 1952, in Bessemer, Alabama, and I was five years old. I was ready to begin my first day of school in the first grade. My emotions ranged from excitement to fear; excitement about meeting new friends and fear of being away from home all day without my mother. I had attended kindergarten, but that was mostly play and lasted only half of the day.

The school I attended, called Hard Elementary School, was the epitome of the absurdity of the segregation principle of "separate but equal." Hard School was so old, it could be called dilapidated. A wooden structure in dire need of repairs and a fresh coat of paint, the floors were often dusty because the immediate area outside the school was all dirt. When it rained, things got worse when the mud and dirt were tracked inside.

If we were lucky, during the winter my classroom had a black pot belly stove. The stove radiated tremendous amounts of heat, but you couldn't get too close or you'd get burned.

There was no organized physical education program. We would go outside during recess and run around the school grounds, chasing each other, or just standing around to pass the time. We didn't have any sports equipment, baseballs, gloves, footballs, or a playground.

The blackboards were so worn down, you could hardly see the chalk writing. Our textbooks were used, having been discarded by the White schools in the area. Often, they were torn, with pages missing.

The saving grace of Hard Elementary School was the teachers. They were there bright and early, and almost everyone I encountered seemed to enjoy teaching. Maybe the lack of sports equipment, the used books, and the inadequate facility motivated the teachers to give us their absolute best, although there were exceptions.

Lucky me, I found an exception on my first day of school. The morning had gone okay, but lunchtime turned into a scary movie. Unfortunately, I had the starring role. For lunch, you could either bring your own from home or purchase a lunch from the school cafeteria. I purchased lunch that day and returned to my seat in the classroom. I was very picky about what I'd eat. After taking a bite or two of my lunch, I decided not to eat anymore. The food tasted horrible to me. I decided I'd always bring my lunch in the future.

When my teacher, Mrs. Taylor, passed my desk, she noticed I hadn't eaten anything and sternly told me to eat. After a while when she saw I still hadn't eaten my lunch, she became upset and had me bring my lunch to her desk at the front of the classroom. This change of scenery, being in front of the class, plus not liking the food, had the opposite effect she'd intended. I still refused to take a bite of food.

At this point, Mrs. Taylor lost it and said, "If you're going to act like a baby, I'm going to treat you like a baby." Before I knew it, she had picked me up and placed me on her lap with my lunch directly in front of me. The entire classroom was silent, and every eye zoomed in on me. First grade, first day of school and I am the show without a dress rehearsal. To add insult to injury, my teacher said that I may be a Momma's Boy at home, but there would be no Momma's Boys in her class.

After placing me on her lap, she took the fork from my plate and demanded that I open my mouth and take a bite of food. Reluctantly, I complied. I immediately started to gag and felt like I wanted to throw up. She wasn't happy and began screaming at me not to throw up on her or I'd really be in trouble.

After this point, I don't remember anything else about this incident. My mind went blank. I don't remember eating the food or returning to my seat at my designated table. It's as though it was a bad dream, and when I woke up, I was back in class the next day with my lunch from home.

I only remember one other thing about first grade. I told my seat mates, Cora Corbin and Richard Long, how to incorrectly write a capital D. I made it backwards, and I was sharply corrected by Mrs. Taylor. Quite a bit of time passed before I provided any assistance to questioning classmates.

I was lucky I didn't become an elementary school dropout based on my first day in that first grade class.

7 THE BACK OF THE BUS

I WAS FIVE years old and minutes away from my first bus ride to the city of Birmingham, Alabama. There was something special in the air that crisp morning as my mother, brother Kenneth, and I walked the few blocks from our house to the bus stop. I remember walking carefully to avoid getting scuff marks on my new Buster Brown shoes. The puddles of rainwater from last night's showers weren't to be sought out, as in the past.

This special Saturday, my mom had combed and brushed my hair and parted it on the left side. Several weeks before she had purchased identical brown suits, with a nice jacket and short pants, for my brother and me.

We waited at the bus stop on Clarendon Avenue that special Saturday for about ten minutes before I spotted the large grey bus with red trim barreling toward us. Its squeaky brakes slammed the vehicle to a screeching halt, as if the driver had considered passing us by.

The White bus driver opened the door. We climbed the three steps to where the bus driver sat stiff in his seat, not bothering to nod or smile hello. My mother deposited three quarters for our bus fare. The bus driver simply shut the door behind us and started driving down the avenue.

Who cared about the silent bus driver? Not me, because I was taking my first bus ride to that far away land of Birmingham. I felt ten feet tall.

I started moving toward a vacant row of seats. I immediately felt my mom tense up. She quickly grabbed my brother and me by the hand, leading us to the back of the bus. I glanced around, wondering what was wrong with the row of seats I initially considered. Were they broken? Were they dirty? What was wrong with those seats in the front of the bus? No one was sitting there. They seemed okay to me.

As we moved to the back of the bus, I saw a sign separating one section of the seats from the other. The wooden sign we passed as we headed to the back of the bus said "Colored." It looked like the word "Colored" had been burned into the wood with tinges and specks of black and brown.

After sitting down, I noticed all of the White people on the bus sat toward the front and the "Colored" sign was behind them. As the bus traveled away from my neighborhood, more and more White passengers got on. So many White people boarded the bus, the driver pulled over and stopped. He got up from his seat, removed the wooden "Colored" sign, and placed it several rows further to the back of the bus, allowing White riders to sit, but forcing Black riders to stand.

Once the sign was moved, if seats became available in the front of the bus, they remained vacant, because Black folks were required to stay put behind the "Colored" sign. How strange, I thought. Even when there were vacant seats in the front and all the seats behind the "Colored" sign were full, Black people still had to stay behind the sign and stand.

My five-year-old eyes noticed an elderly Black man, who looked frail and not in the best of health. As he stood and held on to the overhead bar for support, he swayed back and forth until it seemed he would fall. Then he would catch himself. My gaze would follow him each time he swayed only to stop just before he fell, as though I had some magical powers that could protect him from collapsing.

For no apparent reason, the bus driver started driving really fast, like he decided to have some cruel and unusual fun intentionally hitting bumps so the Black riders would bounce around like bowling balls. For a split second, the back of the bus became heavy with despair and hopelessness which was apparent by the number of downcast eyes. Suddenly, the frail, elderly Black man yelled out with a voice of authority, "Do not pay us no never mind. Don't worry about going fast. There is no one back here."

The bus went silent. We were all suspended in time. The frail, elderly truth teller had expressed the indignity of the moment. My self-respect returned and judging by the faces of every Black person on the bus, so had theirs. It didn't matter that we sat in the back of the bus.

Surprisingly, after the elderly gentleman called out the bus driver, he slowed down. For the remaining trip, the bus with its Black and White passengers stayed quiet. The silence rang out loud and true.

When we arrived in Birmingham, the Whites exited the bus through the front door, and the Blacks exited through the back door. Two races from the same town lived and moved in and out of the city through different doors with different windows. We lived two different lives, one White, one Colored.

8 SURVIVAL SKILLS FROM MOM

GROWING UP IN the segregated South in the 1950s and 60s would shape and fashion my life forever. Shape my life, because early on I remember my mother talking to me about what to expect and how to respond in a world where the deck was stacked against you. Her gift and genius were in making sure I knew it had nothing to do with me as a person. It was because of some White folks' preconceived, ignorant, and racist attitudes. Often, at times, Whites used skin color as a way to affirm their sense of superiority. They might be poor, have little or no education, or be an alcoholic or a criminal, but at least they were White. They weren't cursed to be Black, the lowest of the low, at least in their minds.

The affluent Whites of the establishment set the moral and ethical tones which also reinforced negative Black stereotypes like shucking, jiving, lazy, oversexed, lawless, and no family values. This led Whites of lower socioeconomic status to believe that their pathway to success was dependent on their believing they needed to keep their foot on the back of the Black man's neck.

My mother's first class seminar of things to do and not to do in the White world seemed to come out of nowhere. Had something happened to her that day, some slight, verbal affront, or disrespectful tone? Maybe she was totally ignored at the retail counter. Once, while my mother waited, the clerk continued to talk with a White acquaintance who stood there. Or, perhaps some White store patron, in a hurry to purchase some item for her child, bumped her to the side and acted as though it never happened.

I knew the state of Alabama had rules, regulations, and laws, but I also knew there were unwritten rules that protected how White people treated Black people. This allowed some to physically and verbally abuse Black people and get away with it.

When my mother spoke to me that day, the rhythm of her voice was unlike anything I'd experienced before. There was a tremendous sense of urgency as she began to speak. It was as if she felt that she should have had this conversation with me sooner and was making up for lost time. As she bent down, she cupped my face in both her hands, and pulled me closer with our faces almost touching. This was the first and last time she would do this. Suddenly, she released my face and tapped me on both shoulders and commanded me not to slouch or stoop, especially so when talking with White people.

My mother told me that whenever I went to downtown Bessemer, there were certain things I must remember and do when dealing with White people. I was about five years old at the time, and I had recently begun first grade at Hard Elementary School.

Her first edict involved talking with Whites, and to always look them directly in their eyes. By doing so, she felt I would display my lack of fear. "Always believe that you are as good as anyone else, no matter what people say," she said, adding, "the world may seem unfair at times but that is the way things are." She told me the only thing I had control over was how I handled myself during these situations. She said to always obey the laws, because the police would kill me in the blink of an eye and get away with it. "Avoid them whenever possible," she counseled.

The seriousness of her voice has become fainter over the years in my memory. But the message remains with me and always will.

In September 1952, I entered the first grade, and on October 4, 1952, I celebrated my sixth birthday. On one hand, my formal educational journey had begun, and on the other hand, my mother chose that time to start my instruction on how to best navigate and survive the segregated and racist terrain I would encounter. There was no exit strategy or a third option. The game was on and the stakes could be deadly.

Following this discussion with my mother, I became more attentive and watchful of my parents' interaction with Whites, as well as with other Blacks. I noticed with embarrassment those occasions when some Blacks would literally hold their hats in their hands, heads bowed as they purchased items in the grocery store or other retail outlets. Although my people made purchases with their hard-earned money, it seemed as though the White grocery store owners felt they were doing a favor for Black customers by allowing us to shop there.

White customers would sometimes walk past Black customers to the front of the line. In most instances, no one objected. I remember being in the grocery store one evening when a Black man spoke up. Waiting in line, he said matter-of-factly, "Excuse me, sir, just like you I've worked all day, and just like you, I have been waiting in line. You need to wait your turn like everyone else." You could have heard a toothpick drop. The store became quiet, the tension palpable. The clerk quickly intervened, calling for additional help up front and everyone was taken care of. I wonder what would have happened if the clerk had called the police, instead of asking for additional help at the cash register. Generally speaking, there was no recourse for Blacks who stepped over the imaginary, but very real White line.

9 MEAN STRANGERS

I'm not sure why I felt so happy and light that early spring morning as I skipped from my home to the local grocery store. The store was less than a block away. I was about five years old and felt on top of the world.

I remember this moment well. It struck me in a place where I hadn't been hit before, my male identity. It came at me totally out of left field and staggered me for a moment. This may have been the first time I experienced this kind of haunting criticism as a child growing up in Bessemer, Alabama. This moment made me fully aware of the power of words and how they could change your world in an instant if you allowed them to.

I wore a multi-colored plaid shirt and a dark gray jumper with buttons hidden on the inside. I thought it was way cool, with no exposed buttons. Capping it off was a pair of brown *Buster Brown* shoes.

As I skipped down the street, about to make a right turn at the corner, I looked to my left and saw shadows of figures sitting on the neighbor's front porch. I couldn't make out a single face. The house sat back from the street, the untrimmed hedges and shrubs shielding part of the porch.

Suddenly, someone said, "Why is he so damn happy?" The question sounded menacing, the tone mocking. The comment startled me as I happily floated in another world.

This voice brought me down to earth, and I hit hard. My second reaction was to wonder what I was doing wrong. I'd heard sharp, piercing, and hurtful words before, even if I didn't fully understand them.

The voice continued. "Look, look, look at him! He's skipping down the street like a little sissy."

I knew that a young Black kid being called a "little sissy" wasn't a good thing.

I almost froze in my tracks. I immediately stopped skipping and began to slowly walk down the street at an angle to shorten the time it would take to get away from these folks.

I felt like I had been 15 minutes from the summit of Mount Rainier in Washington State and someone came out of nowhere to snatch my oxygen mask and tank.

My head finally cleared. I arrived at the grocery store, hardly remembering the steps I'd taken to get there.

I decided for my return trip home, as I passed by the house where unseen strangers had shattered my morning, I'd primarily run home and skip just a little to let my skip-hating antagonists know they hadn't totally ruined my glorious morning. My plan worked to perfection. I buzzed by the people on my right as if they weren't there.

Sadly, my skipping days pretty much ended on that day. Maybe a few times as a young kid, I skipped again, but the fun and excitement had been taken away.

PART II

MOVIN' ON UP
TO EXETER AVENUE
1951-1960

10 MOVING TO EXETER AND GRANDMA

Our Black neighborhood on Exeter Avenue was one big extended family, a black oasis. I was five years old when we moved from Gladstone Alley to Exeter Avenue, a few miles away but a world apart. Houses were much bigger, each house had a lawn, and we were on a street, not an alley.

My maternal grandparents, Josephine and Merritt Clark, sold the lot next to their house to my parents for the whopping sum of one dollar. What a deal! What a blessing!

With their savings, and a loan from the bank, my parents could afford to build a small, two-bedroom house. Not a shotgun house. Our new house had a living room (or "front room"), two bedrooms, a bathroom, kitchen, and dining room. Later, a "side porch" was added where we'd hang out in the summer to enjoy a breeze through the screen windows surrounding the porch. Compared to Gladstone, we had really moved up. A gas furnace and gas stove; no more coal. A Frigidaire; no icebox. A washing machine; no clothesline. And no roaches.

It's a good thing we moved next door to Grandma, because then I had my own "safe house." Whenever I was hungry or bored, I knew I could go next door and Grandma would welcome me warmly with a, "Hey, Baby, how're you doing?" No matter how old I became, I would always be her "Baby." Over time I learned that all of her grandkids, nieces, nephews, cousins, and friends' kids were her "Baby" as well. This summed up Grandma in so many ways. She loved everyone and always had a kind and respectful word for all in the neighborhood, and for less known passersby as well. The kindness and love she gave was reflected back to her, sometimes by complete strangers who would call out "Hello, Grandma" as they passed her porch. Her Grandma Fan Club would bring her flowers, volunteer to do lawn work, or run errands for her. Of course, Grandma, being Grandma, insisted on paying them a little something for their kindness. That's just the way she was!

It seemed like my brother Ken and I often stayed at Grandma's, usually playing with my cousin Gean, whose mother (my mother's sister) had died in childbirth so Gean was being raised by Grandma. We three were close in age and as youngsters played together almost every day. And on those few occasions when my parents were angry with me, I knew I could scurry next door to my safe haven.

. . .

Sitting on my grandmother's porch, while only next door, seemed miles away and represented a refuge of love and understanding. My grandmother was the first person who taught me the value of sitting with someone and enjoying their company by simply being with them. Nothing was said or spoken, just comfortable silence. Sitting on my grandmother's porch was how I discovered this easy and peaceful way of relaxing.

As an adult, I now read newspapers and enjoy a cup of coffee as a substitute for sitting leisurely on my grandmother's porch. The newspaper can provide a powerful lens to see and understand a variety of issues and topics, sometimes in high definition. Sips of coffee and quiet time have the ability to take the edge off worldly cares and tensions and to provide another lens to view life a little differently.

Long ago before Starbucks, there was Grandma's porch. Who knew the cost benefit of sitting on Grandma's porch was incalculable. It didn't cost me a penny, simply time, and usually made me feel like a million. I was fortunate to have a Grandma like Josephine Clark.

. . .

One spring morning I was sitting on Grandma's porch step. We had just finished eating breakfast. Fortunately for me that day, biscuits had been on the menu. I had polished off three buttermilk biscuits with the extremely sweet Alaga syrup. The biscuits appeared to have been inflated with air, or a mini-injection of some type, to make them rise to perfection. They looked so tall and fluffy, and the top of the biscuits appeared to have been sprayed with some caramel coloring, with a slight dusting of white flour.

Grandma sat in her swing a few feet behind me. We both noticed a young kid about my age singing as he walked down Exeter Avenue. Little by little, Grandma moved toward the end of the swing on the side of the porch that was closest to the street to get a more up-close look at the young happy camper coming down the street. She thought she recognized him, because she had seen this same young man at a friend's house a week earlier. She immediately started laughing when she thought about her first encounter with him.

This little tyke, who was no more than four or five years old, had taken center stage by saying over and over again in a singsong voice, "The older I get, the bigger fool I get; the older I get, the bigger fool I get; the older I get, the bigger fool I get."

The surprised adults started to laugh, louder and louder. The more they laughed, the faster and louder the little boy went, "The older I get, the bigger fool I get." The kid had no clue what he was saying, other than he was getting more and more attention, while everyone was having a ball at his expense.

Sometimes, especially with young people, we adults encourage the wrong behavior, and when young men become adult men, we wonder how they got that way.

. . .

At the time, it seemed like a once-in-a-lifetime experience. Snow fell one winter night in Bessemer, covering the grass, trees, rooftops, porches, and everything in sight. I believe I was in the fourth grade at Hard Elementary School. Until that morning, I had never seen a hint of snow in our city.

I especially remember this time because I was confined to bed with a serious bout of pneumonia. I knew it was serious, because Mom kept me home and told me I wouldn't attend school for several days. Ordinarily, I would have been excited about missing school, but I didn't feel well and Mom instructed me to stay in bed. I actually wanted my mom to give me a shot of penicillin to make me feel better.

Typically, when nurse mom wanted to give me a shot, I would run away to avoid the deadly looking needle, or I would hit her hand as she tried to inject my rear end. Sometimes, the nurse and patient interplay became so heated, the nurse would say, "Little Brother, if you don't stop hitting my hand, you are going to cause this needle to break off in your behind." I must admit, this warning did get my attention as I visualized the needle sticking out of my cheek. I stopped fighting her.

When my mom said she wanted to give me a penicillin shot in the morning and another in the evening, I pulled down my pajama bottoms without any protest. I felt bad. If I could've administered the shot myself, I would have.

As my mother left for work, she told me my grandmother would come by to check on me. The bedroom where I slept had a window through which I could see our backyard and the worn footpath between our houses. I happened to glance out the window and saw my grandmother walking slowly toward our house. On this unusual snowy day, it appeared still and quiet outside, and I could hear the faint crunch of Grandma's deliberate mini-steps as she carefully navigated the footpath. Grandma had reached the point in her life when walking required a major effort and maximum attention.

Before long Grandma entered my bedroom, greeting me with her ever-present smile. "How are you doing, Baby?"

She walked over to the bed and sat next to me. I noticed she carried a small jar of Vicks VapoRub. She asked me to unbutton the top two buttons of my pajama top, because she wanted to apply the unguent to my chest. Now, I thought my father had hands like sandpaper but as Grandma started applying the salve, her hand took coarseness to another level. Soon I felt the warmth of the Vicks VapoRub, little by little seeping into my skin. In a matter of seconds as she rubbed my chest in a circular motion, the roughness of her hand turned to relief and comfort. I could breathe again with minimum discomfort.

Grandma's hands over her life experiences had been especially tempered for her special gift of applying Vicks VapoRub. Whether it was washing clothes by hand on the washboard; ironing stacks of shirts, pants, and dresses; clearing a vacant lot of excess dirt, rocks, and weeds for gardening; cutting branches and picking up wood to start a fire in the fireplace; or repairing and sewing clothing for her family, Grandma, like my father, used her hands to do what was necessary to provide and care for our family. How lucky we were, and at the same time so unaware of their sacrifices and the never-ending work performed by their hands.

11 GOING NORTH

In 1953, my mother traveled north for her training to become a nurse. I don't remember much about the ride from my home on Exeter Avenue to the Birmingham train station. I was six years old, about to start second grade, and would turn seven that October.

I'm certain someone drove my father, mother, brother, and me to the train station, because we didn't have a car. I remember being squeezed in the back of an unfamiliar car that smelled of gasoline. It was quiet. I don't remember my father saying a single word. However, that wasn't unusual. There were periods of time when he barely spoke. My mother made small talk with the driver, but nothing of any real consequence. Ken tried to take a nap, but the snugness of the backseat and the jostling of the car as we traveled to Birmingham prevented him from doing so.

I had no idea until we arrived at the train station that my mother would be living in Chicago for at least three months. She planned to attend nursing school and become a Licensed Practical Nurse. Up until that time, she'd been a stay-at-home Mom. She needed to work in order to supplement my father's income, especially during those extended periods of time when there were cutbacks or not enough work at the ore mines and the Pullman Standard Boxcar Company. With the periods of time my father was out of work increasing rather than decreasing, a second income was critical to our very survival.

At the train station, my mother talked to my brother and me about being big boys, minding our father, and keeping up with our schoolwork. She promised she would bring us something special back from Chicago if we did these things.

I lost it. I didn't want anything special from Chicago. I wanted my mother to stay home. Why couldn't she go to school in Alabama? Why did she have to go all the way to Chicago? When I saw her two avocado green *Samsonite* bags, I knew things were serious. You didn't need two large pieces of luggage for a four- or five-day stay in Chicago, as I had originally hoped.

When my mother lifted her bags, the fog lifted for me, and I realized she would be away for a long time. It didn't matter to me that my yelling and screaming began to attract a crowd. Why now? Why our family? What had we done to deserve this?

The answer, I came to find out much later, was that Alabama didn't allow African Americans to attend its nursing schools. Once she received training in Chicago, she could work as a nurse in our home state. This time, the unfair racial laws of the state weren't just making things difficult for my family, they were tearing it apart.

While our mother attended nursing school, she lived with Mack Long, my father's son with his first wife, Josie Burns. Our mother was truly fortunate to have this living arrangement, because otherwise the cost of living on her own would have been prohibitive.

My mother graduated from Wayne School of Practical Nursing in 1953, receiving her certificate as a Licensed Practical Nurse. Shortly after returning home, she worked for more than 20 years at West End Baptist Hospital, where she enjoyed a stellar career and became active as an officer in the American Black Nurses Association.

My mother knew what needed to be done to ensure the financial well-being of our family. Leaving her family was a bold and courageous act. If she hadn't made this decision, I am convinced our lives would have turned out very differently. Her family meant everything to her, and no sacrifice was ever too great.

12 LIVING IN A COCOON

In my Black world, Exeter Avenue felt like living in a warm and fuzzy cocoon. A cocoon that expanded and contracted as necessary to insulate, embrace, educate, and protect me, and all those like me, from the prejudices and negativity of the outside White world.

On Exeter Avenue, we often played at each other's home. There was that one house on the block where we gathered most often: the home of Mrs. Charlotte and Mr. Peg Levert. They had a family of three boys and four girls. Next door to the Leverts during this time was a large vacant lot with several trees that provided much-needed shade during the summer months.

Whatever the sport or activity, we would make it happen on Exeter Avenue—from playing stick ball in between the cars passing by, to hide and seek, or to rolling discarded car tires from the top of the hill to the bottom. We also enjoyed the tried and true games of jacks, fiddlesticks, cowboys and Indians, Monopoly, and Spin the Bottle.

Spin the Bottle, when played with some of the girls on Exeter Avenue, ended with a peck on the cheek and lots of laughter and embarrassed faces. The real fun was everyone's reaction to the big smooch.

Sometimes, we would raise the stakes by hiding behind trees on the vacant lot next to the Levert family home and use our BB guns and shoot at one another. Not shooting at one another to seriously injure, but to hit someone with a shot to the body. Typically, those engaged would be wearing thick jackets to protect themselves. I was strictly an observer. It seemed too dangerous to me. I imagined being shot in the eye. That paled in comparison to what my mom would say and what my father would do to me with his weapon of choice, the almighty belt, if I played this game and was injured.

Another high point of living on Exeter Avenue was Mrs. Julia Patton playing bingo with a group of kids during the summer on her front porch. This activity during the dog days of summer brought with it a cool, relaxing breeze filled with fun and laughter.

Few of the parents who lived on Exeter Avenue took the time to play with the kids. That was just the way it was.

On the other hand, if some of us were doing something we shouldn't be doing, a neighbor would speak up quickly. "Hey, you know you shouldn't be doing that. And if you don't stop, I am going to tell your mom and dad." If this happened, a beating of major proportions was the automatic punishment. No questions asked and no explanations accepted by our parents.

. . .

Mrs. Julia was married to a man named Macon Patton, a Clint Eastwood type—quiet, determined, and not to be messed with. Yet, there was this air of kindness about him that made you want to be around him. We called him, with due respect, Mr. Macon.

Mr. Macon had a big truck he used for chores around his home, and it was his primary mode of transportation.

Every once in a while, word would go out in the neighborhood that Mr. Macon would be taking us on a joy ride. No specific destination—just riding around to no place in particular. He would pack as many as 20 kids from the neighborhood into the back of his truck.

The truck ride literally and figuratively elevated us above everything and everyone around us. There was no restaurant where we couldn't eat, no swimming pool where we couldn't swim, no baseball field where we couldn't play, and no water fountain we couldn't drink from. The back of the truck was like being in the front of the bus. We were no longer second-class citizens.

The truck rides made me feel as free as a bird. I could fly. I could soar, if only momentarily. Mr. Macon drove fast as the wind swirled around us, and God forbid if we hit a bump in the road. It was as if Mr. Macon wanted us to understand that the bumps in life's road would always be there and we should get used to them. He increased the speed when he saw a bump, assuring that we would feel the impact and be thrown around. The key, of course, was how we responded and regrouped after the initial impact.

Those spontaneous truck rides were one of the joys, and one of my favorite memories, of living on Exeter Avenue.

. . .

One of my favorite toys as a six-year-old kid was my make-believe horse. This special horse came to life by breaking off a limb from a chinaberry tree. The tree's bright green, pliable limbs could be molded into a variety of shapes. I transformed this particular green tree limb into my pony.

It wasn't just any ole' pony, because as I stripped away sections of the bark from the limb, which gave it a two-tone appearance, my pinto pony emerged. I became quite adept at pulling swatches of green bark from the limb to make the pinto pony pattern.

My pinto pony had great speed and the uncanny ability to detect and jump over any object in its path. Over time, I developed what I thought was my signature move. While proudly astride my pinto pony, in full gallop, I stopped, pulled the reins of my pony until he rose up on his two hind legs, and let out this screeching sound that echoed up and down Exeter Avenue. Then, I patted my pinto gently on the left side of his face to let him know what a good job he'd done. Finally, my pinto pony and I proudly walked slowly up the street, knowing we were in sync and all was right with the world.

· · ·

After seeing some of my friends in the neighborhood roll used car tires down the street, I thought I'd give it a try. My tire rolling experience was short-lived, because when I attempted to roll the tire, I struggled to keep the tire from moving everywhere other than in a straight line. It also made me dizzy. And pretty dirty during my futile attempts. That old tire, with hardly any tread, had enough left to determine the direction it wanted to roll. It was in control, not me.

· · ·

I must have seen someone in the neighborhood transform a regular bicycle into a motorcycle. I worked on my bicycle in the area between our house and Grandma's house. I didn't want anyone to see the finished product with its unique design before it was all done.

I started with four balloons, usually white, to accentuate my black-framed bike with its silver fenders, white-wall tires, silver spoke wheels, and silver handlebars with black tassels. I blew up the balloons almost to their maximum capacity, leaving just enough room to be able to attach them to the bicycle. I fastened balloons on each side of the front and back silver-spoked wheels.

Once I was on my now pedal-powered motorcycle, I started slowly with the vibrations from the balloons and the spokes of the tires creating this muffled guttural sound which became louder and deeper the faster I pedaled. Slowing down decreased the sound and once it became silent, I ramped it back up again.

The downside to the increased sound was that after three or four times of increasing and decreasing speed on my motorcycle, the balloons popped from the friction generated. The sound from this make-believe motorcycle resembled a backfire. It felt so exhilarating, I went through this balloon assembly exercise at least half a dozen times, always knowing it would be short-lived but end with a big, loud pop.

13 YANKEE STADIUM, BESSEMER STYLE

IN OUR NEIGHBORHOOD, a vacant lot with weeds, rocks, and uneven terrain was transformed into a baseball diamond with hard work and
imagination. We considered it our version of Yankee Stadium.

During the 50s and early 60s, Blacks in Bessemer, Alabama, weren't
allowed to use the city-managed and city-owned baseball park, swimming
pools, or any other recreational facilities used by Whites. We paid local
taxes, but we received no benefits from the taxes used for recreational
purposes.

We made the best of this reality by creating and designing our own
baseball diamond. We cut the grass, removed the weeds, and outlined all
of the bases from home plate, to first base, second base, third base, and
back to home plate. Our marker of choice, white lime because someone
in the neighborhood had some. The infield was the most important. We
needed it to be as level as possible to avoid uneven hops and ricochets
of the ground balls. Even on a smooth infield, baseballs can take some
interesting bounces and pop you right in the face. An old fence found on
the vacant lot was reconfigured to make a backstop behind home plate.
However, the configuration had some gaps so some balls missed by the
catcher would roll through our specially created backstop.

To minimize time lost in chasing the balls that got away, we had a young kid who wanted to be on the team hustle the balls. Overall, it worked pretty well with our own farm team system.

. . .

I have a special memory of one baseball game. I swung on the first pitch, and the ball soared over the left fielder's head for an extra base hit. As I rounded first base, I spotted a fig tree with ripened figs. One fig in particular stood out from all others. It bulged, so ripe and juicy it looked like, in a matter of seconds, it might plunge downward to its earthly death.

Mesmerized by this fig, I thought I must save it from falling to the ground and dying amidst the dirt and weeds. If I timed it just right, as I rounded first base, I could snatch the fig from the tree and give it a royal and appreciated welcome to my mouth and tummy before it fell. I reached out and grabbed the fig all in one motion as I headed toward second base. I was so pleased with my daring move that, in my excitement, I tripped and started to fall headfirst toward second base. I did fall just a few feet short of second base and splattered my treasured fig all over my shirt. I started crawling to second base, and barely arrived before the throw from the left fielder reached the second baseman. It was a close call, and my fellow teammates cracked up after observing my misadventure.

I gathered myself and played it as if nothing had happened. I looked to right field and spotted glistening blackberries not too far away. I was quite familiar with this area, because of my lack of skills in catching the ball. I was the right fielder, the one position where my teammates thought I'd do the least amount of damage.

I was on the other side of the blackberry bushes, and the berries looked luscious and inviting. I noticed the pitcher was talking with the catcher about the best way to pitch to Jimmy, aka Sonny Levert, one of the best players on our team. He was a powerful long ball hitter. Because of his focus on Sonny, the pitcher seemed to forget I was on second base. Or, maybe because of my limited hitting skills, he couldn't believe I was on any base.

I was a terrible baseball player. I played when there was a shortage of players. My brother, Kenneth, an all-around good athlete, loved to play baseball. He often teased me by saying, "If you can't play a sport, be a sport."

Ken's love of sports was and is embodied in his son, my nephew, Ny'Ika B. Long. Since early childhood, Ny'Ika always had a love and fascination with sports, especially basketball and football. As a former high school and college quarterback, he translated his love of the game into a professional career, coaching at the high school and community college level.

Back on second base I could see the blackberries weren't far away, and the one skill I possessed was my ability to run fast. In the segregated, racist South, not a bad skill to possess. I darted toward the blackberry bushes, swiftly picked a handful of berries, despite the stickers, and returned unnoticed to second base with a huge smile on my face.

While I watched the pitcher, I noticed he took a long wind-up before releasing the ball toward home plate. Suddenly, with my confidence at an all-time high, third base looked closer than usual. Again, speed was my friend, and off I went, making a mad dash to third base. I took the pitcher and catcher totally by surprise. I arrived at third base without having to slide.

Another reason third base looked so close to me, and motivated me, the new speed demon, was the plum tree right behind third base. It was always loaded during the summer months with big yellow plums, with faint red markings around the seed in the center. These plums were juicy and the skin of the plums, although coarse, was easy to eat with no bitter aftertaste. I spotted the plum of my dreams. Unfortunately, I didn't get a chance to savor the taste of that plum, because long ball hitter Sonny smacked a drive past the center fielder, bringing me home. Sonny ended up on second base with a double.

As I crossed home plate, I was happy to have gotten a hit and stolen a base. And along the way, I had enjoyed the fruits of my labor.

. . .

Thunder didn't crackle in the sky, nor did lightning flash across the heavens on this hot, humid, summer day when the dividing line between Blacks and Whites on Exeter Avenue was crossed. This historic moment in time was initiated by a 13-year old White kid named Billie. He lived in a three-story white house on the corner of 24th and Exeter Avenue. Billie, an only child, lived directly across the street from our baseball field on the adjacent corner of 23rd and Exeter Avenue.

So close, and yet so far, a scant 20 feet separated the White neighborhood from the Black neighborhood on Exeter. Quite fascinating really, that in the segregated South, Blacks and Whites lived on the same avenue, but at the same time were sealed off from one another by invisible dividing lines. The White portion of the avenue was always paved, while the Black section of the avenue lacked paving. We weren't neighbors, we simply co-existed.

One day to our amazement, as we were about to start playing baseball, Billie started walking toward the baseball field. We stared at him in disbelief. We couldn't imagine what he was thinking. None of us had met Billie before, but we all knew him. When he played in his yard, we could hear his parents calling out to him, especially when we were playing baseball at the field so close to his home.

We all stared at Billie, not only because the White kid had crossed the invisible color line, but because of how he was dressed. He looked like a miniature version of White ballplayers we watched on our black-and-white RCA television sets. He was decked out from head to toe with an official looking baseball uniform, including hat, glove, spiked shoes, and a Mickey Mantle Louisville Slugger baseball bat.

There was complete silence for what seemed like an eternity, until Billie asked if he could hit some balls with us. Once that happened, the silence, staring, and awkwardness vanished. We became kids, just playing around and having fun. Billie seemed to be having the time of his life. I recalled that I hadn't seen any other White kids playing with him at his home.

Billie came over to the baseball diamond a couple of more times that summer to play ball with us. The last time he played with us—hitting, pitching, and catching—his mom called him home. This had never happened before. Usually, he played for an hour or so. When he was done, he would just leave.

When I heard his mother call his name, I heard something in her voice. Something changed. The color curtain closed, and that would be the last time Billie stopped by to play baseball. He said his goodbyes and walked away. The expression on his face said he knew this was it. It would be the last time he would play baseball with us. A sad moment.

14 AUNT BESSIE TEACHES ME A LESSON

AUNT BESSIE WAS my favorite aunt. My father's oldest sister, she lived about five minutes from our home. Her full name was Bessie Black, and her brothers and sisters called her "Duke." She was a commanding woman, about five-feet-eight inches tall. She had jet black, long, wavy hair and an extremely fair complexion.

Like John Wayne, also known as Duke, Aunt Bessie took long powerful steps. Whenever you saw her coming it always seemed as though she was on a mission. There was no time to waste; something needed to be done. Aunt Bessie lived a modest life in a three-room shotgun house. She always kept it neat and tidy on a street that, for all practical purposes, was an alley.

Aunt Bessie worked as a maid and cook for a White family that lived about six blocks away. She always wore a white uniform to work. She usually walked because it was a short distance. Aunt Bessie was always generous and kind to my brother Ken and me, and she welcomed us to stop by any time, no appointment necessary.

On one occasion after visiting with her, I saw a small oval shaped glass bowl as I was leaving. This container held several nickels, dimes, pennies, and quarters, and it caught my eye. I was about ten years old at the time. The coins stopped me dead in my tracks. I thought that with so many,

Aunt Bessie wouldn't miss a few. I scooped up several quarters, a nickel or two, and some dimes. It didn't seem like a big deal. I felt perfectly innocent.

Several weeks after my coin caper, Aunt Bessie asked me to go shopping with her at the local A&P in downtown Bessemer. She and I had done this on many occasions. I pushed the cart in the grocery store, and she usually let me pick out a few items for myself. After shopping, I loaded the bags of groceries in the taxicab that took us to her home. When we arrived, I helped put away the groceries. After I visited with Aunt Bessie for another hour or so, it was time for me to leave. I said my goodbyes to Aunt Bessie while she was in the kitchen. As I walked through to her bedroom, the oval shaped glass bowl with coins seemed to have twice as many silver temptations as before.

Well, I thought, I had taken a few coins before and Aunt Bessie hadn't missed them at all. As I walked by, I paused long enough to pick up a few coins and then headed toward the front door. As I opened the door to leave, I heard a voice that sounded like a roaring lion. Aunt Bessie yelled at me and wanted to know why I'd stolen from her. I'd been totally set up. She knew I'd taken some coins previously and asked for my grocery shopping assistance to see if I'd be stupid enough to do the same thing again. Of course, she was correct. I did it. I was a thief.

After being caught in the act, my response was to get out of that front door as quickly as possible. I had nothing to say and my main concern was to escape. Immediately. I ran down the steps, heart pounding and sweat beading, thinking about what I had done. My first thought as I ran for home was my father was going to kill me once he found out. I had no excuses. I knew it would be only a matter of days before I had to face the music, or more realistically, the wrath of the beast and the belt. I wasn't talking about a spanking. In our home, punishment equaled whuppings.

There was no sliding scale of punishment based on the severity of the act. Any and all whuppings by my father equaled maximum physical and emotional abuse. Each time, he went for the gold; neither silver nor bronze would do. The fury of his actions, his contorted and twisted face, made his temporary insanity real. The angrier he became, regardless of me or my brother's mistake, error in judgement, or lack of response in a manner he deemed acceptable, the degree of punishment was always the same—extreme brutality from my father, beginning to end.

I returned to Aunt Bessie's house to see her again in about a month. I figured if she was going to tell her brother, my father, about my stealing change from her, he would have executed his punishment on me by now with this factual information. For some reason, she spared me. Maybe she knew about my father's violent temper and didn't want me to suffer his punishment. Maybe Aunt Bessie was going to take matters into her own hands. As we used to say in Alabama, my ass would be grass and she would be the lawn mower.

Fortunately, Aunt Bessie was calm and soft spoken when I returned to her home, but in a no nonsense way. She expressed her disappointment in me and her surprise at my selfish actions. Aunt Bessie couldn't understand why I would take change from her when she would have just as easily given it to me. As we talked, she shook her head in disbelief.

I had no answers for her questions. I bowed my head, barely able to look her in the face. I promised never to steal from her again. I apologized. This conversation with Aunt Bessie took ten minutes, but it seemed to last forever. After everything was said and done, I felt so relieved. It was like I had been walking around with a dark cloud over my head, a tornado on the horizon. Finally, the cloud lifted, and the storm passed. It felt like Aunt Bessie had saved my life by not telling my father I'd stolen from her.

What I'd stolen from Aunt Bessie was more than her money. I'd stolen her trust in me. No amount of money could replace this valuable commodity. If I hadn't reestablished her trust in me, I'd have no currency at all. From this experience, my relationship with Aunt Bessie became more cherished and special. We quickly resumed our grocery shopping trips and my stopping by her home whenever I wanted. She shared family stories about her brothers and sisters while I sat on her front porch in the evening shade of a warm summer night, or the briskness of a fall evening.

On a couple of occasions, she took me on the Greyhound bus to a place she called the "country." It had to be one of our relative's homes. We stayed overnight. The next morning, I ran between the rows of corn that seemed to go on forever. There were chickens, roosters, pigs, and horses. A special treat at the country farm was breakfast. We had piping hot biscuits baked in the oven of a black stove fueled by wood and coal. I poured on the maple syrup thick and heavy; no jelly to spoil these biscuits. Of course, there were thick slabs of fried bacon and large chunks of ham to make you almost comatose when finished with the meal.

One time, I rode a horse at the farm. After someone helped me onto the horse, I couldn't believe how high up and afraid I was. As I tried to ride the horse in a fenced area of about 30 feet, the horse kept returning to the fence and trying to knock me off by continually banging me into the fence. After this happened a couple of times, I knew the ride was over, and I wanted someone to get me off the crazy horse. Finally, a merciful soul saw my panic-stricken face and took me off the horse. This was the first, and happily the last time, I attempted to ride a horse. This city boy was no country boy.

15 MY DAREDEVIL BROTHER

WHEN MY BROTHER Ken and I grew up in Bessemer, Alabama, during the 50's and 60's, there were public swimming pools. However, there was one main criteria for swimming in those pools and it wasn't whether you could swim. If you were White, the chlorinated "blue" water welcomed you with open arms. However, if you were Black, like my brother and me and thousands of other people in Bessemer and other cities throughout the South, the waters washed us away without a splash.

The one aspect of the discriminatory policy concerning swimming that I appreciated was its total honesty. No "separate but equal" bullshit like school, restroom, restaurant, and drinking fountain usage. The message was clear, no Blacks allowed, and you can count on getting the short end of the stick.

Just because the option of swimming in the local public swimming pools was off limits, it didn't mean swimming somewhere else was prohibited if you were fortunate enough to have color in your skin.

The swimming pool of choice and necessity for most of us in my neighborhood was called the Little Red Hole. This swimming hole was about two miles from where we lived. It was located at the bottom of a hill within 30 feet from an abandoned ore mine, hence the red in the Little Red Hole name. The most amazing part of this swimming destination was the always icy, and I mean icy, cold water.

The trek from Exeter Avenue to the swimming hole was quite an adventure. I reluctantly tagged along even though I couldn't swim, because I'd been hearing about this place for at least two years. I was about 12 years old on this first and last trip. It was a scorching July summer day around noon when we began our walk. The humidity weighed us down with every step we took.

As we made our way deep into the woods, five of us, including my brother Ken, walked slowly up the hilly terrain, at times falling and sliding back down the hill. As we arrived at the summit and then began the walk downward, the bushes, weeds, bugs, and stinging flies became more plentiful. I remember making my way through a dense thicket of weeds when I was suddenly smacked in the face by the bushes the person in front of me had just walked through.

After 30 minutes or so of walking in the intense heat, slippery terrain, thick bushes, weeds, and insect bites, I started to think we were on a wild goose chase, slowly going nowhere. I began to wonder, what am I doing out here anyway? I can't swim, and I'm headed to the Little Red Hole with a group of guys whose best swimming stroke is the dog paddle.

I could almost hear my mother and father scolding me. "Little Brother, what were you doing there in the first place? You know you can't swim. You could have drowned following behind your brother Ken."

Before my logical thinking took over, I regrouped, steadied myself, and thought, *I'm in too deep. If I turn around now, everyone, especially my brother, will tease me about being scared and turning around. Quitting isn't an option.* Out of nowhere I saw a clearing in the woods. Someone called out that the Little Red Hole was close because they could hear the water.

The roar of the water sounded like raging rapids falling off the side of a mountain. Everyone except me started to run toward the sound of water crashing, shedding their clothes as they ran. Here I stood, clothes still on while everyone else sported their birthday suits. As a non-swimmer, I hesitated to jump into the unknown depth of the Little Red Hole. A touch of my toes in the icy water validated my reluctance—too cold for me.

Ken, my brother, was one of the first to jump into this 15-foot diameter swimming hole. He called out to me with sheer delight, "Bup, come on in. It's cold but it sure feels good." By now, he was shrieking and had wrapped both arms around his upper body to try to warm up as he jumped around in the water. Ken smiled broadly, as though competing in an Olympic-sized swimming pool on a tropical island thousands of miles away from Alabama and the oppressive heat, as well as from the institutional racism handed down from generation to generation. Ken's face looked serene and peaceful. He'd found contentment and fulfillment in, of all places, the Little Red Hole.

As I watched Ken swim in the Little Red Hole, I thought about his willingness to take risks. Simply because he hadn't done something before wasn't reason enough for not trying. Nothing ventured, nothing gained or learned.

Immediately, what came to mind was the time about a year prior when he roared down our avenue on a motorbike. When he saw me playing with other kids that evening, he brought the motorbike to a screeching halt. An excited Ken lifted his arm, shouted, and waved me forward to sit behind him. I slowly climbed on, several questions swirling around in my head.

Ken answered one of my questions before I could ask. He shared he had borrowed the bike from the one Black kid who owned a motorbike on our side of town. I then remembered this kid on a couple of occasions riding through the neighborhood as we looked on with awe and envy.

In a matter of minutes, Ken and I arrived at the top of the hill where a streetlight illuminated the stretch of Exeter Avenue we had just rumbled through. Ken slowed, turned the motorbike around, stopped, and exhaled with pride as he looked down the hill to survey his ascent to the top.

With all the excitement, I was almost speechless. Once I regained my senses, I blurted out the one question that consumed me from the moment I saw him on the motorbike, "Ken, when did you learn to ride a motorbike? I had no idea you could."

Without hesitation, he said, "Neither did I!"

During that summer evening, I learned so much about my brother and his approach to life's challenges. Ken thought he could do anything—all he needed to do was try. In many instances, he was right. The motorbike opportunity and challenge became a precedent of how he lived his life.

16 BOUGHT SENSE

I REMEMBER THE first time my mom said, "Bought sense is the best sense." My initial reaction as a young boy was, "What does that mean?" Did I need to go to the grocery store and buy some sense? Or, did I appear senseless? Unfortunately, yet fortunately, over time I learned the meaning of this timeless expression—it meant that you absorb most deeply those truths that cost you most dearly.

My mother used different expressions and sayings to communicate important messages. These expressions, some handed down over the years, resulted from someone who gained knowledge the old fashioned way—they earned it. These sayings, when listened to, served me well, acting as guideposts and barometers in facing and dealing with life's ebbs and flows.

One incident that taught me the meaning of "bought sense is the best sense" started out as what I thought would be a dream come true. The problem, though, was that when it came true, it turned into a nightmare. I was the main character, not to mention the producer and director of this movie. Maybe if I was the executive producer, the person who financed the movie, instead of my mother, the ending may have been different, but I doubt it.

My mother and father, like other parents, wanted to make sure their kids had a better life than they did, even when financially doing so was a stretch. In my brother Ken's and my case, this meant finishing high school with grades good enough to go to the college of our choice. The college of choice couldn't be in Alabama, as our parents wanted us to pursue our college degrees out of state. They didn't want us to go to college and have it be an extension of high school by hanging out with the same people we knew in high school.

They wanted us to broaden our horizons and widen our circle of friends. Also, they wanted us to experience what they hadn't experienced, attending and graduating from college. They felt that attending an historically Black college in Alabama wouldn't give us the independence and freedom of campus life, nor the ability to meet students from all over the world. Meeting students from different economic and social backgrounds was also important to them. My parents were more than willing to work when they were ill, or work double shifts for weeks at a time, to secure the dollars needed to pay for our college educations and activities. Ken and I didn't have any student loans to pay back. Our parents paid for each and every credit hour.

How my learning to play the piano came about remains a little foggy. I do remember one evening Ken talked to our mother about the high school band and his interest in playing the trumpet. He had sophomore high school friends who played different instruments in the band. Ken visited the band room a few times at Dunbar High School, and he was genuinely interested in playing the trumpet.

At some point, the conversation turned to me and whether or not I had an interest in playing some musical instrument. Playing the piano would be cool, but I didn't consider the practice, discipline, and sacrifice it would require. It just sounded good to me. I liked the idea of playing the piano in front of people and everyone standing around marveling at my keyboard skills.

The idea of my brother and I playing musical instruments was another component being orchestrated by our mother. It was part of a larger plan of hers for us to become well-educated and well-rounded young men. The greater the extent of the experiences, the more they would improve and enhance the chances of our being successful in the world. She smiled that night as Ken and I expressed our willingness to expand our outlook musically. It really didn't matter to her what the price might be to achieve this dream. She was thrilled that we were interested, some of us more than others, I might add, in pursuing the musical benefits of life and all they could do to take us beyond the confines of Bessemer, Alabama.

I came home one day from Hard Elementary School, and a new, black, shiny Wurlitzer piano with its glistening white and black keys and matching black bench was sitting in our house.

How and why did this piano come so quickly? I had no time to prepare for its arrival. The first thing I thought about, after recovering from my initial shock, was how much did this fancy looking piano cost? Surely much, much more than a trumpet.

Excitement wasn't the word I would use when I saw "my" piano. How about shocked, scared to death, panicked, and wondering what I'd gotten myself into? My desire to learn to play the piano disappeared as quickly as it had appeared. Gone. I instantly disliked the piano as soon as I saw it. I no longer wanted to play.

What a dilemma! I ignored my initial fears and felt that as time went by and my piano lessons began, I would feel better about this major investment my parents had made almost on a whim.

In hindsight, conga drums or cymbals would have been a more prudent choice. But knowing me, not cool enough.

My parents were hard-working folks doing better than most in our neighborhood, but they didn't have the money to fund a son's effort to keep up or outshine his older brother by asking for a piano. Not many families in our neighborhood, or the entire Bessemer area where African Americans lived, had two brand-new musical instruments in their household.

My mother found a piano teacher, Mrs. Rogers, a music instructor at Carver High School. Within a couple of weeks of the piano's arrival, I had my first lesson with Mrs. Rogers at her studio, about a 20-minute bicycle ride from my home.

Mrs. Rogers could be quite charming and mesmerizing on occasion.

At other times, she could tear you to shreds and seemed to enjoy the idea of mentally and psychologically beating up on you. I never knew which Mrs. Rogers would show up. She kept me on edge. Kind of like receiving a soft peck on the cheek with hearts and flowers one time, then a verbal slap upside your head in front of God and everybody another time.

My piano lessons, which began in the summer of 1960, took place in the music studio located above a former restaurant. The studio had three couches and one fan, bare walls, and lacked any warmth. It reminded me of a punishment room for non-behaving school kids who had been sentenced to piano lessons.

My anxiety and apprehension would begin as soon as I started walking up the 20 steps to the studio. With every step, my heart rate increased to the point of pounding. Sitting quietly on the couch and waiting my turn at the piano translated to real torture. Waiting and thinking about how badly I would play became more difficult than the actual lesson itself.

Piano lessons were on a certain day during specific blocks of time, but there were no appointments. You waited your turn, depending on when you arrived. The amount of time one spent playing the piano during these sessions was totally at the discretion of Mrs. Rogers, who frowned and snarled intermittently. It seemed as though she didn't really want to be there, but the commitment had been made, and she needed to meet her obligation. Like me, sort of.

After the third piano lesson or so, I realized that all of the other students taking piano lessons were female. I was the lone male. Because I was a beginner level student, my piano book was red. All of the other female students had taken lessons for at least a year and had blue or black piano books. Everyone knew I was the oddball male student, just learning to play the piano.

Now, it was my turn, front and center, and all eyes were on me. Mrs. Rogers started the pentameter before I began to play the piece assigned from the last lesson. I froze. I was scared out of my mind, totally out of my comfort zone with no support, or encouragement. Maybe, just maybe, if I'd practiced my lesson before coming, I wouldn't have been so freaked out. You think!? However, during the time leading up to my lesson, I avoided the piano like it was a plague. In fact, sometimes I walked past the piano and stared at it like it was some evil monster from outer space that had inhabited my home to torture me and ridicule my shortcomings.

The tick, tick, tick of Mrs. Rogers' pentameter seemed to increase in speed, and my lack of practice was evident. Mrs. Rogers was clearly frustrated and rightly so because she had gone over the lesson with me a couple of weeks ago. It was obvious that I hadn't been practicing because I was committing the identical mistakes as before. Her patience abruptly ended, and she lashed out at me for my mistakes in front of the other waiting students.

As her frustration grew, so did the decibel level of her voice and tone. She was pissed off and really didn't care who knew it. As I left the piano lesson that evening, I wondered how many more of these sessions I could take. My terror of taking piano lessons, a consequence of a whimsical thought expressed several months earlier now felt like an ever-tightening noose around my neck.

My dislike of piano lessons increased when some of my neighborhood friends teased me about my new adventure. What was up with me? Had I given up riding my bike and grabbing the back of a truck without the driver knowing I was getting a free ride? Were my days as a lookout for my pals when we raided a neighbor's plum and apple trees over? Was I no longer interested in shooting my BB gun at pigeons while they slept in a huge tree at night? Surely spinning the bottle with the neighborhood girls was still in play.

It seemed that whenever I left home to walk to piano lessons, some of my friends were around, just in the nick of time to make fun of "Piano Man." Picture me: very skinny, not the most athletic kid on the block, and the only one taking piano lessons.

The last time I was laughed at and tried to hide my red piano book, I knew I would not return to piano lessons. The relentless teasing, my dislike of the piano, and my humiliating piano lessons were just too much for me at the time.

The next move I made haunted me for a long time, and it still does. I repeatedly lied to my mother, assuring her that I was attending piano lessons, but I spent the two dollars for the lessons on snacks. I made an awful mistake. This sham lasted for at least eight months, until one evening my mother called me from the beauty parlor located on Brickyard Hill in Bessemer, to come and walk home with her.

This request caused no alarm on my part; my mother and I were close and doing different jobs or errands she requested was routine, and usually A-Okay with me. It was a pleasant summer evening, the moon lighting up the night sky.

As I walked into the home of my mom's hairdresser, Mrs. Willie Mae Green, the room went silent. I noticed a look of exasperation and fatigue on my mom's face. I had never witnessed this look before. It was as if she'd been hit in the stomach without any warning. She appeared almost lifeless, no energy whatsoever. I had seen my mom tired before and upset with my brother, father, and me, or some combination thereof, but never an expression of defeat like this.

I soon found out why. As I entered the hairdresser's shop, my mother sat on the opposite side of the room from my piano instructor, Mrs. Rogers, who looked smug and self-satisfied. Busted. No words necessary. Their facial expressions told the tale and revealed the culprit. I had achieved this disgraceful moment all by myself.

The walk home, just ten minutes away, seemed to take an eternity. My mother didn't say much. Her disappointment spoke volumes. I had crossed the line by lying to her. She stated that she couldn't believe I could lie, cheat, steal, and then conceal my actions for an extended period of time. This part of my personality wasn't something she'd seen or experienced before, and she definitely didn't plan to experience it again.

If she'd wanted to strike back at me physically, she could have told my father what I'd done. But she didn't. It was our secret. She knew he would have really put a hurt on me for this unthinkable act of betrayal. Even with my betrayal, she remained my shield and protector.

My father would have gone into a rage, and I would have suffered a severe beating. Factor in his probable lack of support for Mom buying the piano in the first place, and the picture gets uglier. I'm sure my mother made the final decision about buying the piano and trumpet, with or without my father's permission. Nothing cost too much for her sons. He would have been correct though, if he thought I wouldn't follow through on my intent and commitment to learn to play the piano.

Things were eerily quiet for the rest of that evening. For some absurd reason, I thought the next day everything would be close to normal between my mom and me. When I got up that morning and walked into the kitchen where she was cooking breakfast, I tried talking with her. She declined to say a word.

Finally, I asked, "What's wrong, Mama?"

"Please don't bother me." She also told me she didn't know if she could ever trust me again. That statement shattered me. I ran out of the kitchen and into the woods behind our house, crying my eyes out. What had I done? Would my caring, loving, trusting relationship with my mom ever return? I really didn't know. It was the worst possible punishment, which I had clearly earned.

I received the silent treatment from my mom for a few more days. I stayed out of her way and was an especially dutiful son. Eventually, the icy relationship with my mom thawed. Things actually became better between us. She knew I had learned a most valuable lesson about lying and keeping one's word. My mother was someone who, when angry or disappointed, would express her feelings and then move on. Fortunately, she didn't hold a grudge, despite what I'd done.

This experience is one I often recall, because after going through it, I realized in my own mind that "Bought sense is the best sense" especially if you don't make the same mistake twice.

17 THE MANY SIDES OF MACK LONG/WILL LONG

MACK LONG, AKA Will Long, our father, was a very prideful man. He was known for his sense of style and extensive wardrobe. As a young man in his 20s and 30s, my father wore tailor-made suits and shirts. He wore Dobbs hats and had boxes of them for summer and winter. For a period of time, he wore garters on his socks to keep them just so. His shoes were always shined, either by him or the shoeshine man, Jackie Boy, in downtown Bessemer.

One summer Saturday evening as he prepared to go out and about, I noticed he pulled from his right pants pocket a round, maroon, powder puff to wipe away the sweat from his brow. Legend has it that when my father travelled to Birmingham by bus from Bessemer, he stood for the entire 30-minute bus ride to keep his pants from getting wrinkled.

The final accent for my father was his extremely generous application of *English Leather* cologne. Long after he had left home, the fragrance of his cologne reminded us of his strong presence.

On the other hand, this prideful Dapper Dan, with a preference for Scotch whiskey, never flinched when he put on his muckers, as he called them, to do the kind of work that others in our neighborhood wouldn't do, including digging ditches. The most important legacy my father passed on to my brother and me was his work ethic and his personal philosophy about work. Our father believed that if someone really wanted to work, they could always find a job. It may not have been the job they wanted, but it was a job.

Our father took great pride in always being in a position to work and support his family. Anything less than that was unacceptable. No excuses, lack of education or training, or commuting distance to the job ever prevented him from working. Not even overt discrimination, which was problematic and ongoing for a Black man with a limited education in the segregated South, was an excuse to not work. For our father, that was his reality, and he faced it every day of his work life. His core belief was that there was always a job out there. It might take him weeks or months to find it, but he would. He always did.

My father used to joke that taxi drivers were the laziest workers on earth because they sat down all day. In his world if you weren't standing, stooping, digging, moving, or lifting, you weren't really working. My father literally worked in the muck and mire, ditches, and trenches. There were no coffee breaks, maybe a lunch break. The work stopped at the end of the day when the big boss, not the straw boss, said the day was over. If anyone complained, the solution was easy—he was fired. That was the end of it.

As a child growing up, there were several mysteries surrounding my father. One was his name. Sometimes he would introduce himself as Mack Long and other times he would be Will Long. But the one thing that never changed was the way he introduced himself. Regardless of the first name he used, it would go something like this: "Hi, my name is Mack, (pause), Mack Long." When I worked in the field of adult corrections as a probation and parole officer in Seattle during the early '70s, a colleague of mine, Ray Messegee, pointed out I did the same thing when introducing myself. "Hi, my name is Merritt, (pause), Merritt Long." I continue this practice today.

After hearing my father use two different names to introduce himself, I asked my mother why he did this. She said my father had applied for a job at the Pullman Standard, the plant that manufactured box cars for trains. When he initially applied for work at the plant, using the name

Mack Long, he was turned down. Jobs at this plant during the 1960s paid good wages. They were plum jobs for Blacks with limited formal training and education like my father.

My mom said my father was determined to get a job at the Pullman Standard, because he knew this would be a real benefit to our family. A few months later, he applied for another job at the plant. This time he used the name Will Long. He was hired. The second time around his "will" couldn't be denied.

The biggest mystery about my father involved his parents. I never heard him utter one word about his father and mother. It was as though they never existed. It was like he was born an adult, no childhood, hardly any formal education, and no stories or memories from childhood. His father was White, his mother Black. His six siblings came from the same parents.

My mother told me my father's only memory was of sitting on a white horse and there was a White man standing beside him. That was the sum total of what my father knew about his father. I was later told that his father's name was Christopher Wedgeworth. The Wedgeworths were from a prominent family and a town in Alabama was named after them. Years later my niece, LaTonja Long Hunter, found a 1910 Federal census report listing my father and his siblings as Wedgeworth's children.

Even less information was known about his mother. According to the census report, her name was May Long. I've been told she was a very dark-skinned woman who later married a dark-skinned African American. As a result of that marriage, I've heard my family talk about Black Long children born from that union.

The children born from the relationship between Christopher Wedgeworth and my father's mother were sometimes referred to as the White Longs. In talking with my father's oldest brother's son, Bill Long, he mentioned there existed a family dynamic where the so-called Black Longs felt the so-called White Longs didn't care for them because of their darker skin.

My father didn't say much to my brother and me as we were growing up, other than to discipline us when we did something he considered wrong or inconsistent with what he had asked us to do. Most often the punishment didn't fit the crime. If we spoke to him in a tone that he thought was disrespectful, he could and would become irate with veins protruding from his neck. His fair, almost white skin would turn beat red, and he screamed at my brother and me as if we'd just burned the house down.

Our father used his belt, not to spank or discipline us, but to beat us. I don't recall what was worse, the actual beating or the anger and seemingly out-of-body experience our father would have when he was laying blow after blow wherever he could on our bodies. He momentarily became a madman. Maybe all of his frustrations of not having a father, limited schooling, or marketable work skills emerged. Maybe he felt caught in the middle of two worlds, one Black, one White. Some Black people resented him because he looked White, and some Whites resented him because they thought he wanted to be White. Eventually, being caught in the middle took its toll on my father.

For years, and I do mean years, the best thing I remembered about my father was when he wasn't at home. The house had a certain calmness. When he was present, an eruption could occur at any time for little or no reason.

My father may be the most complex person I've ever known. My memories of him stir emotions ranging from love to hate. He could be very mean and even violent, especially if he'd been drinking. Although Ken and I suffered beatings with his favorite choice of torture—his belt— my mother bore the brunt of his violent outbursts.

The one thing that kept me from hating my father was my mother always saying, especially when he would do and say something very upsetting and vulgar, "Your father's doing the best he can." On the other hand, when my brother and I did or said something incorrect, our mother would say, "Your father doesn't know any better, but the two of you should know better." She wasn't trying to rationalize or make excuses for him. She honestly felt that way. And believe it or not, she loved him.

My father's bouts with violence usually occurred after he'd been drinking. He was a tireless, hard-working man who never drank during the week. It was almost always on Friday or Saturday nights. Sunday was off limits, because he would be recovering from his hangover and getting ready for work on Monday.

What a blessing it was that he was such a hard worker and was always, and I mean always, committed to not missing a day of work. This same man, whose picture could be placed in the dictionary to represent "unquestionable work ethic," was the same man capable of verbal, physical, and emotional abuse. A Jekyll and Hyde character, with Hyde lurking just beneath the surface.

One Saturday night stands out from the others. When my father came home after a night of serious drinking, he argued with my mother, about what I don't remember. My brother, mother, and I huddled together in the living room of our house on Gladstone Alley, and we heard the drawer in the kitchen that contained the spoons, forks, and knives fall to the floor. Seconds after this explosion of noise, my mother said, "Let's go, I think Mack is trying to get a knife."

The three of us left in our pajamas in the early morning to go to my mother's parents' house. They lived on Exeter Avenue, just ten minutes away on foot.

The night was pitch black with no streetlights, moon, or stars. The gentle yet strong hands of our mother led us to safety. When she looked back to see if our father was behind us, Ken and I looked, too. We repeated this synchronized action once more before arriving on the doorsteps of Grandma's house.

The day after one of my father's drinking sprees, my mother handled him with kid gloves, spoke in a soft voice, and had food aplenty at the ready. Depending on his condition, she helped him remove his clothes. First his shoes, then shirt, slacks, and jacket if he'd been wearing one.

He would sometimes without any reason or warning become violent, lash out at my mother, and try to hurt her. First with his words, then with his fist. My mother always defended herself. She was no one's punching bag. As Ken and I got older, we did whatever we could to stop this madness. Our timely interventions always kept him at bay. I think we secretly wanted him to act out in some way so we would have an excuse to punish him for his misdeeds. Fortunately, a confrontation like that never happened.

Around 1966, my father quit drinking to excess, which meant his emotional and violent outbursts also diminished. As my brother and I passed into manhood and came closer to entering the work world, the tormented dynamics of our relationship with our father changed.

Our father looked at us differently when we graduated from college. He never said the words, but by the way he looked at us, and started to behave, like teasing around with my brother and me, there was a major positive difference. Also, I think over time and with age, the effects of hard physical work and drinking to excess had caused him to run out of gas.

My father took his own life when he was 76 years old. Years later, I learned he had suffered from depression. Treatment "back in the day" for depression was very limited compared to now when mental health afflictions are considered diseases to be treated, not feared. Excessive drinking and alcoholism were commonplace in Bessemer, Alabama, even considered normal behavior.

I think I can say our relationship had transformed to where we had become friends. I think I had, finally, earned his respect as an independent, hardworking individual, who was experiencing success in the world. A world he had been shut out of. At last, through his sons, he could experience and enjoy some of the opportunities that had eluded him.

. . .

Sometimes my father's racial ambiguity resulted in situations that seemed like a movie script. One such situation occurred when two White salesmen made a cold call to our residence, selling burial plots to the then Whites-only Elmwood Cemetery in Birmingham, Alabama.

Because of my father's light, almost white complexion, some of his friends—men and women alike—jokingly teased him about being White. This was okay with him if it was a friend of his in the truest sense of the word; but if someone called him White and wasn't a good friend and made the statement in a mocking tone, he would take offense. My mother usually intervened to avoid a physical confrontation between my father and the offending party.

The two salesmen selling cemetery plots stopped at our home, assuming my father was White because of his light skin. It would have been extremely unusual, if not impossible, to sell a plot in Elmwood Cemetery to an African American during this period of time, because we weren't allowed to be buried there. My father thought the salesmen were new on the job and, in their enthusiasm to make a sale, hadn't realized they were in the Black section of Exeter Avenue.

My father passed for White that day as the dollar signs blurred the salesmen's eyes and made him who they wanted him to be. My father said he wanted to purchase two cemetery plots at Elmwood—one for him and one for his wife, of course. The salesmen signed him up on the spot and the deal was done.

My father made a financial commitment and signed a contract with specific pay-off terms. This unilateral action by my father was unusual, because on all matters relating to contracts and money management for our household, my mother had primary if not sole responsibility. My father's formal education was limited. His role at that time was as the primary provider. He relished this role, and he easily and quickly turned over his paycheck to my mother. He would work his regular schedule, as well as overtime and double-time whenever he had the opportunity.

When my mother came home later that day and learned her husband, my father, had purchased two cemetery plots at the all-White graveyard of Elmwood, she was shocked, pleased, and amused in that order.

She was shocked because she couldn't believe her husband had made a major decision and purchase without talking with her. She wasn't upset with him for making the purchase because she knew this was a freak occurrence and unlikely to happen again anytime soon.

At the same time, she was pleased and amused that her husband had taken the bold step of purchasing the plots, knowing the salesmen probably thought he was White. My father, like my brother and me, had heard my mother speak with disdain about the cemetery where Blacks and only Blacks were buried. She said the cemetery was poorly maintained, which she knew firsthand since her father and relatives were buried there.

The cemetery resembled a wasteland of throw-aways. The rocky and uneven terrain was overrun with weeds and overgrown plants. There were no shrubs, just patches of grass intermixed with the rocks. There was a general lack of upkeep.

The day following the sale, the "plot" really thickened when my father received a call from one of the salesmen who sold him the two plots. According to my father, the salesman was calling because he had mistakenly sold him two plots that shouldn't have been listed and he wanted to buy them back. My father told him he wasn't interested in selling the plots back and couldn't understand how a mistake like that could happen.

Although I'm not sure what actually occurred, I believe once the salesmen returned to their office, they realized they'd made a huge mistake by selling plots to a Black man they thought was White. I'm sure the cemetery owners weren't happy they'd just voluntarily and unknowingly integrated the cemetery and violated its own practices and the law of the land at that time.

Once again, one of the eager salesmen called my father and tried to wrangle his way out of the signed contract by offering to reimburse him for his down payment if he would release Elmwood from its signed contract. I don't know the reason the salesman gave for wanting to void the deal. Our father listened politely and refused his offer.

Of course, my father knew what they knew, and no way would he give up his right to what he had lawfully purchased. This cat-and-mouse game went on for a couple of months. It finally reached the point where representatives of Elmwood Cemetery offered my father full reimbursement for what he had paid, plus an additional amount of money.

I never learned how much the plots cost, or the additional funds offered, because for our parents it was never about the money or trying to make a profit, it was about pride, dignity, and respect. Also, my father knew how much his wife detested the then Black cemetery given its awful condition.

Our mother was thrilled knowing she would be laid to rest at Elmwood Cemetery. There was no way Mack Long or Will Long would relinquish those two plots. They believed they shouldn't have to be buried in a field of neglect. Elmwood Cemetery was just the opposite of the Black cemetery—well-maintained, a carpet of green grass, no rocky hills or roads, shrubbery carefully planted and meticulously pruned and cared for.

Today, Elmwood Cemetery is totally integrated and has been since 1970 when the family of a Black soldier, who died in Vietnam, won a lawsuit in federal court to force the cemetery to allow their son to be buried there.

My mother and father, despite racial discrimination, rest side-by-side in a place that once prohibited their burial. They simply wanted a decent and comfortable resting place.

. . .

The raindrops coming down that hot summer's day were so large, they plopped with a force that couldn't be ignored. It wasn't a misty rain, but more of a torrential rainstorm, scary and exciting at the same time. Scary because we didn't know whether the wind, thunder, and lightning were very far behind. Exciting because this was the first time, ever, that our father had allowed my brother and I to play in the rain.

This wasn't like our father at all, especially if he thought fun was involved. Typically, it was our mother who gave us permission to go to the local Black movie theater, carnival, Monday night high school football game, baseball game, or an out-of-nowhere opportunity to go for a joy ride on the back of Mr. Macon Patton's truck.

The intensity of the heat, our father's actions coupled with the sweltering humidity, made this summer day, with the rains from the heavens, one to remember for the rest of my life.

Ken and I made a mad dash out our front door before our father could change his mind. What made this moment so special for us was that our father—"Doctor No," "Mister Mean,"—had signed off and authorized our "release papers" himself. This was historic, a first of firsts.

Ken and I wore short pants, with no shirts or shoes as we ran and jumped in the rain. The rain continued to pour like upended buckets of water, but without the crackling of thunder, flashes of lightning, and screeching wind. Added to our good fortune was that, for as far as the eye could see in both directions on our avenue, we were the only two kids playing outside in the rain.

Suddenly, without saying a word, Ken went off script and leaped into a two-foot-deep ditch of dirty water. He was pretending he was swimming, and the ditch was now his personal swimming pool. Because of segregation, neither Ken nor I had ever been in a public swimming pool. You'd never have known this by looking at Ken and his official-looking strokes. He was having the time of his life, his smile electric. He looked so free, without a care in the world.

What seemed like a day of fun and frivolity of playing in the rain with no cares in the world quickly became a nightmare.

Once our father saw Ken "swimming" in the ditch, our front door slammed open and we could hear and feel the fury from our father from 15 feet away. He was livid. He had gone from zero to sixty in a matter of seconds. That wasn't a good thing. Our father yelled out as though he had his own personal megaphone and barked, "Kenny, you better get your butt out of that ditch and come home, and I mean now." Instantly, we both knew "Mister Mean" had returned, and we were in store for good whippings.

We were stunned by our sudden change in fortune. Our father probably thought, I tried to do something nice for you two ingrates by giving you an inch, and you took a dangerous mile.

Once we came inside, our father flew into a rage and beat Ken. The punishment didn't fit the crime. It was as if Ken's action gave our father a legitimate reason to hurt him, above and beyond what was required to make a point. I didn't understand where all of this venom came from. Maybe he had some other demons he was dealing with, but his cruelty is what I still remember.

Because I didn't get into the ditch, I was spared a beating that day. It's still painful to relive this memory of my brother's cries of anguish, and the sound of his voice as he asked, "What did I do so wrong?" I felt guilty that I didn't receive a whipping as well. I can never forgive my father for that barbaric act.

. . .

I had arrived home after my sixth-grade class. It was near the end of the school year, and the summer sun was starting to make its presence felt.

As soon as I opened the front door, my six-foot tall father stood there looking at least ten feet tall. He loomed even larger than ever. His appearance at the front door frightened me. He must have been waiting for me to come home, but why? My father wanted me to turn around and go to the grocery store to purchase a particular bar of soap. He told me the name of the soap to buy, but between him telling me and my arrival at the grocery store, I forgot.

This soap was the one he had used and preferred since previously working in the coal and ore mines, and now working at the Pullman Standard Company. He wanted this soap because it was effective in removing the dirt, grit, and grime from his body. He was extremely adamant that I purchase this soap, and this soap only. I felt sure my father detected my lack of enthusiasm for this errand, which meant walking back down the hill in the hot sun to pick up a bar of soap. My non-verbal cues must have alerted him, because he said, "You better get me the right soap!"

Over time, I had learned to measure my father's bad moods on a scale of one to five. One was the best of the worst. And this day, he was trending to level four with the distinct possibility of maxing out with a five—the worst of the worst.

I placed my schoolbooks on the living room couch and set off to the grocery store on my soap quest. I was familiar with the type of soap my father wanted, although I hadn't purchased it before.

Arriving at the local grocery store, I went to the soap section. I looked at several rows of soap before zeroing in on about three possible soap bars. Which was the magical one? The more I looked, the less certain I became. Since going home with no soap wasn't an option, I made a calculated guess I hoped would save me from the wrath of my father.

When I returned home and gave my father the soap I'd purchased, he was incensed. He immediately accused me of getting the wrong soap on purpose, because I didn't want to go to the grocery store. He spun around, fuming, and said, "I am going to get my belt and whip your butt."

You would have thought I'd shot someone. I started to leave the house. When I heard him say, "You better not leave," my quick steps turned into a fast run out the front door and down the steps. The more he called my name, the faster I ran until I was out of his voice range. I'd decided that getting a whipping for purchasing the wrong bar of soap was out of line. I refused to accept these arbitrary whippings anymore.

I decided that when my mother came home from work that afternoon, I'd go home and make my case to her. Did it make sense to physically punish someone over a bar of soap? My self-imposed banishment lasted about three hours. I returned home about 5:00 p.m. and explained to her what had happened with my father and me. She listened intently to my story with no questions. I laid down on the glider in the screened side porch, relieved and glad to be home under the witness protection program of my mom.

From the side porch, I heard my mother and father talking about what had happened earlier. My mom told my father that I'd been in school all day, and it wasn't unreasonable for me to be tired and not want to go to the grocery store. She stated that she doubted I'd purchased the wrong soap on purpose. My father said because my mother was always sticking up for us, we'd become spoiled and didn't want to do anything to help out around the house.

The soap incident was the last time my father attempted to punish me by sheer brute force. I had been cleansed forever.

. . .

The sound of my father's voice was troubling that day when he came home from work at about 2:00 p.m. He walked into the kitchen through the back door and as soon as he saw my mother's face, he said the following words that I'd never heard him say before or again, "Kate, I couldn't take it anymore." I didn't immediately know what that meant, other than it wasn't something good.

Our father had been working construction on a major housing project about a half mile from our home. This type of temporary construction job was the kind of job he was able to obtain after he'd been laid off from his permanent job at the Pullman-Standard plant of Bessemer, a company that made train boxcars.

I was in the doorway of the kitchen when my father walked by, and I noticed his shirt wasn't tucked in his pants. Although he wore what he referred to as muckers—work clothes accustomed to being in the muck, mire, and dirt—he still tucked his work shirt into his pants. Even in muckers, my father took pride in his appearance.

My mother was home and preparing dinner when he unexpectedly arrived home several hours earlier than usual. As she turned around to greet my father, she saw something was wrong. Her expressive eyes looked pained and worried. I could see her asking herself, before she asked him, what might be wrong. Finally, she spoke. "Mack, what happened?"

I felt uncomfortable being in the kitchen during this conversation, and quietly left the area. I sat down in the living room, still close by. Our house was so small, which meant everything and everybody was nearby. It was about a thousand square feet with two bedrooms, dining room, living room, kitchen, bathroom, and a screened side porch.

My father told my mother that he'd been digging a ditch for over an hour, and it seemed no matter how he dug the ditch his White supervisor wasn't satisfied. My father was an extremely hard-working man, and he took pride in his work, regardless of the job. After a certain point, he said the supervisor started calling him names and screaming at him for apparently no reason.

That August summer day was one of those that was so hot, mothers kept their kids indoors to shield them from the scorching sun.

Even the strength and durability of iron, if hammered on enough, will wear out, my mother used to say. She felt our father, her husband, had reached the point where "iron wears out." He saw two choices: one, knock the shit out of that name-calling "peckerwood," or two, quit the job. He decided to quit and come home. I'd never known my father to quit anything he tried, especially a job. His creed was, if you wanted to work, you could always find a job; it may not be the job you wanted, but if you wanted to work you could always find a job.

This wasn't something he just talked about. He lived this philosophy throughout his life. In the ring of work, he'd never been knocked out and had to walk away from a job. He wasn't wired that way. Supporting his family was his paramount duty. So, for him to quit a job, even under horrible circumstances was an unspeakable act. However, his dignity had been breached; he couldn't go any further. Now, he stood in his home, apologizing to his wife because he felt he had let her down.

I rarely, if ever, observed moments of tenderness or physical affection between parents, but the painfully humiliating experience for my father ironically led to a touching and loving moment.

As I peeked around the corner, my mother was hugging my father as tears rolled down his cheeks. She comforted him by slowly and softly saying over and over, "It's okay, Mack. It's okay, Mack. It's going to be okay."

I went outside in the stifling heat, knowing everything was okay, and for me in some ways, better than ever. I was so proud and happy for my mother and father during this real-life tragedy. My mother and father showed true care and affection for one another at an intense level when everything seemed so bleak. It made me feel good.

How ironic and tragic that a man felt down, because he walked away from a job as a result of verbal abuse. Even though my father was digging a trench for a construction job, he still retained his pride and sense of self. Tragic because, in addition to quitting—a word not in my father's vocabulary—he experienced the pain of letting down his family, especially his wife. Fortunately, my father's self-worth and sense of dignity won over personal verbal abuse at any price. If he'd stayed, I think he would have left part of himself in that three-foot trench forever.

I remember seeing Black men similar to my father in age, education, and work experience, and some appeared to have left their pride and self-respect in a ditch, trench, or the back of a garbage truck, never to be seen or heard from again. Sometimes, the price of doing the right economic thing pales in comparison to the long-term psychological harm that scars one forever.

18 LIFELONG FRIENDS

ALVIN JIMMY MAULDIN and I had known each other basically all of our lives when the defining moment in our relationship occurred. We were both twelve years old and sixth graders at Hard Elementary School in Bessemer.

But before I go there, I need to tell you about the game we created when we were six years old. We called it "Underground Travel." We literally played under our house, which included a system of roads that took us wherever we wanted to go.

These roads were built out of silky-smooth cocoa-colored dirt. When Alvin, our mutual friend Vincent DePaul Allen, my brother Ken, and I went traveling on these make-believe underground roads, we didn't have to worry about anything, especially the color of our skin.

On our knees under the house with the sound of footsteps above us, spider webs dangling here and there, and with the slow drips of water seeping through wooden planks, our world was magical and mysterious. For hours on end, we had this time together during which no one seemed to know or care where we were. We vanished and entered a new world, a world where things such as:

- Water fountains for Colored and Whites didn't exist.

- A seat on the bus was a personal choice.

- Instead of having one movie theater to attend for Colored only, any movie theater could be your theater.

- Baseball could be played on the Whites only manicured playground.

- Hamburgers could be purchased from inside the restaurant, not from the back of the hamburger joint.

When we traveled these roads, whether turning left, right, or even in reverse, we went wherever we wanted. And when we got there, whether for a drink of water, riding a bus, watching a movie, playing baseball, or enjoying a tasty hamburger, the only thing that mattered was finding the right road to get to our next destination.

However, years later, the days of Alvin, Vincent, my brother Ken, and me playing Underground Travel was a distant memory after our sixth-grade class, taught by Mrs. Emmons, defeated Alvin's class, taught by Mrs. Colquitt, in a game of touch football. Alvin was furious after the game as we lined up at the entrance of the school. Alvin was so incensed over his male classmates' loss, he challenged our entire class to fight him. He believed the touch football loss was a fluke and there was no way we should have won. To further make his point, Alvin stated he could kick our ass on a one-on-one basis, or he could beat all of us at once if anyone had the nerve and courage to fight him.

After Alvin's outlandish challenge to our entire class, we were shocked. My classmates and I hadn't even had time to savor our victory, when out of nowhere came this challenge, not just about the touch football game, but to our manhood. Alvin's pride and self-respect had been eroded by this simple win of touch football. Not even tackle. Touch. When you view yourself as "King of the Hill," regardless of the game being played, loss isn't acceptable. He decided he needed to show his dominance and kick some butt, and it really didn't matter whose butt.

Once the gauntlet had been thrown down, our class became eerily quiet, not even a whisper. Alvin was a known brawler and was willing to take a punch to land a punch. One's size or reputation didn't matter; he was fearless. In addition, he intimidated with his loud voice, facial expressions, and self-assuredness. No matter what price he had to pay, he was going to come out on the winning side of the battle. The bigger the crowd became, the more bombastic he became. He relished the spotlight.

However, in the classroom and in the academic ring, he was generally quiet and wanted to be invisible. But, in the fighting ring, he was front and center and roared like a lion.

Alvin had a couple of nicknames. One was "Wop" and the other was "Good Ni Boy." How ironic, I thought. I wondered to myself where the "good" in the "boy" had gone, as he was about to reign terror on an unlikely subject, me.

Here I was, Mr. Goody Two Shoes, almost afraid of my own shadow, but I felt the need to speak up and not let Alvin's challenge to our class go unanswered. Alvin thought his class had more tough guys than ours, and he couldn't understand how his team had been defeated.

Before I knew it, I had an out-of-body experience and my other self, whom I had seldom if ever seen, emerged out of nowhere. First, I jumped out of the class line where I was standing near the back. Alvin was front and center, still ranting about our accidental victory. I slowly made my way toward him and my right and left hands had magically turned into fists. Before I knew it, I stood directly across from him. When he saw me, he looked as shocked and surprised as I felt. Like me, he couldn't believe that of all my classmates, I had dared to accept his challenge. Alvin started to smile. He immediately suggested I get back in line to avoid the whupping he was about to put on me if I continued to pretend I wanted to do battle with him.

Maybe I didn't like being called a zero to my face and in front of everyone. It was like a public shaming. Alvin called me Bub, which was one of several nicknames I had. Alvin, in his own way, reminded me of our long history and how on many occasions we'd played as kids with minimum hassles. As the years passed, we spent less and less time together, but our relationship remained cordial.

Being a fan of Friday night boxing matches, my first instinct was to move away from Alvin and to continually circle around him. Another way to look at this, of course, was that I was afraid of Alvin and didn't want to engage in physical contact, unless it was inevitable. He became infuriated with me and demanded I stop running around in circles and fight like a real man. Seriously, I had no intention of fighting Alvin. The more I circled around him, the angrier he became, and some of his own classmates started to laugh. Brain and speed, at least for the moment, was winning over brawn.

Fortunately, the class bell rang, which meant the "fight" was over and everyone had to go inside to their classes.

What a relief. My prayers had been answered. The fight was over, I hadn't been hit, and my personal pride was still intact. However, as Alvin and I walked up the steps to return to class, he said that he still was going to kick my ass for running away from him, which prevented him from kicking my ass in the first place.

Fortunately, after school that day, our altercation was history. Alvin had his sights on someone else. Many years later, we had some great laughs about our "fight." He often reminded me how lucky I was that he hadn't caught me.

Alvin's mother liked the fact we were friends, because from the ninth grade through high school graduation, he attended classes consistently. We hung out with Richard Long, Richard Horn, Wayne Hill, Augustus Chambers, Ronald Banks, and David Hood. The social aspects of this group meant a lot to Alvin, and if attending school on a regular basis to maintain these relationships was required, school it was. Once he was your friend, he was always your friend.

Alvin had a quick and wicked sense of humor. On one occasion when I stopped by his house, unannounced, he was holding a telephone over a record player that was playing some jazz music. This was several years after our almost fisticuffs, and we were good friends. It was 1963, and we were in the 11th grade. I was surprised because I didn't think Alvin was a jazz fan. I was puzzled why he was holding the phone over the record player.

He looked up at me with a sheepish grin on his face, and in a quiet whisper said, "Soothing music to quiet the angry beast." He then grinned with a million-dollar smile.

I was totally in the dark. I had no idea what he was talking about. He shortly hung up the phone and told me he was playing the jazz music for the boyfriend of the young woman who he'd literally kidnapped and brought home with him for a couple of days. The boyfriend wasn't a happy camper.

The next day, I heard gunshots ring out on our avenue. Alvin and I lived one house apart from each other for about 15 years. The angry boyfriend was in the neighborhood to reclaim his girlfriend. He had positioned himself across the street between the houses of Mr. and Mrs. Macon Patton and Mr. Sheff. When he saw Alvin on the front porch, he took his best shot at him. Fortunately, he missed. Later that evening, Alvin suggested to his new friend that she should return home to make sure her boyfriend didn't get hurt. The girlfriend left under the cloak of darkness, returned home, and Alvin's legend and reputation increased. He was unscathed and experienced great joy from telling this story to anyone who'd listen. As the story was told again and again, the number of shots fired increased from two to six and the bullets got closer and closer to hitting him, but his quick reflexes and bravery saved the day. Without throwing a punch or pulling a knife or razor to defend himself, Alvin's bewildered foe had retreated into hiding.

Alvin's own well-being was always secondary to "having my back." Alvin knew fighting wasn't my game of choice, while he seemed to relish moments of conflict and potential fights. Alvin seemed to get a little taller and his features became more pronounced when he was ready to do battle. I don't remember him provoking a fight, but I never saw him walk away from one.

Alvin would be the last to admit it, but I think my standing up, or more truthfully, my running from him that day in the sixth grade was our connection point for the rest of our lives. You might be tempted to conclude that Alvin was a bully and always looking for a fight. Not really. Beneath all the bluster, he was an extremely kind-hearted and generous person who always, regardless of the odds, looked out for his friends. I was blessed to be one of them.

I was fortunate growing up to have a wide circle of friends, Alvin aka Wop, among them. We had delightful, innovative, comical, and astounding nicknames in our group.

To appreciate the smorgasbord of names, I've listed several below.

Animal-Related Nicknames
Ratman, Rat Killer, Dog, Dog Catcher, Deputy Dog, Crow, Coon, Pig, Piglets, Rooster, Bull Tail, Frog, Froggie, Freddie Frog Stank Garly

Insect-Related Nicknames
Bumble Bee, Fly

Large in Stature-Related Nicknames
Tree Top, Big Man, Lard Ass, Lead Belly, Blimp

Small in Stature-Related Nicknames
Straw, Stick, Stick Man, Slim, Boney Maroney, Little Man, Little Brother (my mother's name for me)

Color of Skin Color-Related Nicknames
Red, Ole Yellow, Blue, Black Bugger, Smokey, Shoe Polish, White Boy

Hustler Type Nicknames
Slick, Fastman, House, Housecoat, Houseman, Barnyard Pimp, Ronnie Too Bad

Your Guess Is as Good as Mine Related Nicknames
Lowdown, Wop, Applehead, Sheriff, Pun Jam, Punza, Pun Jam Jellies and Preserves, Bay Boy, Scrap Iron, Bup (me), Bub (me), Man (my brother Ken, pronounced "Main"), Brogs, Jackie Wilson, Arthur Prysock, Bay James, Poot, Fart, Good Ni Boy

Nicknames in my hometown and the South, in general, was an art form, not always understood but always enjoyed.

. . .

What started out as an easy way to escape from my sixth-grade class at Hard Elementary School, go home and miss the rigors of class didn't end up that way.

The rainy season had arrived that February 1958. The accumulation of rain over the weekend soaked the school grounds, puddles formed everywhere, and the rain continued to fall. Our elementary school resembled a small prison from the outside. There were no flowers, shrubs, trees, sidewalks, benches, chairs, or even grass. We did have a slide with sand at the bottom and a teeter-totter, as well as a long slab of concrete about 125 feet long and 5 feet wide. We often used this concrete strip to run sprints from one end to the other. It was usually two of us racing with the understanding that we'd run side by side, at a leisurely pace one way, then when we turned around to run the other way, we'd run at full speed. It was all done with good sportsmanship. I don't recall anyone breaking the informal rules of how the race was run.

No one complained about what we didn't have. We made the best of the situation by playing with one another, which mainly meant pushing and shoving each other around in a fun way. We also chased each other and played tag. Sometimes, a group of girls would chase one of the boys. If they caught you, down you went with all of them laughing uncontrollably. This happened to me a couple of times when I was in the third grade, and it scared me. I received a few bumps and bruises from their capture. Following recess, I was taken to the fourth-grade classroom where a few band aids were applied, and then all was well.

Once the fourth-grade teacher said, "Is this who all the girls were chasing?" I realized the question wasn't about identifying the object of the chase, which was me, but it was like, "You must be kidding, they were chasing you?"

My good friend and cousin, Ronald Banks, aka Ronnie Too Bad, was a fun-loving, adventurous guy who'd try almost anything. He taught himself how to cut hair by practicing on friends like me as guinea pigs. He played baseball with the ninth and tenth graders by learning to be the catcher on their baseball team. Ronnie was a good hitter, even though he held his bat in a cross-handed position. In high school, his grandparents purchased a 1966 Chevrolet. Believe it or not, no driving lessons for Ronnie Too Bad. He taught himself how to drive and never had an accident.

Ronnie's grandparents raised him and treated him like a king. There wasn't anything they wouldn't do for him, and they had the money to do so. They loved his spirit and lust for life. He made them laugh and created fun memories for them.

One winter's day, Ronnie came up with a plan to legitimately be excused from class and go home. His master stroke of genius was to take place during recess. He purposely jumped over and over again in the puddles of water surrounding the school until his pants became very wet. He figured that if he got wet enough, our teacher, Mrs. Emmons, would allow him to go home and change his clothes. Surely, she wouldn't let him stay in class in his wet clothes. Ronnie lived on what was called Brickyard Hill, about a 15-minute walk from school.

After he thought he was wet enough, Ronnie went upstairs to Mrs. Emmons' classroom. When he got her attention, he didn't say a word. He just looked down at his extremely wet jeans and pulled his jeans up just enough for her to see his soaking wet socks and squeaky, soggy shoes. He added a few well-timed shivers, coughs, and sneezes for effect. Masterful, I thought. Ronnie played it out perfectly. Ronnie Too Bad was making the magic happen.

Mrs. Emmons, after witnessing this performance and without Ronnie even making his request, demanded that he leave school immediately and go home and change his clothes before he caught a cold. She also suggested he have lunch while at home, because the lunch period was in 30 minutes and he would miss it. After he finished lunch at home, Mrs. Emmons said he should come directly back to school.

Ronnie Too Bad walked past me as I stood there in shock, having watched his Academy Award winning performance. He looked over toward me with his back to Mrs. Emmons, gave me a wink, and with a big smile on his face, headed for home.

I sat at my desk, thinking about how I could come up with a scheme like Ronnie to be able to leave school and go home. I didn't bring my lunch that day, so I had to go to the lunchroom to eat. Perfect, I thought as our class was dismissed. I started walking to the lunchroom by first standing in the pouring rain for a minute or two. Afterwards, I found the deepest, biggest puddles to splash around in. I entered the lunchroom and quickly gobbled a ham sandwich and potato chips for lunch.

After leaving the lunchroom, I again stood in the pouring rain for a minute or two, happily splashed in a couple of puddles and imagined my slow walk home after I pulled this off. I was pretty wet and very pleased with myself.

When I entered the classroom, Mrs. Emmons was sitting at her desk, grading papers while classmates who had brought their lunches were eating. The classroom was very quiet. As I walked toward her, I noticed that when she saw me, she frowned. I suddenly felt as though I was walking in cement. I wanted to turn around, but I couldn't. As she looked at me, I thought she might be wondering if I was dumb enough to try this tactic after Ronnie's success, and would she say, "I thought you were a little smarter than that."

I knew I'd been busted in front of God and everyone, but what could I do at this point other than make the request to go home. By now the entire class was watching me make a total fool out of myself. I tried to sweeten my request by saying I was only ten minutes away and could return to class in about twenty minutes. I was desperate.

After I made my feeble, half-hearted request, Mrs. Emmons looked at me for a moment. Then she pointed to the hot, black pot-bellied stove in the back of the class and told me to stand in front of the stove until I got dry.

While standing in front of the stove wet with soaked socks and shoes,

Ronnie Too Bad returned from his mini-vacation. He avoided looking at me directly because he was so tickled, he could barely control himself. He quickly went to his desk and put his hand over his mouth to keep from laughing out loud. By now, my embarrassment had diminished, and I was starting to laugh at myself when Mrs. Emmons wasn't looking.

I was standing, soaking wet almost from head to toe in front of the raging hot, black pot-bellied stove laughing at my own "feat." I realized there was only one, and I mean one, Ronnie Too Bad. Merritt Too Bad never had a prayer—he just ended up all wet.

During the fall of 1963, our senior year in high school, Ronnie Too Bad, Alvin, and I had been visiting Richard Horn and some other friends on the north side of town. Ronnie drove us home to the south side. As we were traveling down Clarendon Avenue in Too Bad's 1966 Chevrolet, which was lavender with white accents and had whitewall tires with silver rims, the unimaginable happened.

Without any warning, the hood of Ronnie's car came loose and popped up with the entire hood right in front of us, totally blocking our view. Suddenly, our leisurely drive home had turned into a bad movie on black-and-white TV.

Ronnie Too Bad made an all-time Too Bad move. First, he looked at Alvin and me and started to laugh. He was having fun and we were scared to death, cursing with words that our mothers would not approve of. His second move, which convinced us that Too Bad was losing it, was when he took his hands off the steering wheel and thrust them skyward mimicking the front hood. This was followed by an even wilder move when he said, "I can't see anyway, I might as well close my eyes." He did. All the while he laughed until tears rolled down his cheeks.

Seconds later, he opened his eyes, pulled over, braked the car, and then soundly closed the hood. After I recovered, I got a kick out of Ronnie Too Bad's antics. He had a blast, and we simply went along for the ride.

19 PAYING A PRICE FOR GETTING WHAT YOU WANT

As SCHOOL CAME to an end at Hard Elementary School in mid-May, I was excited about the traditional field trip sixth graders took to Dunbar High School prior to starting classes as seventh graders. (We returned to Hard Elementary for eighth grade.) It felt like a rite of passage. Instead of having one teacher for all of our classes, seventh grade began the process of experiencing different teachers for each individual class. For grades one through six, I'd been accustomed to and comfortable with being taught by a single instructor. During an academic school year, I'd become familiar with the expectations of my individual instructors and learned what not to do if you wanted to stay in their good graces.

In addition to two sixth grade classes from Hard Elementary, there would be several more sixth grade classes from surrounding elementary schools also transitioning to seventh grade at Dunbar High. Before I knew it, the excitement of the much-anticipated rite of passage began to ebb. How would I get to know and get along with the new students from outlying school districts? What would happen if I got lost going from one class to another and ended up in the wrong class or was late? My head started to swirl with my anxious thoughts.

Out of the blue, Mrs. Emmons announced that our class wouldn't take the Dunbar field trip. Everyone looked stunned; a hush fell over the classroom. We expected Mrs. Emmons to share the details about the trip. Just as quickly and easily as Mrs. Emmons announced the cancellation, it was over. She segued to another topic as we all shook our heads in disbelief.

Mrs. Emmons was a thoughtful instructor and I thoroughly enjoyed being one of her students. However, after hearing about the cancelled field trip, I decided not to take "no" for an answer. My only recourse would be to talk to the Principal of Hard Elementary, Mr. Walter Branch, Mrs. Emmons' boss.

A few days following Mrs. Emmons' announcement, I passed Mr. Branch's small cubicle of an office under the stairs leading to the second floor. I noticed his open office door, and I looked inside to see him sitting at his desk. Although surprised by my unannounced appearance, he invited me inside. He asked me what was on my mind. I'm sure not many students sought him out. When teachers sent students to the principal, it wasn't to exchange pleasantries or be praised for their outstanding scholarly work.

I asked about the recent cancellation of the traditional sixth grade field trip to Dunbar High School. He seemed surprised the trip had to be cancelled. He also promised to look into the situation.

Several days after my conversation with Principal Branch, Mrs. Emmons asked me to stay after class to meet with her. The school year was almost over, and I'd never been asked to stay after school to meet with Mrs. Emmons. My first thought was that this wasn't a good thing and unfortunately, I was right.

Mrs. Emmons was one of those rare teachers who went above and beyond to recognize the positive attributes of all students even when some experienced academic difficulties. She always endeavored to encourage and motivate her students.

She would recognize students who willingly shared their lunches with those who hadn't brought a lunch from home or lacked the money to purchase one from the school's cafeteria. Mrs. Emmons also praised students for safeguarding younger and smaller students from being bullied by the fourth and fifth graders. The attributes of kindness, selflessness, and courage to speak up were as important to her as academics.

I admired Mrs. Emmons for these traits. She wanted her students to succeed. She wanted them to be able to raise their heads and hands with self-assuredness, inside and outside the classroom. She never made excuses or voiced complaints about the classroom being overheated during the summer or severely cold during the frigid winter months. Nor did she speak ill of the lack of books or the torn and out-of-date books. She always moved forward with the lesson, as though in possession of the best supplies and equipment.

My respect and admiration for Mrs. Emmons made me wonder if I'd caused her a problem by questioning Principal Branch about the field trip. I knew Principal Branch and Mrs. Emmons discussed the cancellation. I knew going into this meeting with Mrs. Emmons would be a "lose-lose" proposition for me.

Without any fanfare, she brought me up-to-date on her conversation with Principal Branch about the field trip being cancelled. Mrs. Emmons didn't yell at me for going over her head without even talking with her. Her low-key approach made me feel about two-feet tall, and I heard the disappointment in her voice and saw the pain in her face. Her body language resembled someone who'd been gut-punched by a friend.

Now it was my turn to get a taste of my own well-deserved medicine. My older brother Ken had been in Mrs. Emmons sixth grade class two years earlier. He was well thought of by her and helped pave the way for me to be regarded as a very good student. Now, Mrs. Emmons reached into her medicine bag and gave me a double-dose of medicine by declaring, "I'm not sure what motivated you to pull such a stunt like this, Merritt, but I'm sure your brother Kenneth wouldn't have gone to see the principal without speaking to me first." Mrs. Emmons threw up her hands in disgust, asking, "How could you do this without talking to me first?"

I walked away from Mrs. Emmons, stunned and embarrassed. I asked myself what had just happened? How did a routine field trip that I pursued end up hurting one of my favorite teachers?

I had made the field trip all about me. Students hadn't come together and decided that I should be the spokesperson for our class.

From first grade to sixth grade, the last thing on my mind was questioning persons in authority after a decision had been made. Why then, in this particular instance, did I decide to stick my neck out? When I faced the hurt Mrs. Emmons experienced over my actions, I knew I had lost face with her. In a matter of seconds, I knew our relationship would never be the same because I had violated her trust.

The following day after my meeting with Mrs. Emmons, she announced she had good news because the field trip would be occurring in a couple of weeks. Everyone in the class, except me, smiled with excitement. My reaction was complete silence. If there had been a way to disappear, I would have left, the destination unimportant. I never mentioned my role in the rescheduling of the field trip to anyone.

Mrs. Emmons stated that Mrs. Colquitt's class, the other sixth grade class at Hard Elementary, would also participate. Then she explained the purpose of our trip was three-fold. One, to become familiar with the overall campus setting since Dunbar's footprint was five times the size of Hard Elementary School. Two, to meet some of the teachers who might be our instructors in the fall. Three, to shadow students in current classes at Dunbar High School as they moved from one class to the other.

The day and time finally arrived that third week in May when some 72 students were lined up and ready to see the wizard at Dunbar High School. Naturally, we had our two teachers to keep us in line.

At the designated hour of 9:00 a.m., we were ready to trek our way by foot from the south side of Bessemer to the north side where Dunbar High School was located. This journey of about two miles started from the front of Hard Elementary School on the gray dirt that surrounded the entire school. Our journey ended a little over two hours later in front of Dunbar High School similarly surrounded by dirt but more dirt. The only difference between the two schools was that since the high school was more expansive, the dirt covered a wider swath, no grass to be seen anywhere.

[87]

When we began our walk that summer morning, it was pleasant under mostly overcast skies. The sun peeked through and the humidity was not to the "I feel sticky all over" level yet. Mrs. Emmons and Mrs. Colquitt got everyone lined up and made notes on who was absent. Typically, Mrs. Emmons' face was creased with a morning smile for everyone with a little twinkle in her eyes. However, on this step-by-step journey to the other side of town, the smile and twinkle unfortunately had not been packed.

After walking close to 45 minutes, the earlier pleasant May morning changed for the worse. First, the sun blazed its way through the clouds. The temperature seemed to have zoomed from the low 70s with a slight breeze to almost 80 degrees and no breeze. The humidity tagged along as well. These weather-related factors were compounded by having to walk on the edge of the roads. No sidewalks. The number of cars traveling on the road increased as time passed, kicking up dust with small pebbles and rocks occasionally bouncing off our legs.

Mrs. Emmons and Mrs. Colquitt's journey was made especially difficult because even though they weren't in the classroom that day, they dressed as if they were. No sneakers, shorts, jeans, or informal wear for these well-respected teachers. They both wore high-heeled shoes with stockings, and dark blue and black dresses.

We didn't take a school bus, because we didn't have one. The first time I remember having access to a school bus was as a sophomore at Jackson S. Abrams High School.

When the two sixth grade classes started out there was an air of excitement, the sound of laughter from time to time and smiles here and there. However, by the midpoint of the journey, the joy, laughter, smiles, and sense of adventure evaporated as the heat, humidity, and dust appeared.

In the midst of the dismay taking over, I made eye contact with Mrs. Emmons. If looks could kill, I would have been seriously wounded. Fortunately, we soon arrived at Dunbar High School. Although dirty, sweaty, thirsty, and tired, our sense of pride allowed us to successfully complete our trek without any accidents or injuries.

However, with the mission accomplished—at the cost of letting down,

embarrassing, and hurting the feelings of one of my favorite instructors—
the aroma and taste of what I had envisioned for this special day had lost
all of its flavor. This experience was one of the first times I'd experienced
and gotten exactly what I wanted, but I didn't feel good about myself
because of how I achieved the desired results.

The lessons I learned from this experience have stayed with me into
adulthood and throughout my life:

- Bypass the chain of command and you may get what you want
  for the short term, but it may dampen or ruin your long-term
  possibilities.

- Be prepared to pay the price and accept the consequences for your
  actions.

- Always accept blame and responsibility for actions taken that
  adversely affect others.

20 GOOD THINGS COME TO THOSE WHO WAIT

I WAS IN the eighth grade at Hard Elementary School in Bessemer, Alabama, in 1959. I was one year away from entering my freshman year in high school. There were two eighth-grade classes at our elementary school with about 35 students in each class. Most of us had known each other since first grade, and in some cases, we'd known each other since kindergarten.

Grades one through three were dismissed from class at 2:00 p.m. instead of 3:30 p.m. To help these younger students arrive home safely, there were safety patrol guards placed at busy intersections and armed with a yellow stop sign outlined in black on a pole about the same size as a street stop sign. The safety patrol guard would bring traffic to a halt by walking to the middle of the street with this stop sign. This would allow the younger students to safely cross the street with no fear of oncoming traffic.

In addition to carrying the stop sign pole, patrol guards also wore a white belt that crossed their chests at an angle. It resembled something a cadet attending a military academy might wear.

A former teacher of mine from the seventh grade, Mr. Dudley, was in charge of the School Safety Patrol Program and made the decisions about who would be on the Patrol. Mr. Dudley taught math and other seventh grade classes. I considered him to be one of the new breed of teachers.

He was strict about how you should behave in class. The rules were: no talking when he was talking, pay attention, and speak up when asked a question. But he had a dry sense of humor and enjoyed having fun in class, too. One of his specialties, if he became annoyed, was to throw an eraser at someone misbehaving in class. He was the first and only teacher I knew who did this. The first time he wound up and threw the eraser, the class was totally blown away. We couldn't believe a teacher would actually throw an eraser at someone. I never remember him hitting anyone, but just the idea of it held everyone's attention, for a while anyway.

I appreciated how he balanced being serious about his subject matter, assignments, and attendance, but didn't take himself as seriously as some teachers did during this era. He wasn't afraid of revealing his humorous side.

Seven of us expressed interest in being on the school patrol. Mr. Dudley gathered us together in his classroom to make final decisions. One by one he called out the names of who would be on the school patrol: Ronald Banks, Charles Curry, and so on. When he got to the final name, I was starting to get nervous. I was bold enough at this point to say, "Mr. Dudley, what about me?" I couldn't believe I'd done this. I felt that I should be on the school safety patrol and, somehow, he'd forgotten I was there. Mr. Dudley, in a very low-key way, said, "Hold on, Long, hold on." To my astonishment, he called out the name of the last patrolman and it wasn't me. It was Robert Charley. How could this happen?

My grades were excellent, and I hadn't been involved in any type of disturbance at school. Nor had I been disrespectful of any other teachers. Plus, Mr. Dudley knew me from his seventh-grade math class, and I believed he thought highly of me as a student.

It was in this moment that I learned, much to my surprise, there was another position Mr. Dudley appointed, the captain of the school safety patrol.

Mr. Dudley said, "Long, I want you to be the captain of the School Safety Patrol." He reached out to me while smiling, placed the badge in my hand, and closed my hand around it. The thing I remember most was that the captain badge was outlined in blue instead of being all silver like the rank and file patrolmen.

I didn't know there was a captain of the Safety Patrol. I thought I was being overlooked and just the opposite was true. Mr. Dudley had seen me as someone with leadership qualities, someone who could be trusted and counted on to make sure the job was done correctly. This appointment caused me to view myself differently, a definite boost to my confidence. It felt good to be recognized.

This was my first taste of power and influence, and I loved it. Or maybe it was the cool blue outlined silver badge and white belt that I kept sparkling clean. I was the captain, and I liked the sound of being called "Captain." Perhaps this was a portent of things to come.

PART III

HIGH SCHOOL YEARS
1960-1964

21 MARILEE'S FLOWER SHOP

I WAS OUT of school for the summer after completing the eighth grade, excited about beginning my freshman year that September 1960 at Jackson S. Abrams High School.

When I stopped by chance at Marilee's Flower Shop to inquire about work, the man in charge—Mr. Bob Wright—said he would decide if he needed someone to help with different jobs at the flower shop. Duties would include sweeping and mopping floors, delivering flowers, cleaning windows, watering flowers, assisting with flower displays for funerals, and helping out in other ways as needed.

I thanked Mr. Wright for the consideration and walked the two miles from downtown Bessemer, Alabama, to our home on Exeter Avenue. It was summertime, the month of June, and the Alabama sun and humidity showed no mercy. It reminded me of an open-air furnace. My mom would often say, "It's summertime, honey, what do you expect?"

After I reached home, I told my father about my job search and meeting with Mr. Wright of Marilee's Flower Shop. He paused for a moment, then said he knew Mr. Wright from having dry cleaning done where Mr. Wright had previously worked. My father asked me if I was serious about the job, and I said, "yes."

Daddy decided we should go back to the flower shop, and he would put in a good word for me with Mr. Wright. My first thought was about having to walk back downtown again in the scorching hot sun. But we made the trek together. My father told Mr. Wright I would be a good worker and it would mean a lot to him if I was hired. It worked. I was hired on the spot.

Mr. Wright felt comfortable hiring me, because of my father's reputation and standing. Mr. Wright, my father said, had occasionally delivered his dry cleaning to him personally to our house when we lived on Gladstone. I would later learn that Bob Wright was a master at providing personalized customer service even to Black people. This was my first experience of using one's relationship with someone to benefit themselves or others in a business transaction. Mr. Wright, because he knew my father, decided to hire me, and I started work the following Monday.

My salary for working during the summer, Monday through Saturday, from 8:00 a.m. to 6:00 p.m. was $11 a week, less than $2 a day. When I worked after school from 3:30 p.m. to 6:00 p.m., Monday through Friday, and all-day Saturday, I was paid $7.50 per week.

The first thing I was told about my new job was that under no circumstances was I to use the restroom at the flower shop. Mr. Wright instructed me to walk around the corner and use the restroom at the Jefferson County Courthouse. This was the early 1960s and all public facilities were segregated. There was the "Colored" water fountain and "White" water fountain. At this time, all of the downtown restaurants catered to Whites. If Blacks were served, it was at the back or side of the building, generally on the outside.

For the first three months I worked at the flower shop, I dutifully adhered to Mr. Wright's two requests: one, I wouldn't use the restroom in the flower shop; and two, I would walk to the courthouse and use the restroom marked "Colored." Initially, leaving the flower shop to use the "Colored" restroom at the Jefferson County Courthouse was no big deal. It gave me a chance to leave the job. I didn't hurry to and from the courthouse. It was a good way to kill a little time at the boss's expense.

On the other hand, I resented the fact I was being told there was something so awful about my shit and piss that they needed their own special toilet. It also made me question my self-worth and value as a person. My mother and father, especially my mom, always stressed that I was inferior to no one. By going to the county courthouse, I felt like I was acknowledging that I was less than the White employees working at Marilee's Flower Shop.

My remedy was to occasionally use the restroom at the flower shop and still go to the Bessemer County Courthouse to use the "Colored" restroom. This accomplished, at a minimum, two things. By using the restroom at the flower shop, I exercised my independence and freedom by not letting someone make me feel less than a human being. Use of the "Colored" restroom at the county courthouse gave me the freedom to take a break from work and goof off for a while.

· · ·

Mr. Bob Wright was the face and voice, and seemingly the owner, of Marilee's Flower Shop. In reality, the business was owned by Mrs. Gladys Wright, his wife. Her parents initially owned the business. Mrs. Wright was the principal designer and architect of the various flower arrangements crafted at the flower shop. Her work ethic on a scale of one to ten was a fifteen. She was a working dynamo—fast, skilled, direct, no-nonsense, and bottom-line oriented.

While working at Marilee's Flower Shop during my high school years, I learned the art of excellent customer service. Although the various flower and floral arrangements that were designed, sold, and bought were of superior quality, I discovered that the difference between "just okay" sales and consistent sales and profits, hinged on how each customer was treated.

Here's where Bob Wright excelled as the husband of the owner and primary floral arranger, Gladys Wright. He had the knack and gift of treating all of his customers with reverence, appreciation, and a million-dollar smile. Also, he had a little twinkle in his eye as a bonus especially for the females who made up the majority of his customers.

Bob Wright was the epitome of customer service with just the right dash of Southern charm. He had a genuine interest in seeing that customers got the best of what they wanted. In my four years working at the flower shop, Mr. Wright hardly ever designed or put together any flower arrangements. However, repeat customers would call and request that Bob arrange some flowers similar to the ones he did last time. Everybody loved Bob, and I mean everybody. He was a very likable person, who treated "Colored" customers with respect and dignity. That wasn't the norm among White merchants in Bessemer, Alabama, during the 1960's era.

Bob was an active listener who always seemed interested in what his customers had to say. He never dominated the conversation unless they asked his advice. I loved watching him talk with his customers. I could tell by his animated behavior that he enjoyed the exchange. When he was with them, he exhibited laser-like attention and they were the center of his bullseye.

Whether it was the first or fiftieth time, there was always a ready handshake and a warm, but not too warm, embrace especially for the ladies. He observed his customers. Bob noticed and acknowledged a female customer's new hairdo, earrings, or a particular dress he thought looked good.

Bob had that unique ability to make every customer feel special and important, because to him they were. He emphasized to them that, if for some reason a purchase wasn't to their liking, they should let him know and he would make it right. In those rare instances when this did happen, he always remedied the situation promptly and with a smile.

Given the caste-like system in Bessemer, I was always intrigued by how Mr. Wright interacted with his Black customers versus the White ones. Unlike most White merchants in downtown Bessemer, he generally treated his Black customers with respect. Black folk came to the flower shop primarily to purchase seeds and plants, such as tomato plants, for their gardens in the summer and fall. Occasionally, a Black person would come into the flower shop to buy a potted plant or bouquet of flowers but not often.

Mr. Wright would meet and greet each Black customer with a friendly hello and ask, "How can I help you?" Although nice enough to his customers, it seemed as though he was holding back by not being as effusive as he would be to a new White customer he didn't know. I wondered if he was thinking he'd already crossed the line of perceived decorum between Blacks and Whites with his impish smile and easygoing manner.

Purchasing goods and services from Marilee's Flower Shop wasn't like most other White-owned stores where after you bought something, the change and dollar bills would be often slammed on the counter as though you'd just committed some offense. A clerk in an establishment of this type would be quick to ask in a condescending voice, "What do you want?" A "thank you" and "please come back" was out of the question. These establishments made customers feel as though they were doing them a favor by allowing them to purchase items from their store.

I was a sponge around Mr. Wright, listening and learning everything I could about managing a successful small business. The following are examples of principles I learned from him and in some instances, reaffirmed messages and lessons from home:

- Everyone wants to be heard.

- You might learn something if you listen.

- A thoughtful word goes a mighty long way.

- Your chances of benefiting from the glow increase when you shine the light on others.

- You never know when someone is watching the work you do, so always do your best.

. . .

I saw a different side of Bob Wright one summer day. I cannot forget that lovely summer morning when I walked from home to work and eagerly entered the front door of Marilee's Flower Shop. Bob Wright sat in his favorite chair, reading the newspaper. After the bells above the door announced my arrival, the first thing out of his mouth wasn't 'hello' or 'good morning.' Instead, he called out, "Merritt, I see a nigger was shot last night."

Bam, right between my eyes. Right then, I felt like I had been "shot," not by a stranger or a stray bullet, but by someone I'd been working for over the past two years. Caught off guard, I was hurt by this unprovoked attack, but not mortally wounded.

After my initial shock, I knew I couldn't let this insult go unchallenged. I walked over to Mr. Wright, stood over him, and said emphatically, "That word is Negro, Mr. Wright." His response was, "That's what I said," again pronouncing the word "Negro" with a slight variation that sounded this time like "negra" versus "nigger." Instead of pronouncing the word "Negro" again, I spelled it out letter-by-letter for Mr. Wright, emphasizing each and every letter.

Then, I turned around and walked to the back of the flower shop to one of my two workstations. I had nothing else to say. I thought that whatever else I said wouldn't change his odious pronouncement of the word "Negro" anyway.

I didn't see this disrespect toward Black people coming at all from Mr. Wright. He had always been courteous, kind, jovial, light-hearted, and fun to be around whenever we delivered flowers around town. Sometimes, he would stop by my high school and pick me up before we delivered flowers in the Birmingham area. After work, he often gave me a ride home. He encouraged me to do well in school and occasionally attended some of our high school football games.

I had heard other White people in Alabama pronounce the word Negro as "negra" just as Mr. Wright had that day. Maybe, they believed they were being more respectful and civilized to Black people. This seemingly enlightened public persona quickly vanished when talking among themselves and not having to worry about what others thought—Black or White—and the word negra became full-throated nigger, their word of choice.

As a 15-year old African American, I believe my exchange on how the word Negro was pronounced was my first *mano-a-mano* experience with an adult White male regarding race. Mr. Wright was probably around 50 years old. That summer Saturday morning workday in 1966 was the first and last time I heard Mr. Bob Wright attempt to pronounce or utter the word "Negro" again in my presence. We never talked about the incident again. It seemed as though on our little flower shop island the word ceased to exist, which was fine with me especially if the best he could do pronunciation-wise was what I had experienced earlier.

I don't know why Mr. Wright thought he had to use the N-word. Maybe it was his way of letting me know or reminding me that no matter how well things were going for me, I was still a nigger in his eyes and the world's, regardless of how the word Negro was pronounced.

. . .

Several months following the exchange with Mr. Wright about the pronunciation of the word Negro, I was outside the shop, watering flowers and plants when I noticed an African American man sweeping the street. I had seen him in town, and he was well-known for sweeping sidewalks and streets. He didn't work for the city, had some mental challenges, and was slightly disabled with a noticeable limp.

When I walked back into the flower shop, Mr. Wright, who'd also been watching the man sweep the street, remarked, "Merritt, that boy must be crazy, right?"

I responded, "Mr. Wright, he's not a boy, he's a man." I didn't take the time to deal with the question Mr. Wright had asked about the man's mental health. I was so pissed about him calling a Black man a boy, which was common during that time. White men and White women often referred to Black adult men as boys.

Our conversation ended as quickly as it started. He and I just stood inside the flower shop, the air conditioning system humming in the background. He and I intently observed the movements of an obviously mentally ill African American man, probably in his mid-30s. He swept the streets directly in front of the flower shop, the scorching Alabama sun blazing down on him with temperatures in the 90s.

The man was capable enough to be completely clothed from head to toe to protect himself from the intolerable heat that day. He had a beige baseball cap on his head, blue denim long-sleeved shirt and pants, along with what looked like steel-toed boots, black in color. Also, the man wore beige leather gloves with a white handkerchief tied around his neck.

This volunteer street sweeper was also prepared with the necessary tools to accomplish his task. He had an aluminum garbage can with a lid, a push broom, and a device he'd constructed that enabled him to push the garbage can down the street without having to carry it.

Over the next two summers, I saw this man sweeping the streets in downtown Bessemer as if he was a full-time city employee. Cars traveling by would stop and let him pass by, or drive around him, without even a honk as he swept the streets. I wasn't aware of him being arrested or anyone giving him a hard time. He was visible to everyone in town, but invisible as well. I wish I would have said something to him, if only a hello or some thanks for keeping the streets so clean. He wasn't a boy...but a hard-working, dedicated man.

. . .

While delivering flowers one fall afternoon, I learned something new about the special skills and abilities of some of the dogs owned and trained by some Whites in the segregated South.

After getting no response when I rang the doorbell several times to deliver flowers to a family on Clarendon Avenue in the then White section of town, I started to return to the car where Mr. Bob Wright waited. He got out of the car, pointed toward the back of the house, and suggested we walk to the rear of the residence to get someone's attention and try to deliver the flowers. He thought he saw the owner of the residence, a friend of his, working in his garden.

At first, this delivery seemed routine until I saw this horse-sized dog approaching and eyeing me like I was a walking piece of meat. He was black as coal, with menacing red eyes and appeared to be a mix of Doberman Pinscher and Great Dane. The closer he got to me, the quicker his gait became, to the point where his pace had increased to a slight trot. This beast of a dog trotted toward me, eyes glaring, teeth gnashing, and trickles of foam coming from both sides of his mouth. Not a pretty or encouraging sight from where I stood.

Suddenly, this routine delivery was turning into a horror movie. The owner called out twice to his dog, aptly named Killer, to halt. Fortunately, the dog was well-trained and stopped immediately after the second command by his owner. The owner then approached me, without any apology for his dog's behavior, stating, "For some reason, Killer doesn't like niggers and whenever he sees one, he reacts this way."

I decided this was not the time or place to give the dog owner a lesson in how to pronounce the word Negro.

This was a startling reassurance by the owner that his dog's response to me was nothing personal, I just happened to be a nigger and Killer didn't like niggers. It was comforting to know that it wasn't me that he wanted to rip to shreds, but niggers in general.

Well, I thought if he was born this way, he couldn't help himself. Another "reassuring" moment that it wasn't me, but the color of my skin. I could breathe better now, knowing that mankind and womankind were safe, unless they happened to be Black and in the proximity of Killer.

After the flowers had been delivered and I arrived home unscathed, I appreciated the safety of my home. I reflected on my surreal encounter with the dog named Killer. I started to think about how this dog learned to hate and to attack Black people. I wondered if there were certain characteristics Black people exhibited that Killer responded to. Was it our skin color, smell, voices, or manner of walking? Or was it simply the hatred of its White owner, who trained his dog to attack Black people?

. . .

A side of Mr. Wright I appreciated was his kindness towards me at times. Without being asked, he would periodically drive me home after work. This was especially true when we worked past 7:00 p.m. during exceptionally busy periods such as Mother's Day, Valentine's Day, and Christmas holidays. This wasn't something that he had to do. When he did drive me home, I think he wanted to make sure a young kid got home safely after dark. At the end of the workday, he would say, "Merritt, can I give you a ride home?" or "Come with me, Merritt," as he left the store.

A route Mr. Wright and I took often was north on what was called the Bessemer Superhighway to deliver flowers in the greater Birmingham area. It included West End Baptist Hospital, Birmingham University Hospital, Calloway Methodist Hospital, and Lloyd Noland Hospital. Unexpectedly, one day while going to the Birmingham University Hospital and West End Baptist, Mr. Wright took a new turn off of the highway.

I had no idea where he was going, and he gave me no clue until he headed toward a hamburger and barbecue diner. The car kicked up small bits of gravel and rocks from the unpaved road and created a pinging melody as we traveled in the two-toned, light green and dark green station wagon with the funky sounding V-8 engine. As he slowed, a dusty mist flowed over the car, and when he stopped, the dust continued on its path to cover other cars in the parking lot.

Mr. Wright exited the station wagon without saying a word. It wasn't complicated to figure out as he headed to the sandwich shop that he was going to have some lunch. It was around 1:00 p.m. I lowered my window part way down and laid my head on the seat where I was sitting to chill out and relax. I relaxed in the wagon for about ten minutes when I saw Mr. Wright returning with a small white bag in his hand. When he reached the wagon, he extended the bag to me and said, "Try this, I think you'll like it."

He then turned around and walked back to the two-story white building that housed the sandwich shop. It wasn't fancy, there were just signs listing the menu items of French fries, hot dogs, hamburgers, milk shakes, onion rings, and barbecue pork sandwiches. The signage in the front of the building bragged that the barbecue sandwiches were considered some of the best in the state.

As I opened the white bag, I noticed the sandwich was wrapped in waxed paper and some of the sauce was seeping through. As I unfolded the paper around the sandwich, I discovered it was a barbecue sandwich, still warm, with tiny wisps of steam floating up and an aroma that called out for it to be eaten.

This sandwich shop catered to Whites only, and I felt self-conscious in the parking lot, eating this delicious sandwich that some Black person had probably seasoned, cooked, and prepared. How ironic, I thought, because like me, the cook couldn't eat at his own place of employment other than in the kitchen. If he tried to eat in the dining area, he'd run the risk of being arrested.

From where the station wagon was parked, I could see the rear of the sandwich shop. Unlike some sandwich shops and restaurants that were for Whites only, this sandwich shop did have a small window for Black folks. This allowed them a place to stand if they wanted to purchase something to eat. This meant that Black folks were required to wait in the scorching summer sun and intense humidity, torrential rain and thunderstorms, and frigid bone-chilling cold in the winter for their food.

I opened the sandwich and eyed the crispy but not too crispy pieces of barbecued pork on the top of the lightly-buttered toasted bun. Some of the pieces of pork were falling off the edges of the bun as if they were making a break to escape the confines of the bun, but they wouldn't make it past me. Once I had inspected the pork, I could see the other sandwich ingredients: coleslaw made of cabbage and mayonnaise, topped by two thin slices of dill pickles. The bun had been grilled in butter and the sandwich was topped off with a little mustard and ketchup.

After my inspection, I took my first bite and it tasted as good as it looked. All the condiments came together in a harmonious way, a little sweet, a little sour, and crunchy. I knew I had hit the motherlode when the juices combined with grease dripped down the side of the bun onto my hand.

By the time Mr. Wright returned around 30 minutes later, I had finished my delicious sandwich and was starting to go to sleep. He got back into his station wagon with a toothpick on the left side of his mouth, let out a belch, started the vehicle, and off we went. I thanked him for the barbecue sandwich and let him know how much I'd enjoyed it, thinking to myself that it would definitely be okay if this became a routine stop on our flower delivery route.

In addition to being treated from time to time with barbecue pork sandwiches, Mr. Wright had a favorite milkshake place located off the Birmingham Superhighway. It was just a few minutes from the sandwich shop.

Mr. Wright would go to the outside counter and return to the station wagon with two tall milkshakes, taller than any milkshakes I'd ever seen. I'm sure my mouth was open, because I was hoping one of those shakes was for me. As Mr. Wright got closer to the wagon, I noticed that some of the contents were spilling down the side of the white plastic container. The first thing I noticed was that it wasn't chocolate, but I wasn't quite sure of the contents because the valuables were concealed in the white plastic cup. In a few seconds, the shake surprise was over as Mr. Wright said, "Here's your strawberry shake." I took my first sip of that luscious pink and white concoction of milk, strawberry ice cream, strawberry syrup, bits of strawberries, and a generous portion of whipped cream with a cherry on top.

It was a sight to behold. Before having a strawberry milkshake, my shake of choice was a chocolate malt. I walked away from chocolate malt land quite easily and was sip-by-sip enjoying my new adventure into strawberry land with no regrets. I became a strawberry milkshake fan on the spot.

The ice cream place was for Whites only, but it didn't seem to bother Mr. Wright. It didn't bother me since I had survived the segregated barbecue pork sandwich shop. Once we were on the Superhighway, Mr. Wright was like a big kid, slurping down the milkshake while driving and enjoying this treat as much as I was. Typically, he would stop at the ice cream stand during the summer months and when the weather was warm in the spring or fall.

Although the walk from the station wagon to the ice cream place was no more than fifteen feet and Mr. Wright only had to wait in line for five minutes in the summer heat and humidity, he'd return to the wagon drenched in sweat. Mr. Wright was about five foot seven and weighed more than two hundred pounds. I'm sure his weight didn't make it easy for him during those times when he needed to stand in the hot August Alabama sun. However, he never complained about the weather conditions and how hot he became.

I was glad Mr. Wright loved ice cream. Strawberry ice cream, especially a strawberry milkshake, continues to be my favorite and is a special treat.

. . .

Working four years at the flower shop from the summer of 1960 to the summer of 1964 offered me the opportunity to almost on a daily basis work with, observe, and listen primarily to White people in Bessemer, Alabama. This was a learning experience that provided a first-hand account of their personal everyday lives, habits, fears, and ambitions.

Generally, this experience was candid and unvarnished by my White colleagues, because they usually communicated with each other as though I wasn't in the room. It was like I was there but not, or it didn't matter to them that I was present. This arrangement worked well for me on those occasions when we weren't busy—nothing was going on and everybody was doing nothing, including me. Mr. Wright, Mrs. Wright, and Mrs. Lucille Cummings, the other full-time staff person, would sit in their designated chairs in front of the flower shop.

I would stand behind the main front counter in front of five bins filled with different types of bean and pea seeds, which were sold to customers for gardening. I kept my left leg raised high enough for it to be positioned atop the bin's edge. I didn't feel comfortable sitting with the others.

Black employees didn't sit or chit-chat. They stayed busy, especially if they wished to remain employed.

While at my workstation in the middle room of the flower shop, I listened to the two women who worked there, Mrs. Cummings and Mrs. Wright, chatting while they made floral arrangements. I overheard Mrs. Cummings praise then-Governor George Wallace for his stance against the eventual admittance of Black students into the University of Alabama.

"We're so proud of him for all he's done to try to stop this day from coming," she said to Mrs. Wright.

Governor Wallace had stood at the doorway of the University of Alabama to block the entrance of Black students.

It wasn't what Mrs. Cummings said, but how she said it. She asserted that the inevitable had happened and there was no turning back the hands of time. She knew segregation had been replaced by the unknown world of integration. It was as though, in her heart-of-hearts, a way of life had ended and a future like she'd never seen or experienced or even imagined was about to begin. The many knowns of segregation would be replaced by the unknowns of integration and the gigantic steps of one Black man and one Black woman at the University marked the opening steps of systemic change. I was energized by her comments because they sounded like a realization of the change ahead.

After hearing the sentiments and feelings expressed by some of the employees of Marilee's Flower Shop, I was reminded of a comment made by Mr. Wright on one of the few occasions when he talked about race relations in Bessemer. He stated that if God wanted the races to mix, he never would have created black birds and white birds. "You never see those flocks of birds flying together," Mr. Wright said.

. . .

When I started working as a 13-year old boy in the summer of 1960 at Marilee's Flower Shop, I had no idea I would learn so much during those four years I was in high school.

In addition to the work fundamentals of being on time, being dependable and reliable, and completing a task thoroughly and in a timely manner, my work experiences afforded me a first-hand view of how some White people in the South viewed segregation and their way of life. Essentially, their respective sentiments reflected the mores and values of most White southerners.

The prevailing sentiment seemed to be one of segregation today and segregation forever. White people thought, "It's always been this way, why change. It works for me. What's the problem?" The two-tier racist system of White people being in absolute power and African Americans being at the absolute bottom in Bessemer, Alabama, was akin to the relationship between "peanut butter and jelly" or "ham and eggs." This was the preferred formula perpetuated even after the Emancipation Proclamation freed the slaves in January 1863. Segregation and racist attitudes toward Black people and other people of color in the South were considered a birthright.

From the first time I met Mr. Wright, he was someone I liked and grew to grudgingly respect. However, over time there were comments he made and words he used that caused me to dislike what I thought was his true self. I admired his ability to connect with people and how positively they responded to him. He was never verbally abusive or threatening to me. He was kind to me in many ways, driving me home, occasionally treating me to BBQ sandwiches and strawberry milkshakes.

He occasionally upset me with comments he made about Black people, comments I considered offensive and inappropriate. Like all of us, he was a product of his times and culture. He was not evil, but the racist attitudes and practices he held surely were.

. . .

In December 1971, I was visiting my parents in Bessemer, having come from Seattle, Washington, where I lived at the time. My father had asked me to drive him to downtown Bessemer to his bank, which was located on the opposite side of the street from the flower shop. Mr. Wright conducted his personal and business transactions at this same bank.

As I walked into the bank, the first person I saw was Mr. Bob Wright. To my immediate left as I entered the door, I saw him talking with one of the bank employees. Without any hesitation, I approached him. When he saw me, he paused and looked directly at me. I said, "Hi, Bob Wright. How are you doing?"

I didn't say Mr. Wright or Mr. Bob. In my mind, we were on the same footing, no deference necessary. Just calling him by his first name was my way of letting him know that I was speaking to him man-to-man.

Surprised, he nodded and seemed to mouth, "Hello."

I asked, "Do you know who I am?"

"Yes, I know who you are." After this brief exchange, I walked away. It may have been the first time a Black person in Alabama had addressed him by his first name and didn't put a mister in front. I felt liberated from the negative feelings and experiences I'd endured while working at Marilee's Flower Shop! It was amazing to feel the relief.

As I turned around, I noticed my father had completed his banking business. We left the bank, got into the car, and drove away. After a few seconds, my father asked me what I'd said to Mr. Wright. I said I called him "Bob Wright." My father surprised me by saying, "That must have felt good." I said it did.

I wasn't aware my father had been watching us, and I was taken aback by his question. By his response, I could see that my calling the former Mr. Bob Wright "Bob" was important to my father, too. I am sure that all the years he had known Bob Wright, he was Mack Long, and Bob was Mr. Wright.

We looked at each other, smiled, and never talked about the incident again. Never. It was done. Time to move on.

22 MY MOTHER'S SMILE

DELIVERING FLOWERS TO the area hospitals was a win/win situation. The person sending the flowers felt good about making the gesture, and those on the receiving end were happy to receive them, regardless of the color of the person delivering them. Going to West End Baptist Hospital was my favorite delivery destination, because it meant I might see my mother. The possibility was just that, a possibility, but the uncertainty of not knowing made the occasion extra special when I did see her.

Her crisp white nurse's uniform would be starched and ironed to perfection. Her white nurse's hat would be creased with precision, allowing a small portion of her hair to show. Mom always polished and buffed her white shoes so they had a reflective sheen on the toe. Her white seamed stockings completed the ensemble. Mom's face of cocoa brown skin, accentuated by just a touch of powder, blush, and a hint of red lipstick would welcome me whenever I appeared.

There was a different energy, and oddly enough, a carefreeness, about my mother at work. Maybe at work, she had only one thing to focus on, rather than the myriad responsibilities she embraced when at home, as mother, wife, church member, and community activist. My mother seemed so at peace with herself at work; she moved with confidence, in control. At home, she always seemed to be in a hurry with little time to spare.

Sometimes, when we were home, we would all be together, but she seemed to be lost in her thoughts. I remember once I came into the kitchen and had tears streaming down my face, crying quietly. She never noticed I was crying because she never looked into my face; she was absorbed with her own thoughts. Maybe that's why I enjoyed seeing her so much at work. She would look directly at me. I could instantly tell what was going on with her by looking into her face. She could do the same with me. Maybe at home, as I grew older and started hanging out with my friends, I became lost in my thoughts and my world and stopped looking at her other than when I needed or wanted something.

The most important thing I remember from when I saw her in her work world, and I was in mine, was her smile. It was a smile that said:

- I love you, Little Brother, no matter what.

- Your future is bright, and I know you are on the right path.

- The sacrifices your father and I made for you and your brother were worth it, and we would do it over again.

There's no greater gift of love than a mother's love.

23 GUESS WHO CAME AFTER DINNER

Mom, Dad, brother Ken, and I were relaxing in our living room one fall evening at 2317 Exeter Avenue, watching The *Ed Sullivan Show*. This Sunday night ritual was one of the few occasions, other than dinner, when we were all together. It was 1961, and I was a sophomore at Jackson S. Abrams High School.

Earlier that day, immediately following church, we had feasted on one of my mom's special Sunday suppers. She routinely prepared Sunday dinners the day before. That way she relaxed on Sunday, because all she needed to do was to warm the various dishes. Once in a while my father would cook during the week, but Sunday dinner was hers alone. It was a big deal, and we all looked forward to this treat.

My mom actually prepared two meals on Saturday. One for my father, who was extremely picky about his food, which meant my mom tailored one meal specifically to him. My father had his own small table in the kitchen where he ate all of his meals. My mother, brother Ken, and I would eat together around the dining room table, enjoying the second meal she prepared to satisfy the limited palate of her two sons. I know exactly what you are thinking. How spoiled and pampered the men of the Long household were. You are absolutely correct, and we enjoyed every morsel and minute of it.

This particular Sunday, Mom had prepared one of my favorite pots. It consisted of green beans, with chopped white onions, green onions, and chunks of white potatoes that had simmered around ham hocks for a couple of hours.

I have relived eating this amazing dish many times and when doing so, the saliva in my mouth starts to get in the ready position. I have imagined a little grease from the ham hocks gently burning my lips. Not too much, but just enough to get my attention.

During previous meals, the grease from the fixings would speak to me, saying, "Calm down, slow down, the food is not going anywhere...act as though you have had this before, which you have. Each and every time you have this dish, I have to remind you to slow your roll!!"

Of course, there were extra onions available if you wanted to add them and small green peppers on a little plate looking up at you, saying, "I betcha you want to try me but, beware, I am too hot to handle."

Mom also prepared T-bone steaks in such a way that I have never experienced anything close to them since. Actually, I'm not quite sure exactly what went into her preparation and execution of this dish. Execution is indeed the right word because she literally killed it! With the exception of baking certain pies and cakes, I never saw my mom use a recipe. Her recipes, I am sure, came from her mother and the lessons learned from trial and error.

Here we go...on that Saturday, Mom began by seasoning, to her taste, at least three T-bone steaks. This seasoning consisted of black pepper, salt, celery and garlic salts, and a splash or two of Worchestershire sauce. Then she'd let the meat marinate for four to five hours. I knew magic was about to happen when I heard her tearing the aluminum foil to cover the pan of steaks before placing them in the oven at 275 degrees. I don't know how long the steaks would originally cook on Saturday, but on Sunday she would put those bad boys back in the oven until she felt they were ready to serve.

The meat was like butter, cooked past well-done, but still juicy, flavorful, and cocoa brown in its own sauce. Once the dishes were served up, the real dance began. The juices from the ham hocks, beans, and potatoes would slowly wind their way to intersect with the steak. What a wonderful and glorious collision. I'd momentarily stop eating—as suggested to me earlier and wisely by the pot grease—and just savor the moment. Nirvana is rapidly approaching. Remember, act like you've had this before.

My mom was not big on saying "I love you." She showed and gave her love to you by doing things with you and for you. That could be cooking, baking, making sure you knew how to properly use a knife and fork, instilling a sense of pride and confidence that you were special when everything around you said differently, and pushing you to be stronger when you became discouraged.

As we were relaxing after Mom's wonderful dinner and thinking about dessert, we didn't know we were about to have unexpected guests.

My family's evening of TV watching changed dramatically when out of nowhere came the sound of horns honking. Not a honk to let someone know you're there, or a honk to say hello to a friend you haven't seen for a while. This honking was different. It was the sound of many cars honking saying, "Come take a look at me. I'm coming down your street, and the reason I'm honking is for you to see and fear me!"

I got up from the sofa, walked over to the front door, and looked through one of the three small windows in the door to see what was going on. To my shock and amazement, I saw at least ten cars, one behind the other. Horns blared, and the inside lights of all the cars were on, illuminating two people in the front seats and two people in the back seats. They wore what appeared to be white sheets with hoods. As I watched from a distance of about 20 feet, the hoods looked like an upside-down V-shape or cone head, similar to the Conehead Family on Saturday Night Live with Dan Aykroyd and Jane Curtin.

This was no joke, though, and no one in our household laughed. Even though this Klan caravan incident occurred over 50 years ago, the image of that experience is as sharp and clear as when it happened.

However, I am quick to remind myself that Klansmen driving through the neighborhood, while not your usual Sunday night experience, paled in comparison to some of the horrific acts of brutality, lynching, and murdering of primarily Black men in the South as well as the North.

For a moment that seemed like an eternity, I was stuck at the small window watching and not knowing what to do.

Should we call the police? I didn't think so. Policemen were probably a part of this Ku Klux Klan caravan.

Should I run outside and let them know I wasn't afraid of their antics? No, not if I wanted to live, given the history of the Klan.

I thought I'd let the Klan know I was watching them and turned the porch light on. As soon as I hit the switch, Ken called out, "Turn that porch light off. Let's not bring attention to ourselves. Come back over here and sit down." Ken was right. I sat down, dazed that the Klan was making such a public display of their existence.

After the Klan drove away, I wondered why our neighborhood and why that night. As a family, we never discussed this incident that night or in future days. At the same time, we didn't need to discuss it. Everyone knew what time it was—time to remind the Colored folks what their place was in the White world of Bessemer, Alabama.

The "Colored" and "White" water fountain with its specialized plumbing to provide Colored water for "Coloreds" and specially distilled White water for the "Whites" wasn't that long ago. The Klan and other masked Whites wanted to preserve the past and shape the future based on a racist past.

Ken, who had worked in my place for one week that summer, said it was Bob Wright, our boss from Marilee's Flower Shop, and his homeboys coming by to let me know I needed to step up my "yes, sirs" and "no, ma'ams" and tilt my head more downward when talking to him and other Whites at Marilee's Flower Shop. Ken had reported to me that Mr. Wright told him I needed to be more respectful of White people at the flower shop. Even though my behavior did not change when I returned to work, Mr. Wright never said anything to me. Maybe he had heard me flush the toilet in the forbidden "Whites only restroom" on those occasions when I refused to walk the three blocks to the public "Colored" restroom at the county courthouse.

You know, Ken may have been right.

24 A TEACHER MAKES A DIFFERENCE

I'm sure that, like me, you've heard the expression that there was probably at least one teacher who made a difference in your life. This doesn't imply that all your other teachers were ineffective, but there was one teacher who caused you to want to work a little harder, helped you to believe in and expect more of yourself, someone you looked up to and didn't want to disappoint. For me, it was Daisy Pearl Chapman, my homeroom and English instructor from ninth grade through my senior year in high school.

As a ninth grader, I was in the college prep track instead of general education. The classes such as chemistry, physics, geometry, biology, and advanced English composition were rigorous and designed for students who might have the opportunity to attend a four-year college. Mrs. Chapman taught English to college prep students.

I remember quite clearly the first time I sat in Mrs. Chapman's classroom. It was located on the first floor of Jackson S. Abrams High School. What I remember so vividly is how serious and no-nonsense she looked. It was crystal clear to me that this woman, Mrs. Chapman, was all business. No playing around in here, I thought.

Before saying a single word, she seemed to take the time to measure each and every student by looking at us one by one. My time under her microscopic gaze seemed like forever. If her method was to intimidate, she achieved her objective. I knew then my school life would change, but I wasn't sure if that would be a good thing.

During my freshman and sophomore years under Mrs. Chapman's instruction, the class focused on learning the basics for composing structured sentences and paragraphs, along with punctuation, dangling participles, spelling drills, the conjugation of verbs, and more.

Mrs. Chapman maintained our interest and also kept us on our toes with a periodic pop quiz. After we completed a certain portion of the curriculum, she'd announce she was going to give us a pop quiz to see if we truly understood and had mastered the subject matter. The results were immediate, because we exchanged papers with one another and scored the exams right away. Everything was done on the honor system, each person's score was their score; it wasn't recorded for winners or losers. Mrs. Chapman wanted all of us to know how we were doing individually and what we needed to improve on when it came time to take the actual exam.

The pace and beat of Mrs. Chapman's class was unlike any class I'd ever experienced. Classes would often start rather leisurely with her slowly and deliberately providing a general overview of what was planned for that class day. Mrs. Chapman sometimes would take long pauses between saying one word to the next. I literally hung on every word, wondering when the next one would drop. Other times, in the middle of a statement, she'd just stop and look away from the class. It was like she was taking a side trip to refresh, regroup, and come back to us in full focus mode.

Then, out of nowhere, the tempo would pick up and she spoke louder, her cadence was faster, and she talked so fast covering so much ground I could hardly keep up. The 45 RPM record had been jettisoned for a 78 RPM. It was as if she was saying to us, "So you think I was moving too slow earlier, how do you like me now?" And, just as quickly as her pace had sped up, she slowed down dramatically and I, for one, was relieved because I could now keep up and take notes accordingly.

During my freshman year, whenever Mrs. Chapman called on me, I was terrified. She was so exacting, precise, and wanted no fluff, just the facts. Even when I knew the answer, I'd second guess myself because I felt the pressure of her strong presence. Over time, I adjusted to her style, prepared more thoroughly for class, and eventually gained her respect for my scholarly efforts.

Having covered the more technical aspects of writing and composition, Mrs. Chapman moved to a subject she stressed over and over again throughout our junior and senior years in high school—the art and importance of public speaking. Mrs. Chapman believed that being comfortable speaking in front of groups, both large and small, was an important ingredient for our future success regardless of our individual career choice.

Mrs. Chapman stressed and expected each class member to demonstrate many attributes in the multiple presentations we gave throughout the school year. These included: being familiar with the material you were presenting, avoiding the practice of reading word-for-word and line-by-line, making consistent eye contact with the audience, maintaining good posture by standing tall with chest out, smiling, and using self-deprecating humor to get you and the audience to relax.

The repetition of preparing and giving various oral presentations served me well while in college, but especially helped prepare me as I entered the professional world of work, whether as a beginning employee, manager, administrator, state agency director, or bank director. The skills I learned from those high school days in Mrs. Chapman's English class were the foundation for future success in the public speaking arena. Initially for me, public speaking wasn't a piece of cake, but with Mrs. Chapman's tutelage, once I had that first bite, I wanted more.

As a small child growing up in Bessemer, my first name "Merritt" was different from other common names and its pronunciation was often butchered. I was called Mary, Meredith, Mead, Melvin, and Merrill, to name a few. The first time Mrs. Chapman called my name, it bounced off the walls, made me sit up straight in my chair and take notice. I was impressed by the way she called out my name with her rather husky voice. I realized then that I had been given a very special name, having been named after my grandfather, Merritt Clark, my mom's father. I never quite figured out why Mrs. Chapman would alternate by sometimes calling me by my first name and on other occasions by my last name.

During my junior year in high school, I started thinking about what college I should attend. There were three colleges I was most interested in: Clark College and Morehouse College, both in Atlanta, Georgia; and Tuskegee Institute in Montgomery, Alabama. I narrowed my choices to these colleges because, with the exception of Tuskegee, the other two colleges were out-of-state, and my mother wanted me to broaden my horizons beyond Alabama.

I visited with representatives from Morehouse and Clark Colleges when they talked to potential students at Abrams High School. Most importantly, my brother Ken was a freshman at Clark College. He was also quite familiar with Morehouse because it was just across the street from Clark College. Without any hesitation, he strongly encouraged me to attend Morehouse; he pointed out that Morehouse was recognized as one of the leading and prominent Black colleges in the country. He didn't say this, but I got the feeling that if he had the opportunity again, he'd have attended Morehouse. Essentially, he wanted me to have the best college experience possible.

His endorsement was all I needed. Morehouse was my first and only choice. Fortunately, it worked out that I was accepted at Morehouse because it was the only college I applied to.

Prior to applying and being accepted at Morehouse, I was so excited about the prospect of attending the college, I started carrying around the school's materials with my high school books and notebooks. I thought I was being super cool by having college materials while still a junior in high school.

As I was leaving Mrs. Chapman's English class one morning, the newly appointed principal of Abrams High School, Mr. Walter Branch, walked down the hallway. I first met Mr. Branch when he was the principal at Hard Elementary School. When I was in the sixth grade, my interactions with him were limited but positive, unlike some other school principals I'd met. He was more approachable and his first method of getting a student's attention wasn't physical punishment.

Mr. Branch and I spoke briefly as we walked down the hall together. He immediately noticed the Morehouse brochure I was carrying and stopped mid-stride. Initially, I thought maybe he'd attended college there and was pleased to see I was considering attending. I was totally off base. We stood in the middle of the hallway while Mr. Branch scanned the Morehouse College brochure. After a cursory review, he returned the brochure to me and asked, "How long do you plan on attending Morehouse?"

His question surprised me. I wondered if Mr. Branch questioned my ability to successfully study and graduate from Morehouse. It seemed as though he was questioning my intellectual capacity and fortitude and I felt he was being insulting and disrespectful. Mr. Branch knew I was one of the top students in the high school. I expected him to be more encouraging concerning my college pursuits. Maybe he thought I was reaching too high and would fail, because I would soon wade into a college setting that was beyond my depth.

After taking a few moments to regain my composure, I responded slowly but sincerely to his question by saying, "I plan on attending and graduating from Morehouse College in four years." Since my ability was being questioned, I couldn't resist emphasizing my point by counting out four years on my fingers. As I raised each finger, I looked him directly in his eyes. By the time I reached three, I thought Mr. Branch, the principal known for being reasonable, would blow a gasket. Fortunately, he just stood there and simmered in place for a while. I was thankful we were in the middle of the hallway with students milling all around.

Now it was Mr. Branch's turn to show me his finger by pointing and instructing me in a firm and angry voice to go to his office, take a seat, and not move until he told me to do so. I turned around and started to walk to Mr. Branch's Office, which was only a few feet away. At first, I thought the entire incident was pretty silly, and I had to maintain my composure to keep from laughing. I'd never been to the principal's office for any type of offense throughout my educational experience until then, the eleventh grade. To make matters worse, this was all about a student wanting to attend college and planning on graduating in the expected time frame.

I must have sat in the principal's office for more than an hour, waiting for Mr. Branch to return and dole out my punishment for what? Insubordination? As I sat in the designated "bad boy chair," I gained a different perspective on the high school.

Students walked by the principal's office and pointed me out in utter disbelief, taking a look and then double takes. I overheard one student saying, "I can't believe Merritt Long, Mr. College Prep, has been busted. I always knew he was up to something, but I never knew what it was." Another student chimed in. "Well, it must be something. He wouldn't be sitting in that chair for nothing." Off they went, laughing down the hallway. As time continued to pass and more students went by, I sensed the word was spreading that an unlikely offender was on display in the principal's office. For a while I enjoyed my new persona of getting a new reputation as a "Bad Boy" one-day wonder. I took my sunglasses out of my pants pocket and put them on, just for emphasis.

I continued to wait in the principal's office, wondering what specific punishment I'd receive for my verbal insurrection. I squirmed in my chair, having difficulty reconciling being recently dethroned as an Honor Student to becoming a newly acclaimed Bad Boy.

All of a sudden, there she was, Mrs. Daisy Pearl Chapman. Where did she come from? I didn't see or hear her approach. She simply asked, "Long, what are you doing in the principal's office?" Embarrassed, I tried to paint the best picture I could. I explained that Principal Branch saw my Morehouse brochure and asked me how long I planned on attending Morehouse. This had occurred over an hour ago when I left her class and was headed down the hall to Ms. Minor's history class on the second floor. I told her I had responded by only saying I planned to be there four years and somehow that resulted in my being sent to the principal's office. Mrs. Chapman looked at me in disbelief. She asked, "Long, are you sure that's all you said?"

Busted, I thought to myself. No wonder you're in the principal's office if that's the best excuse you can come up with, College Boy Wanna Be.

I unburdened myself with the truth and provided Mrs. Chapman with the sordid details of my finger-counting demonstration of one year, two years, three years, four years to Principal Branch. After she heard my second response, she shook her head, turned around, and started to walk out of the principal's office. Then she turned around to look at me once more. She continued to shake her head while exiting Mr. Branch's office.

There was one residual benefit of my exchange with Mrs. Chapman—I knew for sure that whenever she called me by my last name, she wasn't a happy camper.

A few minutes later, Mr. Branch finally returned to his office. I guess he figured I'd stewed long enough, and it was time to put a fork in me. He walked into the office as if he had 15-pound weights on each of his legs; his steps were beyond slow. At the rate he was moving, my stay in his office would be an overnighter. Let's get this over with, Mister, I thought. Of course, for dramatic effect, he had a solemn face, hands clasped behind his back as though he was about to press the button on an execution.

The slow-walking principal finally reached his office, took a seat in his high-back chair behind his worn brown wooden desk, sighed deeply, and waved at me to come in.

As I started to sit in the small squeaky grey chair facing his desk, Mr. Branch propped both feet sideways on the right side of his desk. This placement allowed him to look directly at me while having his feet not quite in my face. My punishment was slowly being administered. Mr. Branch told me he thought my response to his question was uncalled for. To give me time to think about my actions, he had a special assignment for someone like me with such a get-up-and-go attitude. He uncurled himself from the desk, stood, and opened a green storage cabinet that looked like Army surplus. After a couple of failed attempts, he finally opened the sticking door and brought out a wooden stick.

He walked around the desk and said he wanted me to use this tool, i.e., stick with a nail attached, to pick up paper and other garbage that had been discarded by students on campus. My work area was on the west side of the school, and he wanted me to spend the next three hours carrying out this task. He asked if I had any questions. I shook my head, said "No," and didn't count any fingers.

I was halfway out of the principal's office when Mr. Branch stopped me and handed me a matching green Army surplus-looking wastebasket and said with a smile, "You might need this." He walked away with considerably more pep in his step than earlier. Lesson learned: force meets force but student's force pales in comparison to the principal's force.

Clearly, the principal was the boss and as long as you were under the principal's roof, you'd treat him with dignity and respect. Also, the principal decided where the dignity and respect line was, and if and when you crossed it.

Alone with my thoughts again and out of Principal Branch's eyesight, I still couldn't believe this embarrassing punishment was really happening to me. After leaving the principal's office with my two new best friends, the wooden stick with nail attached at the end and a green trash can, I was convinced it was really happening. And that many of my classmates would see it.

The west side of the school was located on about two acres of land. The area closest to the side double doors that exited from the lunchroom got the most debris as students frequently used this pathway throughout the day. Also, the further you went toward the railroad tracks on the outskirts of the acreage was the area used for touch football during physical education classes.

As I began to pick up paper with the wooden stick, I soon realized as I surveyed the area that there were half-scribbled pieces of notepaper, milk cartons, portions of books, newspaper clippings, and wads of paper I'd never seen or imagined in this quantity. Sizing up the job, I thought maybe I needed two sticks with multiple nails to be efficient. Fortunately, on this spring day it wasn't raining, and the temperature seemed to be in the high 60s with a faint breeze from time to time. I must have cleaned up the immediate area outside the side double doors in about 30 minutes.

While walking to the next debris and paper-filled area, I turned around and faced the high school, realizing the principal wanted my classmates to witness my punishment because I'd talked back to him. For an additional 30 minutes, I continued to do my job, only stopping when I needed to dump the wastebasket full of paper into the large campus dumpster.

Out of nowhere, I heard someone call my name over and over again. I looked up and realized Principal Branch was motioning me to come back inside the building. After more than one hour of punishment, Mr. Branch fired me on the spot and took back my former two best friends—the stick and the wastebasket. He provided no explanation for his change of heart and, trust me, I neither wanted nor needed one. He said to me, "Boy, I'm not sure what class you should be in, but you better get there as fast as you can." "Yes, sir," I eagerly replied, smiling as I quickly went down the hall and up the stairs to Mr. Dawson's chemistry class.

By the time I was almost to the top of the stairs, I heard a familiar voice say, "Long, Long, come see me now." What a rollercoaster ride. I'd been freed by the principal and within minutes of my newfound freedom, I was being called out by a more powerful and influential authority, Mrs. Chapman. I stopped in my tracks and walked back down the stairs. I felt like a balloon with its air slowly escaping. By the time I reached the bottom of the steps to face Mrs. Chapman, I felt totally deflated and embarrassed. I knew she was going to read me the riot act, because as I picked up trash, she would have seen me with a stick and trash can in hand—not an inspiring picture of one of her college prep students.

Mrs. Chapman stepped closer, placed her right hand on my shaking shoulder, and in a calm, low voice talked to me like no other teacher had ever done before. Mrs. Chapman told me that next year I'd be a senior and she expected more leadership qualities from me. She said that other teachers felt the same way, and she was depending and counting on me. Mrs. Chapman asked me not to let her down.

She didn't say anything about my encounter with Principal Branch, but she didn't need to because her message was clear. How can you be a leader, inspire others, and be depended on if you are walking around picking up paper and garbage like a school troublemaker?

I stood there—lifting my somewhat bowed, shameful head—stunned, surprised, and speechless for a long moment. I thanked her for the vote of confidence, turned around and ran up the stairs to my chemistry class. As I went to my seat, all eyes in the class were on me. I sat a little taller in my seat, shoulders erect and straight, spoke with more confidence, and was willing to ask questions about things I didn't completely understand without fear of embarrassment.

What a day it had been, from public shaming and humiliation to validation and recognition by Mrs. Daisy P. Chapman. The day that initially began as one to forget, eventually ended up as one that forever shaped my perception of myself.

25 RUDE AWAKENING

When I rode my bike to downtown Bessemer in the early 1960s, there was only one place in town where I could have lunch or dinner inside. McLellan's Five and Dime Store. There was one lunch counter for Blacks and one lunch counter for Whites. The lunch counter for Blacks was almost identical to the one for Whites, and the fact it was located toward the rear of the store and next to the exit doors was a non-issue. When you have nothing, certain things seem less important.

The Black women who worked there wore the same uniforms as their White counterparts and everything about the lunch counter was spanking brand new. It was a place where you could have an enjoyable lunch and not be concerned about standing in the back of a restaurant or waiting outside, wondering if and when you might be served, how to protect yourself if a thunderstorm occurred, or how to stay warm during winter.

It was amazing and satisfying to witness and experience Black folks, my family included, sitting at a lunch counter, ordering food, and having lunch or dinner with a sense of pride and dignity. Black families certainly appreciated the separate, but equal, access and opportunity for customers provided by the local merchant.

However, I had a different experience in Bessemer at another food establishment. My good friend and cousin, Ronald Banks, had parked in the lot of a hamburger place on Ninth Avenue. It was a lovely Sunday evening during the early part of summer when the humidity wasn't high, and the temperature must have been in the 70s. Before we arrived at the hamburger stand, we'd been at Ronnie's house, laughing and talking, having a little get-together. He lived with his grandfather and grandmother. They'd recently added a new room to their home, and we thought it needed to be christened.

As Ronnie turned the car engine off at the hamburger place, the car became deafening quiet. When we arrived at the hamburger joint, we looked through the front window of the glass-enclosed stand. It was as though we were at a drive-in movie, seated in our car with no sound as a film unfolded before us. There must have been 20 customers in the restaurant, a mix of White guys and girls. They looked to be juniors and seniors in high school, as several of the guys wore letterman sweaters from Bessemer High School, an all-White school located within walking distance of my home. Even if Bessemer High School had been located directly across the street from our home, I couldn't have attended courtesy of segregation.

Everyone gathered at the hamburger stand seemed to be having a good time, judging from the big smiles on their faces, apparent laughter, slaps on the backs, and hugs all around. Even from Ronnie's parked car, we could see baskets of French fries everywhere. Instead of Alabama's number one drink, Coca-Cola, being consumed, milkshakes were the king and queen drinks for the evening. It was like a TV commercial was being filmed of this lovely utopian summer evening in Bessemer, Alabama, 1963, except it was for Whites only. Not me and Ronnie.

In a synchronized move, Ronnie and I turned our heads and looked to the right of the hamburger stand. We saw a faded, dingy looking sign affixed to an old building, which announced, "Colored Only." The earlier carefree moments Ronnie and I enjoyed collided head-on with the reality of living in two worlds: one White, one Black. It was like being slapped in the face by an invisible hand.

26 BUSINESS IN THE BLACK COMMUNITY

Typically, on Sunday from after church until around 8:00 p.m., various Black-owned and operated small businesses flourished.

In today's terminology, these businesses would be called start-ups, and the ones that had operated for at least three years were viewed as established ventures. The business model was based on the premise that the business wouldn't pay the typical fees, i.e., licensing, state and local taxes, salaries, rental cost, and employee benefits such as insurance and retirement funds. When a business of any size, small or large, eliminated these customary expenses, the businesses' road to profitability was accelerated.

These businesses stayed off the radar as far as local elected officials and law enforcement were concerned. By and large, the White power structure could care less as long as these activities weren't in their neighborhoods, and they kept the Colored people quiet and satisfied.

The benefits of working in and/or owning one of these small businesses, which were located on various streets, avenues, and alleys, included the ability to sample products and offered discounted purchasing power. The business activity was usually operated from the owner's residence, so the owner received a percent of profit, commonly referred to as the "house's cut." Also, workers usually had flexible work hours and owners could shrink or expand their business without requiring city, county, state, or corporate approval. The businesses were agile and could quickly adjust to changes in the marketplace.

Often these businesses operated on Saturdays and Sundays because the owner and employees held down full-time jobs during the week. Barbershops were a common business. Some were started by a licensed barber, but some were operated by individuals who learned their trade and craft practicing and experimenting by cutting their relatives', neighbors' and friends' hair for free. The most revealing aspect of a haircut is that it speaks for itself. There's no hiding how it looks. Over time, your work is seen throughout the neighborhood and community. I can recall asking acquaintances and strangers, "Where did you get that haircut?" This type of respect and admiration for certain barber's work was more valid than a license or a diploma, which really didn't demonstrate up front the barber's ability and skill level.

As the barber shop business began to thrive on the weekend, mainly supported by African American men and boys, there was always a line of people waiting to have their hair cut. Some enterprising barber shop operators started barbequing ribs and frying fish to sell to waiting or departing customers, as well as to others in the neighborhood. Takeout was readily available.

In a matter of months, the proprietor of the barber shop expanded his business to include food and beverages for his loyal customers. The two revenue streams served to whet the appetites of the newly minted business entrepreneurs.

Sometimes, gambling activities became a third element added to the business model. The most common form of gambling was rolling dice. I had a rudimentary knowledge of the game at the time, but that didn't stop me from rolling the dice one Sunday afternoon after I attended the First Baptist Church on the South side.

After I received my haircut, I entered the dice game room. I got down on my knees on the floor with everyone else in one of the bedrooms and waited my turn. I knew very little about the rules of rolling dice, only that throwing sevens or elevens were winners and if you rolled snake eyes, you crapped out. I was nervous when my turn came, although some of my friends already playing encouraged me.

Believe it or not, on my first roll out comes a seven followed by an eleven on my second roll and a seven on my third roll—all winners. My friends wanted me to play, because they thought I was having beginner's luck, which to my amazement I was. My next roll of the dice was a six so I had to make this point until I crapped out. My beginner's luck continued and I was consistently making my point for a while until I finally rolled snake eyes and crapped out.

My neighborhood friends were making different side bets that I had no clue about, and overall, they did quite well. I was just happy to walk away with a few dollars. This was my first and last game of dice in the neighborhood, although it was pretty exciting. I mainly wanted to play to show my non-church-going friends that, just because I went to Sunday school, church, and was a dutiful student, I wasn't a square.

The barber shop, food and refreshment bar, and/or gambling activities have been staples of the Black community for many years. These businesses continue to this day, whether on the south side of Bessemer, Alabama, or the south side of Chicago, Illinois. These mini-businesses and social centers emanated from segregation and provided more than just a way to earn additional money.

27 A FIELD TRIP TO REMEMBER

IN 1963, DURING my junior year at Jackson S. Abrams High School, our class took a field trip that proved to be historic for all of us. Historic in that we had the opportunity to visit an African American owned and operated bank. Prior to this adventure, I'd never been in a bank where Black people worked in jobs other than as a custodian. The very idea that Black people founded and managed a bank seemed totally foreign.

My frame of reference for businesses owned and operated by African Americans in the South was of the Mom-and-Pop variety. These businesses, whether in Birmingham or Bessemer, tended to fall in the following categories:

- Dry Cleaners
- Beauty Salons
- Flower Shops
- Soul Food Restaurants

- Upholstery Shops
- Barber Shops
- Record Stores

One unique and ironic exception to the Mom-and-Pop businesses operated and owned by African Americans during this era was the funeral home business. The business of managing and coordinating the needs and affairs of the deceased appeared to be quite lucrative. Funeral home enterprises that existed during the 1960s, such as Chambers Funeral Home in Bessemer and A.G. Gaston in Birmingham, still thrive to this day.

The trip on the school bus that spring from Abrams High School to Birmingham lasted a little more than 30 minutes, but it seemed like an eternity. The temperature outside was perfect—somewhere between the high 60s to low 70s. Flowers had begun to bloom, and here and there you could hear the chirping of birds and smell the freshly cut grass that had changed to green from the winter's brown.

Inside the bus, everyone talked faster than usual; it was as if we'd gone from low to fast. We were so juiced. If the energy from all of us in the school bus had been harnessed, we could have charged several homes with electricity for the remainder of the day.

As the bus driver made his way to the parking lot, we weren't sure which building was the bank because there were three similar buildings right next to each other and no visible signage. By now, we were looking in every direction with much anticipation, trying to figure out which building housed the Black-owned bank.

What a relief as we walked from the parking lot to Building A and entered through the double glass doors with mahogany handles. As I walked through the entryway of the bank, I felt a little taller and held my head higher. I began to smile with pride, as though, for a fleeting moment, I was one of the founders and the bank was a part of me. What a historic day for my classmates and me as we observed African American men and women handling the financial affairs of primarily Black customers at the teller lines and desks. The notion of never being in a Black-owned bank or Blacks working as professionals was quickly replaced by these positive images.

The bank, modest in size, contained the customary counters for the five bank tellers, desks and chairs for the additional staff, and two private offices for executive staff.

The bank staff were impeccably dressed. The men all wore suits with white starched shirts and ties with hints and splashes of color, understated while still making a statement. Two of the male employees had pocket watches that added flair and a dash of sophistication to their ensembles. One of the men wore a three-piece suit, his gold pocket watch safely tucked in his vest pocket. The other man I noticed appeared to have a silver pocket watch in his right pants pocket, judging from the silver chain dangling across his vest. I couldn't miss their shoes, either, and wondered if I got close enough, could I see my face in the tips of their glossy shoes.

The female bank employees wore tailored dark suits with blouses in vivid colors of blue, orange, and yellow. It was quite a sight to see as they carried themselves with casual elegance.

After informal conversations with the bank staff and a tour of the president's office, the president provided an overview of the bank that included when it was founded, the total number of employees, bank assets, the customer base, and plans for the bank's future. He concluded his presentation by stressing the need for Black people to pool their collective resources and become more than just consumers, but business owners. He thought this would enable the Black community to help one another and expand the Black business base beyond the typical Mom-and-Pop type of operation.

At the conclusion of the tour, we received a bonus when our instructor, Mrs. Chapman, informed us we were on our own to have lunch in downtown Birmingham. She asked us to form into small groups and to return to the bank at 1:30 p.m. It was about noon, so we had time for a leisurely lunch in the "Big City."

My group consisted of Gwen Dudley, Leslie Cephus, Alvin Mauldin, Barbara Owens, Shirley Lewis, and Eloise Green. We started to walk toward the central part of town where there were a number of restaurants and department store lunch counters. The big question was whether we'd be served. Although lunch counter sit-ins began in 1960, discrimination in restaurants wouldn't be outlawed until the Civil Rights Act was passed in December 1964.

The McLellan's Five and Dime Store in Birmingham had only one lunch counter, not two like the Bessemer store. So this lunch counter was for Whites only. The four of us spotted four vacant seats and nervously moved toward them. Before we even sat down, the White waitresses eyed us as though we were from outer space. Several whispered to one another, but loudly enough for us to hear them. The whispers went something like this:

"I don't believe it; these niggers are going to try to eat here."

"They must be crazy. I'm not serving their Black asses."

"What in the hell is the world coming to?"

Once we sat down, we became invisible. No one who worked behind the counter would make eye contact with us. They began hurrying and scurrying in every direction except ours.

After an excruciating five minutes or so, I got the attention of one of the White waitresses. She responded immediately. "We don't serve your kind. Why do you want to start trouble by sitting at this lunch counter?" I said, "We simply want to have lunch."

You would have thought I'd just made a declaration of war and an attack was imminent at the lunch counter. At the top of her lungs, she screamed, "The niggers want to have lunch, what are we going to do?" Two White waitresses about to serve White customers became so disoriented after the screaming alert, they crashed into one another with dishes, forks, spoons, water glasses, and food going everywhere except to the people intended.

By now, the screaming, crashing of dishes, and general mayhem coming our way had attracted quite a crowd to the lunch counter. Someone in the crowd shouted, "Let's call the police and get them all locked up."

At that point and time in the skirmish, we decided to get up and leave, retreat if you will, and wage our battle another day. By trying to eat at the lunch counter, we had made a declaration not of war but of our rights. They knew we and others like us would be back. A new day had begun. Although we didn't eat lunch that day, when we returned to the bus and traveled home, we felt full. It had been a good day "banking my way" to the lunch counter.

28 CLARK COLLEGE HOMECOMING WEEKEND

IN THE FALL of 1963, we were going to go to Clark College in Atlanta, Georgia, where Ken was a sophomore. Clark College is a HBCU (one of the Historically Black Colleges and Universities) and a member of the Atlanta University Center which also included Morehouse, Spelman, and Morris Brown Colleges. It was homecoming weekend, and we looked forward to seeing him and participating in Clark's homecoming activities.

Prior to our road trip, my mother and I, for about two weeks, had been involved in a tug of war concerning what I should wear to the various homecoming festivities. My mother was adamant that I should wear a suit and tie. I was totally against this idea, which was quite unusual. Seldom did I take issue with my mother's wishes. She was pretty cool and usually very reasonable. I believed the idea of wearing a suit and tie would cause me to stand out like a sore thumb, stifling my cool entrance on the college scene.

I wanted to wear something more casual and hopefully present myself as a believable college boy, not a high schooler, even though I was a big-time high school senior. I wanted to look like I belonged on the Clark College campus, rather than some country bumpkin from a little town outside of Birmingham, Alabama.

My mother and I continued to discuss my wardrobe. I saw the frustration on her face. I knew her patience was wearing thin; if I kept protesting against her wishes, the hammer would come down and I might be axed from the trip altogether.

Time to cut a deal, in other words, compromise. I proposed the idea of my wearing a cardigan sweater, shirt, tie, and dress slacks, instead of a suit and tie. The drama concluded, and I felt good about the end result. I sensed my mother's relief at ending this debate.

After driving for about three-and-one-half hours from Bessemer to Atlanta, we immediately made our way to Clark College. Ken arranged for our stay on campus for the two nights we'd be staying in Atlanta. While walking from the campus dormitory where we were staying to dinner that evening, the first thing I noticed was the attire of the male students on campus.

Suit and ties everywhere. Most students looked like they were going to a fashion show, not just to dinner. Some students had taken the basic suit and tie formula to a whole new level. They were resplendent in three-piece suits, with pocket watches, tie bars, and an assortment of colored silk handkerchiefs, depending on each person's fashion sense. For the first time, I saw different fraternity pins adorned on one's vest, creating another level of sophistication and coolness by the wearer.

Now, here I was looking exactly like what I was trying to avoid, a country bumpkin. All I needed was a little straw dangling from the corner of my mouth. I was the only person that day and evening wearing a sweater, shirt, tie, and nice dress pants. I guessed I might be viewed as a pace setter and ahead of the curve, or perhaps, behind the curve.

Of course, my mother noted this in serene silence. She didn't need to say a word, because the scene around us screamed, "Next time, listen to your mother, dummy!"

She ended my silent suffering by saying, "Little Brother," one of the names she calls me, "everyone looks so nice in their suits and ties, don't you think?" She followed up with a jab to my chest and a punch to the head, smiling broadly all the while. "Suit and Tie Gate" concluded with my mom certain I'd gotten the message.

The dinner before the homecoming game at Clark College was extremely special for a number of reasons. The setting had a majestic feeling similar to an old black-and-white Humphrey Bogart and Lauren Bacall movie. The only thing missing was Bogie saying, "Play it again, Sam." The dining hall, its lights muted, created an intimate and personal ambience. For this moment in time, everyone seemed to move with elegance and grace. Also, the servers—smartly dressed in black slacks, white shirts, black bow ties, and freshly starched white jackets—were posted throughout the dining room and added to the overall elegance of the dining experience. I don't remember what was served for dinner, but I felt special to be there. From that moment on, attending college wasn't something I wanted, but something I knew I needed to experience firsthand.

A college's homecoming game and weekend, I learned, was a really big deal. It was the party of all parties. There was the school marching band, which had practiced for weeks to outdo the other school with its spectacular homecoming performance during halftime of the football game.

Everyone attending the game dressed in their best attire, nothing being spared. When you looked to your left or right, everyone seemed happy and at peace with themselves. The moment was now and nothing else mattered.

Fraternity brothers, whether they be Phi Beta Sigma, Kappa Alpha Psi, Alpha Phi Alpha, or Omega Pi Phi, wore a colorful array of fraternity sweaters, fraternity pins, suits, and ties. At the right moment, during the game, pledges from the respective fraternities made their grand entrance, all decked out in identical outfits, because by this time of the year they were in the final stages of pledging and were required to dress identically.

My mother, brother, and I walked to the football stadium from Clark College behind Clark's marching band. The walk to the stadium took about 15 minutes.

Just seconds after taking our seats, someone in front of us started jumping up and down and pointing toward the back of the stadium. When I looked back to see what all the excitement was about, I spotted the Heavyweight Champion of the World, Muhammad Ali. The first thing I noticed was the size of his head, which appeared unusually large, but not in an odd or strange way. What a majestic man. His skin positively glowed. His erect posture emphasized his height and bearing. He resembled a Greek God.

The weather on that day of sighting Muhammad Ali was cloudy and it looked like rain was in the offing. The Champ seemed well prepared as he was wearing a long black raincoat. Muhammad's Hollywood good looks were polished off with black sunglasses. He could see you, it seemed, but you couldn't see him, which seemed in some way, the way it should be.

Capping off my first sighting of The Champ was the fact that the once threatening rain clouds were floating away from the stadium as if in a movie script. The good guy, The Champ, enters the scene with threatening clouds and rain, pauses for a moment, the clouds break, and the sun with all its radiant glory shines upon The Champ. Just like on TV. This time, it was real.

I was proud to be Black and related—perhaps very distantly—to Muhammad Ali. He represented not only victory, but victory on his terms. He was his own man.

Merritt, Gean and Ken. My mother had dressed Ken and me in our Sunday best for this picture with our cousin, Gean (née Ford) White. I thought I was ready! circa 1951, Bessemer AL

My parents, Will "Mack" Long and Katie Clark Long, on a trip to Atlanta where we watched a Braves baseball game. This was the first and only trip to Atlanta for my father. circa 1974, Atlanta, GA

My mother, Katie Clark Long, is on the far left, 2nd row. She very proudly graduated from the Wayne School of Nursing in Chicago so she could work as a Licensed Practical Nurse in Alabama. circa 1953

My brother, Ken, as a young man in Bessemer. He was sharp! circa 1961

My older brother, Mack Long, Jr. and his wife, Iris. My mother stayed with them while she attended nursing school. 2003, Olympia, WA

Ken, his wife Jacque, daughter LaTonja, and son Ny'Ika at Tonja's ballet recital. circa 1973, Seattle, WA

Ken, LaTonja, Ny'Ika and me at the ballet recital. circa 1973, Seattle, WA

Ken and Tonja's husband, David Hunter, enjoying a good laugh. Photo by Nate Naismith 2009, Olympia, WA

Governor Gary Locke, my wife Marsha and me. We both served on Governor Locke's Executive Cabinet. circa 2005, Olympia, WA

*Marsha and me with Governor Chris Gregoire and First Gentleman Mike Gregoire at a
holiday reception at the Governor's Executive Mansion.
Photo by Weldon Wilson circa 2005, Olympia, WA*

*Governor Gary Locke commemorating the 15th year anniversary of the Learning Seed
Foundation at the Governor's Executive Mansion.
Photo by Nate Naismith 2016, Olympia, WA*

Governor Jay Inslee and First Lady Trudi Inslee with Learning Seed Scholar Brianna Ogunsemi-Dorsey at Learning Seed dinner at the Governor's Executive Mansion. Photo by Nate Naismith 2018, Olympia, WA

Our daughter Merisa and I greet golfers at the 1st Learning Seed golf tournament at Indian Summer Golf Club. 2002, Olympia, WA

Merisa, age 3, wearing Marsha's Arizona State Fair hat from back in the day. 1983, Olympia, WA

My beautiful family on our back deck: (from left to right) granddaughter Eden,
son Dan, daughter Merisa, Marsha, me, and grandson Marcus.
Photo by Cortney Kelley Photography, 2018, Olympia, WA

PART IV
MY COLLEGE YEARS
1964-1968

29 MOREHOUSE COLLEGE

It was fall 1964, and I was a freshman at Morehouse College in Atlanta. Everything was new, exciting, challenging, and slightly uncomfortable, all at the same time. I was no longer a big fish in a small pond, but a little fish in a very big pond, many times bigger than high school. There were more than 1,200 male students from throughout the country, indeed the world, attending Morehouse. Each student was a star or superstar from their respective high school. Several students, because of their scholastic abilities, attended Morehouse after completing only the tenth grade. It was the first time I'd met anyone from Africa. The freshmen from Africa were very confident, verging on arrogant.

I remember once during my political science class, I didn't understand what the instructor had said and asked an African student, "What did the instructor say?" His response was, "This is your language, man, and your country, don't ask me." Also, during freshman orientation, we were individually asked to tell why we came to Morehouse. Another African student proudly said that the only reason he came to Morehouse was because he wasn't accepted at Harvard or Yale, and Morehouse was his third choice. How do you like me now?

The mystique surrounding the Men of Morehouse is as prevalent today as it was over 50 years ago when I was a freshman. There are those who say,

"You can always tell a Morehouse Man…but you can't tell him much." I am sure, Marsha, my wife of over forty years would wholeheartedly agree. Where did this notion about Morehouse Men come from? Possibly from the atmosphere of quiet confidence that radiated throughout the campus with the presence of some of the best and brightest students from across the country and world. There was a sense of competition but not with each other. Rather, there was a feeling and belief that each of us had to strive to achieve our personal best for we would be compared to the rest of the world. Our professors pushed and challenged us by talking about the differences we could make if we applied ourselves fully, not halfway. You were either in or out, no in between. Because our professors held such high expectations for us we believed we were special and meant to do extraordinary things.

I'll never forget my experience at the local dry cleaning store. I had walked from Mays Hall (Mays Hall is named after Benjamin Mays, the esteemed former President of Morehouse) to the dry cleaners on Hunter Street, a few blocks from Atlanta University Center. As the young lady wrote out my laundry slip, I noticed that she seemed to be checking me out from head to toe. It felt like I was under her personal microscope. As I turned to leave, she called out in a booming voice, "Are you from Morehouse College? I was taken aback, and after a few seconds, replied, "Yes, I attend Morehouse." She smiled and said, "I knew it, I can always tell." I don't know what hints or tells I might have given for her to sense something unique about me. Maybe it was that mystique about being a Morehouse Man.

. . .

One of Morehouse's goals was to develop the whole man, not just academically, but spiritually, physically, and socially. Morehouse was preparing us to move in any circle once we graduated for we were expected to do great things in the world. As freshmen we were required to attend a weekly lecture with Dean of Students Brazeal who covered a wide range of topics, from the proper etiquette of using the correct knife, fork and spoon to being a gentleman, such as walking on the street side of the sidewalk when escorting a woman.

Dean Brazeal was a real character, the opposite of a stuffy academic. He had a wicked sense of humor, and sometimes he was funny without even trying. During one of Dean Brazeal's lectures he stressed the importance of giving flowers to the person you were dating and suggested giving chrysanthemums. "Let me spell that," he said, "C-R-S... Well, give her some roses. R-O-S-E-S." All of us started laughing at the instantaneous change in flowers. The more we laughed, the redder his face became. The dean was not a happy camper with a room full of freshmen laughing in his face.

Dean Brazeal brought the hammer down after a few minutes and we had quieted down. For this class we were assigned seats alphabetically. Dean Brazeal told us to look to our left, then to look to our right. He explained that based on historical data, one of the three of us would not be there next year. Silence reigned supreme as we took to heart this stark reality. I distinctly remember looking to my right and seeing fellow student Michael Lomax, one of the top rated freshmen in our class. Michael has had a very distinguished career as President of Dillard College, Fulton County Commissioner, and President/CEO of the United Negro College Fund. I knew Michael would not be in danger of flunking out of Morehouse so that meant me and the student to my left were in jeopardy. This reality check from Dean Brazeal was a wake-up call that added fuel to my study habits.

. . .

While walking from my room on the second floor of Graves Hall to the bathroom and shower facilities directly across the hall, I looked to my right for some reason. I stopped for a moment to look through the large plain glass window to see a group of primarily African American males walking toward Brawley Hall, Morehouse College's auditorium and gymnasium.

Immediately, I remembered that the Reverend Dr. Martin Luther King, class of 1948, would be speaking. Seconds later I recognized Dr. King, who accompanied three other individuals to the auditorium.

It was my freshman year, 1964, and fall was turning into winter. There was a slight mist or fog that almost obscured the face of Dr. King. He was wearing what appeared to be a light grey topcoat over his suit.

Dr. King's hair was closely cropped, and he strode up the sidewalk with a serious look on his face. Dr. King seemed to be, from a distance, self-absorbed and singularly focused. My first thought when I saw him was that I thought he would be taller in stature, like over six feet tall versus his actual five feet seven inches. Probably because of his previous accomplishments and what he represented, Dr. King was larger than life in my mind. As quickly as I saw him, he was gone.

I knew Dr. King was scheduled to speak that day, and I had thought about going to hear him speak the night before. But when I woke up the next day, I was tired from staying up most of the night to study. My freshman year challenged me, my college studies more rigorous than I'd ever experienced. Some of my fellow freshman, who lived on my dorm floor, would tease me by saying, "Merritt, when you are in your room, you are either sleeping or studying." They were correct. That first year, I was all business.

As Dr. King passed out of my view and faded into the fog, my moment with him—although from a distance—concluded. I felt bad for not getting my butt up and doing what I needed to do to be there, being in the presence of the man of our times—Dr. King. I didn't fully realize his greatness that day in 1964.

The next time Dr. King visited the Morehouse College campus was May 1968. He was being eulogized as the College's most distinguished alum, following his assassination in Memphis, Tennessee. In his relatively short life, he had demonstrated his greatness in so many ways through his courage, perseverance, vision, compassion, political savvy, oratory speech, and humility. The campus was bursting at the seams with mourners and admirers from all over the world.

. . .

As I left my dorm, Graves Hall, headed to the dining room on campus for dinner, I heard a voice like no other voice I'd heard before. It was a baritone laced with southern sweet molasses. Every word was delivered slowly and methodically with a special cadence that made you want to hear more. By the time I got to the bottom of the steps, I could see about 30 students surrounding the person I could hear.

On the front lawn of Graves Hall, I gently pushed my way to the front of the students who were gathered. I soon learned the voice, the voice that had captured my attention and later captured America, was the voice of Julian Bond. He was running for a seat in the Georgia State Legislature.

Julian Bond looked like other students at Morehouse, dressed in blue jeans, light blue button-down shirt, penny loafers with no penny, no socks, and no belt. His hair was cut the way most of us wore it then, and the way President Obama wears his hair. The close-cropped cut was known in the African American community as a Quo Vadis.

In one respect, he looked like a typical Morehouse student, but when he spoke, it was obvious to all of us the word "typical" and Julian Bond didn't go together. He was the first African American I'd ever heard, in person, running for elective office.

The details and whys for his running for office weren't what impressed me the most about Bond. It was his easy-going style and his ability to make everyone feel as though he was speaking directly to them. What a gift, I thought, admiring his obvious comfort in his own skin, his calm, his wit, and his tinder-dry sense of humor. It was an unforgettable moment in my life.

The second time I had this type of experience was at the Westin Hotel in Seattle many years later when then-President Bill Clinton spoke to about 500 people at a fundraiser for Gary Locke, who was running for governor of the state of Washington. Like Bond, President Clinton had everyone in the room mesmerized, including some of my friends who came in support of Gary Locke. Prior to the event, they'd made it clear they didn't care for President Clinton. Of course, that was before he talked to everyone in the room with his sweet southern drawl, just trading and sharing stories with good friends. Like Bond, when I heard Clinton speak, I thought, what a gift. As my grandmother would say, "It was just in him."

Bond's legacy of activism is long and deep. After enrolling at Morehouse College in 1957, he and John Lewis (who was later elected to the U.S. House of Representatives from Atlanta) formed the Student Nonviolent Coordinating Committee (SNCC) at Morehouse College. He served as the communications director of SNCC, leading student protests against public facilities and Jim Crow laws in the deep South from January 1961 through September 1966.

Bond was elected to the Georgia House of Representatives by a landslide vote of 2,320 to 487. Ironically, and sadly, the Georgia House voted 184 to 12 not to seat Bond because he publicly opposed the Vietnam War. On December 6, 1966, the United States Supreme Court ruled nine to zero, in the case of Bond versus Hoya, that the Georgia House of Representatives had denied him his freedom of speech and was required to seat him. On January 9, 1967, Bond took his seat in the Georgia House of Representatives where he organized the Georgia Legislative Black Caucus and served until 1974.

History was made by Bond when on August 29, 1968, he was nominated for vice president at the Democratic National Convention. He declined the nomination because at 28 he was 7 years shy of the age requirement.

Julian Bond, a Morehouse man, returned to Morehouse in 1971 where he earned his degree in English. He was eventually awarded 21 honorary degrees from various colleges and universities.

Upon Julian Bond's passing, President Obama shared, "Julian Bond was a hero and, I am privileged to say, a friend. Justice and equality was the mission that spanned his life from his leadership of the Student Nonviolent Coordinating Committee, to his founding role with the *Southern Poverty Law Center*, to his pioneering service in the Georgia Legislature, and his steady hand at the helm of the NAACP. Michelle and I have benefitted from his example, his counsel, and his friendship, and we offer our prayers and sympathies to his wife, Pamela, and his children."

Little did I know during my freshman year, within my first two weeks of being on campus at Morehouse, I would see the political beginnings of an icon.

. . .

For some reason each and every time I think about my political science professor, Dr. Robert Brisbane, I hear tapping. Tapping from Dr. Brisbane's thick-soled, black, wing-tipped shoes. As the magic hour for Political Science 101 drew near, we would hear the melodic, tap, tap, tap of his shoes in the hallway. The closer he got to entering the classroom, the louder the tapping, and he would enter the classroom with a brisk flourish, as if he'd been propelled by his own personal gust of wind.

The classroom was quiet as Dr. Brisbane placed his trusty briefcase on his desk with a loud thud. This thud was his official announcement that class would soon start and he was open for business. Dr. Brisbane made it clear to his 40 students, supposedly among the best and brightest from across the country, that he was the sole owner of this proprietorship.

Typically, during the fall and winter months he wore dark suits, often with a vest, white shirt, and a tie of subdued colors and patterns. A dark colored fedora accented with a colorful feather in the hatband topped off his somewhat conservative outfit. When the weather turned cooler and wetter, he wore gloves and a topcoat or raincoat. As spring and summer rolled around, his suits became lighter in color with a splash of a seersucker suit added into the wardrobe mix to withstand the hot and humid summer. As you might surmise, Dr. Brisbane was all business, with a dry sense of humor and no flash or dash.

Miles Davis is often credited with the "birth of cool" with his music, how he carried himself, how he dressed, and equally important, his air of certitude and assuredness. He was just cool. My introduction to the "birth of cool" officially occurred in September 1964, in Atlanta, Georgia, in Dr. Robert Brisbane's class. Born in Jacksonville, Florida in 1913 and moving to New York City as a toddler, Dr. Brisbane was greatly influenced by growing up during the Harlem Renaissance, which brought him in contact with some of the leading artistic and philosophical luminaries of the time. His heroes during this enlightened era were W.E.B. Du Bois, James Weldon Johnson, and William Trotter. Dr. Brisbane was greatly influenced by attending and then graduating from Harvard, the prestigious, button-downed, Ivy League university.

I can't overemphasize the enormous influence Dr. Brisbane had on me from the very beginning as he subtly instilled in me confidence and self-esteem. Ironically, I didn't even know it was occurring but fortunately it did. The power of a role model! I found myself sitting on the edge of my seat so I wouldn't miss one of Dr. Brisbane's pearls of wisdom or golden nuggets of inspiration. Dr. Brisbane's confidence in a young colored boy from Bessemer, Alabama, the kissing cousin of Birmingham, Alabama, two of the most racist and segregated cities in the country, proved invaluable.

While at Morehouse, I majored in political science with a minor in history. My goal at the time was to attend law school after graduation, like so many of my political science classmates. In retrospect, the idea of going to law school may have been similar to my notion of playing the piano. It sounded really good at the time, generating positive responses and approving praise from adults. This balm of acceptance and recognition felt great each and every time I mentioned my intention. My mother loved telling her best friends that I had the goal of becoming a lawyer. After a while I began to feel a little guilty and embarrassed because I knew deep inside, I had no burning desire to go to law school. Unlike the piano scenario, though, prior to making the final decision, I decided that I needed and wanted to go work to earn some money and to pursue a career. I knew if I went to law school only because it sounded good, the chances of things working out were not favorable.

Dr. Brisbane always seemed comfortable in his own skin and resolute in his thinking. If he had been in a quandary about a particular topic or issue, by the time he arrived for his lecture he would have resolved it in his mind. Dr. Brisbane, to my recollection, never waffled or contradicted himself. His only retrospective was to reference a historical event to help us understand the present state of affairs and give a perspective on possible future developments. He was unapologetic in his beliefs and was definitely not a "would have, should have, or could have" kind of guy.

My initial introduction into Dr. Brisbane's world was unforgettable. Why, you might ask? Before he started his first lecture, he informed us of the following insights to success in his class:

- If I were you, I would take copious notes and write down everything I say.
- My exams will be based solely on class lectures.
- Your knowledge of the subject matter is limited or nonexistent.

Like most of my classmates, I was initially taken aback by his proclamations regarding note taking and exams. However, the more these concepts soaked in, I realized Dr. Brisbane's edicts played to three of my major strengths at that time: my ability to memorize, retain information, and take excellent notes. I knew going forward I should fare quite well when tests were given.

Dr. Brisbane was a man of his word and, thankfully, his exams throughout the year were always based on his class lectures. Being in Dr. Brisbane's class for nine months, observing how he carried himself, how he communicated verbally and nonverbally, and how he effectively got his message across was very instructive to me. I learned the impact of one's presence on how others perceive you and accept your point of view. I learned more fully the value of preparation. However, preparation doesn't just include information from textbooks, research materials, and periodicals but also the reflection of experiences from one's own life.

Dr. Brisbane taught at Morehouse College for over 40 years, serving as a role model and mentor to thousands of students. His department produced more Black Ph.Ds., lawyers, judges, and government officials than any private college in the country. Among his more illustrious students are Julian Bond, former Georgia State Senator and Representative, and Maynard Jackson, former mayor of Atlanta.

Personally, I am thankful to Dr. Brisbane for teaching me so many things, just from his example: *if you look good, you'll feel good, and you'll do good.* If you are confident, this confidence will spread to others. I learned about the personal power that each of us has and how to put that personal power to good use and for the benefit of others.

. . .

I found myself homeless when I arrived on campus for my junior year. I had the money to pay for campus housing but I chose to help a good friend instead. You see, this good friend of mine and fraternity brother was one of several Morehouse students who maintained an apartment off campus strictly for parties and other social activities. No one actually lived there. The rent was due and my friend didn't have his portion. Me, Mr. Big Time, who had no money to spare, loaned him my housing funds.

Fortunately, Thomas Sampson, another Omega Psi Phi fraternity brother, and his roommate, E. Clayton Wade, allowed me to sleep in their dorm room until I could secure alternative housing off campus. The dorm rooms were not spacious; barely enough room for two people to sleep and study. Compounding the space situation was the fact that another good friend, Howard Gary, needed a place to stay. Tommy and Clayton would take the mattresses off their beds and place them side by side on the floor between the two beds. That allowed them to sleep on the box springs and Howard and I to sleep on the mattresses. After a few weeks, I left the homeless rolls when I found a one-bedroom apartment I could afford not far from campus.

Tommy and I are still good friends and we keep in touch to this day. He is the Managing Partner of Thomas Kennedy Sampson & Tompkins LLP, the oldest minority owned law firm in Georgia.

Several years ago, while watching the news from around the country I saw a familiar face that I hadn't seen in many years. It was Howard Gary, my sleeping-on-the-floor buddy. Howard was being interviewed about the riots in the Liberty City area of Miami where there were complaints about police brutality. As Miami's first Black city manager, he was responsible for this major city. I was proud to see the success of my temporary roommate who had left the floor and risen to great heights.

30 MUHAMMAD ALI

IN 1967 WHEN I was a junior at Morehouse College, I was leaving the campus of our sister school, Spelman College, when I noticed an immaculate, white, four-door Cadillac making a left turn to enter Spelman College campus. Seldom would you see a car entering the campus during the day; usually it was in the evenings when those Morehouse students fortunate enough to have a car would arrive at the Spelman campus to pick up their dates, especially on Friday and Saturday nights.

The Cadillac screeched to a halt, and the black-tinted window on the back-seat passenger side rolled down. To my surprise, Muhammad Ali poked his head out of the window and asked, "Do you know where Spelman College is at?" My initial thought took me back to my ninth grade English teacher, Mrs. Daisy Pearl Chapman, who would have responded to The Champ by saying, "You should never end a sentence with the preposition 'at'."

I quickly realized my responsibility wasn't to correct Muhammad's English, but to give him directions as requested. Once I came back to my senses, I let The Champ know he was heading in the right direction, that he should just keep going, and he would reach the heart of the campus. "Keep going, You can't miss it." I thought, "Sorry, Mrs. Chapman, English lessons would have to be given another time to The Champ."

One of the advantages of attending one of the colleges in the Atlanta University Center—comprised of Clark, Spelman, Morris Brown, and Morehouse—was that you could attend classes at any of the participating schools to meet your graduation requirements. During my four years at Morehouse, I took classes at Clark College, as well as Spelman College. In addition to having the opportunity to meet students from different schools, access wise, it was a piece of cake because Clark and Spelman were a stone's throw away.

The day after I gave directions to Muhammad Ali at Spelman College, he walked into my religion and philosophy class led by Dr. Rogers at Clark College. We suddenly had a visiting professor.

Ali just took over the class by simply walking into the room. He greeted our instructor, shook his hand, and Dr. Rogers, right on cue, moved from the front of the classroom to the side of the room. He instantly knew it was The Champ's class now.

Muhammad Ali proceeded to give the class a lecture about the negative connotations associated with the word "Black" and the positive attributes associated with the word "White." His observations included the following:

- White hat – Good guy
- Black hat – Bad guy
- Angel food cake – White
- Devil's food cake – Black
- Blackmail – Bad
- Bad hair – Nappy, curly hair

- White lie – Good
- Black Magic – Evil
- Black cat – Bad luck
- White angels – Good
- Good hair – Straight hair

This impromptu lecture provided by the former Heavyweight Champion of the World, Muhammad Ali, focused on how he felt some White people tried to consciously and subconsciously influence the thinking and self-concept of Black people and the perception of Black people by associating negativity, and in some cases evil, with the word "Black."

I don't recall very many questions being asked of The Champ. Like me, most of the students had never heard the perspective that Ali shared that spring day. It was as if he was going behind the meaning of the word "Black" and how one's psyche is influenced by something that, on its surface, may appear harmless.

Little did I know as I sat in my religion and philosophy class, that I was less than an hour away from being quizzed by The Champ. The questioning involved about ten Morehouse students, hanging out with other students from the Atlanta University Center at a store called Yates and Milton. This popular gathering place was the go-to spot for school supplies, toiletries, cold medicines, envelopes, stamps, and, of course, hot dogs and hamburgers, which really weren't that good, but the price was right! But this location wasn't about the food; it was about the bevy of female students who were there.

It was indeed the spot, located just across the street from Morehouse on one corner, Clark College on the other corner, and Spelman College just a few minutes away. Rounding out this cosmic explosion of Black intelligentsia and beauty was Atlanta University, Morris Brown College, and the International Theological Center.

Yates and Milton, on the day Muhammad Ali arrived, was humming as usual. I don't recall anyone saying, "Here he comes." or "Is that Muhammad Ali?" Suddenly, he stood in the middle of the room, making eye contact with each of us who quickly formed a semi-circle around him. He looked at us with the stare of a lion about to feed upon its prey. Seemingly, his most difficult decision was deciding which one of us he would devour first.

Then Ali asked the following question in a firm, commanding voice that clearly said: when you answer this question, you must be truthful, because if not, there will be real consequences.

The question posed by Muhammad Ali was one I'm sure no one expected. "Who is the Baddest 'MF' in the room?"

Without a moment of hesitation, we chorused, "Frank Redding."

There was no reason for debate or a recount. Frank was born and raised in Atlanta. He was someone the students on campus called a "city boy." His personality was larger than life, and he loved being the center of attention. We gladly surrendered it to him. He always had some wild story to tell and usually had us all cracking up as he held court.

Frank's reputation always preceded him. He was known as someone you didn't want to mess with. He looked like an adult among young boys. Frank seemed to be someone who had been around the block a time or three, while most of us were still trying to locate the block. He was a real man about town who fascinated some of the ladies from Spelman. A popular bad boy, Frank was a bad boy before it became fashionable.

Frank was the nicest and most generous person you'd want to meet. He had this huge infectious smile and whenever he saw you, he seemed glad to see you. I loved being around Frank. It was usually fun, and a party was sure to happen. I remember being out and about one night with Frank and one of his partners, Butch Wainwright, another city boy. We had been partying pretty hard. Butch and Frank decided that they had too much to drink, and I was in much better shape to drive. The thought of driving in Atlanta at night horrified me, especially not knowing my way around and with two inebriated passengers.

Frank insisted, and that meant compliance. Somehow, we made it back to campus safe and sound. After that night on the town with Frank and Butch, I became better friends with Frank. Almost everyone on campus seemed to respect and want to be around him. He was like the Pied Piper of Morehouse.

I was sorry we had to "rat" Frank out to The Champ, but he'd asked us to tell the truth, and if we'd called someone else's name, Frank would have been pissed off, too, because we'd have disrespected him. Also, when Muhammad Ali asked the infamous question, I looked at Frank. He appeared apprehensive. I even noticed his lips moving to form his name, "Frank Redding."

Following the unanimous decision by everyone at Yates and Milton, including Frank, that Frank Redding was indeed the Baddest "MF" in the room, Muhammad Ali slowly walked toward him and hooked his middle finger on the middle rear belt loop of Frank's jeans. He then carefully and slowly escorted Frank out the front door, much to everyone's amazement. All the while, Frank displayed this sheepish grin on his face that I'd never seen before or since.

Muhammad Ali looked to be about six-foot-three and two hundred fifteen pounds of sculpted muscle. The Champ towered over Frank, who wasn't a small person. Frank, I believe, was close to six feet tall and weighed about two hundred pounds. He wasn't a muscular guy, but he had a stocky build and looked like a Brother you didn't want to mess with. If you were in a street fight, Frank was the person you wanted on your side.

As Frank was being escorted from the building, he looked toward The Champ and said something like, "Come on, Champ, I'm your boy." Once The Champ deposited Frank immediately out the doorway, he spun around with a smile on his face. Frank wound up standing outside, wondering what happened and if he should reenter Yates and Milton. Inside, all of us were cracking up and having the time of our life. During this period of uncertainty by Frank, and glee from onlookers, The Champ posed the question, "Now, who's the Baddest 'MF' in the room?"

Muhammad Ali had been stripped of his Heavyweight Champion title and barred from boxing earlier in 1967, because he opposed the Vietnam War and refused to be drafted. He was still the "People's Champ" and his courage in standing up for his convictions made him an even bigger hero, especially to us in the African American community. I didn't know a single person who didn't revere him. He represented the Black male we all aspired to be.

A few years later though, Muhammad Ali disappointed me as he prepared for his championship fight with Joe Frazier, the reigning champion in March 1971.

For Ali, it seemed that when he was marketing, promoting, and hyping a fight there were no boundaries, regardless of who he was fighting. Muhammad relished, loved, and thrived in the spotlight. The TV camera seemed to be as fascinated with him as he was with himself. He was made for TV and TV was made for him. This love affair lasted until his death.

Sometimes, there can be too much of a good thing. For Ali, his first fight with Frazier fit that description. At one press conference, Ali hurled insult after insult at Joe Frazier, calling him an Uncle Tom, ugly, dummy, and a monkey. Up until this point, Ali had been my unflawed hero, but these antics crossed the lines of decency and respect. Ali upped the ante for insults during this press conference by pounding and pounding upon a toy monkey. As he mercilessly struck the toy monkey, he said in a loud mocking voice that this was the way he was going to beat up Frazier.

I later learned that when Ali had been banned from boxing and stripped of his title, Frazier was one of the few boxers who continued to be supportive of him, both financially and with words of encouragement. Frazier, who befriended Ali during his hour of need, was repaid with a barrage of personal attacks and insults about his abilities and character.

For many in the general public, Cassius Marcellus Clay went from being a handsome,—with movie star good looks—playful, witty, Olympic Gold Medal winner to a draft dodger, yellow communist, un-American coward named Muhammad Ali. Ali knew there were fight fans of his who didn't want to miss a boxing match—whether in person, on pay-for-view, or radio—because they wanted to experience and savor his defeat. Muhammad knew his legions of fans around the world and his dedicated detractors equaled a box office bonanza. His axiom seemed to be, "Love me or hate me, just pay me."

One of the qualities I most admired about Muhammad Ali was, whenever he lost a fight, which was infrequently, he never made any excuses for his defeat. His immediate reaction was to acknowledge the defeat and seek a rematch to avenge his loss. No excuses!

Ali would taunt Frazier by saying that although Joe Frazier was the Heavyweight Champion of the World recognized by the boxing establishment, he was the Peoples' Champion, and until Frazier beat him, Frazier wasn't really the true Heavyweight Champion of the World. Ali became a constant cloud over Frazier's head. Ali was like a shadow, always lurking—never too close, never too far away—as a constant reminder of his powerful presence even when he was absent.

Going into the "Fight of the Century" between Ali and Frazier at Madison Square Garden in 1971, both fighters were undefeated. Frankly, I think Ali would've had to kill Joe Frazier to win the fight that night. I believe his strategy of trying to unnerve Frazier and getting into his head had backfired. Ali's insults and antics, and Frazier's prior personal and financial support of Ali, fueled the "Left hook from Hades" that sent Ali sprawling to the ring's canvas in the 12th round, red tassels swirling in every direction on his once glistening white leather boxing shoes. The canvas provided a perfect landing strip for Ali and a glide path of redemption and validation for Smokin' Joe Frazier.

Even in defeat, Ali demonstrated his warrior spirit by getting up off of the canvas and mounting a brief rally before the end of the round. Boxing experts to this day wonder and marvel as to how Ali was able to get up from such a devastating left hook. Throughout his boxing career, Ali was vulnerable to the left hook.

In Joe Frazier's locker room after the fight, a number of reporters claimed that Frazier was literally out on his feet. He kept asking his boxing team who had won the fight. Imagine the fight is over, Frazier has won and is in his dressing room, not knowing the outcome of the fight. Frazier was so locked and loaded the night of the fight, "Smokin' Joe" was much more than smoke. He was on fire with embers that became hotter and hotter as the fight progressed and, on that night, he destroyed the ominous shadow of Muhammad Ali.

Muhammad Ali was someone people either loved or hated—no in-between. Those who loved him hung on his every word like honey from the heavens. One taste always led to another, and then another. There is no such thing as getting full on only brief moments of satisfaction. Ali's fans became a part of his mojo; their love, loyalty, energy, smiles, and constant adulation provided that boost to take his skills and endurance to another level when facing a very formidable opponent. The connection between Ali and his fans resembled a two-way power surge. First, he would power up his fans, then the fans would send their energy to him. A winning combination!

From the evolution of the Louisville Lip named Cassius Clay to the draft-dodging communist named Muhammad Ali to the enduring legacy he left behind, Ali's life and times embodied the period in which he lived. He personified an era that questioned authority, demonstrated the power that one person can exert, and helped to dispel the myths and stereotypes of being Black in America.

He was instrumental in causing me to rethink how I thought about myself, the world, and how I might make a difference in the broader world. A true role model, he exemplified the truism that one person can make a difference!

31 GRADUATION

IT WAS MY senior year at Morehouse College, May 1968. I was, believe it or not, three weeks away from college graduation. I had triple-checked my credits for graduation, and everything was A-Okay. For the remainder of my time at Morehouse College, I had a grand total of 12 more class hours to complete. I stood in that sweet spot and savored every moment.

Capping this remarkable journey and celebrating my accomplishments, my mom traveled from our home in Bessemer, Alabama, to Atlanta for my graduation. I had booked a room for her about ten blocks away from the campus at the Black-owned and operated Paschal Motel Hotel. The Paschal brothers, who also owned the Paschal Restaurant and Coffee Shop, provided a meeting place for civil rights leaders, and would often post bond for arrested protestors.

One of my family's goals for my brother and me was to broaden our horizons by graduating from a reputable four-year college, preferably located outside of Alabama. But most importantly, my parents wanted us to have as many options as possible for obtaining employment and that our major assets would be the ability to think and reason.

Because of their vision, values, commitment, and willingness to sacrifice for my brother and me, their aspirations came true. I received my

Bachelor of Arts degree in political science from Morehouse College in Atlanta. My brother Ken attended Clark College in Atlanta for two years, then graduated from Miles College in Birmingham, Alabama, with a bachelor's degree in sociology.

Our parents had gone above and beyond by providing the financial resources and encouragement we needed to enroll in and complete college. At an early age, our mother often stressed to us the importance of not letting anyone or anything, including blatant racism and discrimination, prevent us from achieving our dreams. She often said, "If you want it bad enough, go get it. No one can stop you but yourself."

I remember my freshman year at Morehouse. Midway through the first quarter, I called home to talk with my mother. I was getting my butt kicked in geometry, a course I'd avoided in high school, and my reading retention skills were below par. I'd never been "looking up the hill" like this before, and I didn't like the view. I thought my mother would listen to my tale of woe and, with words of wisdom and a special elixir of sympathy, soothe and ease my pain.

After waiting my turn in the line of fellow students on the third floor of Graves Hall, I placed my call. Thankfully, my mother was home and answered the phone right away. At first, we talked about mundane things, such as getting my clothes laundered, not hanging out with the wrong crowd, and not staying up too late. Finally, I—now a college boy, the former high school honor student who was in the top ten percent of my class—admitted I was having a rough time with a couple of courses and doing satisfactorily in three others. I wasn't excelling as in the past. I told her I wasn't sure what to do.

Her response took me by surprise. Without missing a beat, she said two words. "Study harder." She spoke bluntly and clearly. No other words necessary. That was the end of the conversation about my underachievement. The prescription had been written: "Study harder." Now it was my job, as the patient, to accept the prescription, take it to heart, and everything would be okay. I followed her prescription and brought my studying to another level, and I never looked back.

My mother's advice was her personal credo: Study and work harder. Whether it was traveling to Chicago to earn a Licensed Practical Nurse diploma or studying for the voting test. I remember her studying into the early hours of the morning to prepare for the Alabama voting literacy test. She passed it on her first attempt with flying colors and was one of the first people on our block, and one of the few Black people on the south side of Bessemer, who had dared to take the test, not to mention passing.

32 JAIL TIME

WHAT A SPECIAL night it had been. In Bessemer, August evenings could be hot, but that evening there was a slight breeze with temperatures in the low 80s, and the humidity was bearable. Earlier that evening, I'd been to see my girlfriend. We'd made tentative plans for a party at one of the downtown hotels in Birmingham with some other friends later in the summer.

Better yet, her mom and dad left the living room, giving us a chance to have a few hot and heavy moments. Life was good as I drove my cousin's car to pick him up at his girlfriend's (and future wife) home. As I turned left from North Avenue, aka, the Bessemer Superhighway, to 22nd Street, I noticed a police car traveling in the opposite direction. Nothing to be alarmed about, I thought. I wasn't speeding, and I hadn't been drinking. I was merely on my way to pick up my cousin, Ronald Banks. This sense of innocence and calmness soon vanished. In my rearview mirror, I saw the police car quickly spin around with its lights flashing.

Within seconds, the police car was almost touching my rear bumper, and the police officer on the passenger side frantically waved me to the side of the road. I was in total shock. What had I done in the nanosecond from the time the police saw me and then whirled around and advised me to stop?

The policeman who was driving the car immediately asked to see my driver's license. As I handed him my license, my question was, "Officer, could you please tell me why you stopped me?" At this point he just looked at me and walked away to the patrol car, without saying a word. The other police officer just stood there, looking at me as if I had robbed a bank. I was particularly interested in the placement of his right hand. It wasn't on his gun, but it was pretty close, signaling to me, "Don't try anything, because if need be, I can get to it quickly."

By now, his partner had returned and he must have found out I didn't have any outstanding warrants. For the second time, I asked, "Officer, why did you pull me over?" Finally, he indicated the reason he had pulled me over was because as I passed him, I had failed to dim my lights. My first response was disbelief and I thought, "You mean I'm getting all this grief for supposedly not dimming my lights? I mean, we're not talking about speeding, driving without a license, driving while under the influence, assault, burglary, or carrying a concealed weapon, but failing to dim my lights?"

Once I got past the shock of why I'd been stopped, I informed the police officers, not in a confrontational way, that my lights weren't set on bright or high beam. I suggested that they must be mistaken. I was adamant about this and mentioned that if this was the case during my travel from Birmingham, someone driving on the Superhighway would have flashed their lights alerting me that my lights were on bright. I told them this hadn't happened.

It was 1967 and I was a senior at Morehouse College in Atlanta, Georgia, majoring in political science, with a minor in history. At this time, my plan was to graduate with a Bachelor of Arts degree and attend law school. As a result, I'd taken a number of law and law-related courses. This education boosted my confidence. Believe it or not, I wasn't intimidated by the police, but I was respectful. On those few occasions when I've been stopped by the police for some minor traffic infraction, I always thought about what my mother told me as a kid, "Respect the police, and remember they can kill you for no reason and get away with it." Knowing my rights, according to the law, was one thing; the law and Alabama was another.

As cars buzzed by while I was interrogated by the police, I studied the two policemen who had stopped me. One appeared to be in his late twenties and was about five feet eight inches or so. I noticed his trousers were much too long and dragging on the ground. His shoes looked spanking brand new. He also fidgeted with his hat. One moment he would have it on; and the next moment he would take it off. Essentially, he seemed uncomfortable wearing his hat. It seemed too much for him to shoulder. However, whatever he lacked in comfort within the confines of his uniform, he made up for with his excitement at pulling me over for supposedly not dimming my lights. He was the driver and the first out of the police car. He walked toward my parked car with a real sense of pride and purpose. I believe he was a rookie police officer, and on the police force for a limited period of time.

I thought maybe he was someone who wasn't taken very seriously when he was in high school; maybe he was teased or bullied or was an outsider. Now, as an officer of the law, he could decide who was in or out of bounds. He had to be listened to, whether you wanted to or not. He enjoyed and relished every moment.

Some of my assumptions about this officer were confirmed by the presence and appearance of his partner that evening. The other police officer seemed to be in his late forties or early fifties, and he stood a little over six feet tall. He had a certain swagger and air of confidence about him. I could just tell this wasn't his first rodeo. His hat rested on his head, tilted to the side. This tilt wasn't accidental or happenstance. It was placed that way for a reason, it made the statement—I got this!

The lights of cars passing by illuminated the sheen of this officer's uniform, which showed that it had been worn and cleaned a number of times. Just the opposite of the young apprentice with him that evening.

The senior officer's shoes looked like modified combat boots that had been issued during a different era. This officer did most of the talking, and I saw that the younger officer looked to his partner for his cues.

The two White police officers were really checking me out. I think they didn't especially like the fact that I was questioning their judgement, not once, but twice. One of the police officers had a flashlight, and he started shining the light on me from head to toe. I had a large Afro, framed by a full black beard. I wore prescription sunglasses, and it was about 10:00 p.m. Rounding out my look was a gold knit, short-sleeve sweater with brown stripes, gray slacks, and brown sandals. Sort of an Eldridge Cleaver look.

After being inspected from head to toe, the police officer who was on the passenger side of the car, out of nowhere, asked me if I was funny. Not "ha, ha" funny as in being a jokester, but funny at that time in Alabama meant, "Are you a sissy, faggot, punk, or did you have sugar in your britches?' Without missing a beat, my response to the police officer was, "Are you funny?"

As soon as I uttered those three words, I thought, "Merritt, you must be crazy. So much for all the training you've received from your parents and relatives over the years. Get ready for the ass whupping you are about to receive."

Instead, and fortunately for me, the two policemen decided that I needed to be locked up. They placed me under arrest and drove me to jail in downtown Bessemer. Once I arrived at the jail, and before being placed in a cell, I was allowed to make one phone call.

By now, the absurd had become ludicrous, and I thought this surreal experience was indeed funny—and I mean "ha, ha" funny. I called Ronnie at his girlfriend's home, explaining that I was in jail in downtown Bessemer for failing to dim my lights. Initially, he didn't believe me and thought I was playing a joke on him. After I convinced him that it was no joke, he started laughing and cracking up, which meant I started laughing and cracking up. However, the arresting officers didn't appreciate my sense of humor. They pulled the telephone from my hand and ended my call.

Because of my bad attitude, I wasn't locked up in a regular jail cell, but the cell at the jail known as "The Hole." This cell had a small opening at the bottom of the door, just large enough for a food tray to be slipped through. The cell was in total darkness, the walls padded.

Here I was, Mr. College Boy, Morehouse Man, in a padded cell in my hometown of Bessemer, Alabama, for failing to dim my lights, questioning authority, maybe being funny. Worst of all, I couldn't stop laughing my head off.

Now that I was in "The Hole," I needed to demonstrate I was worthy of such esteemed placement in the jail. I started banging on the door and in the loudest voice I could render, demanded my release because of being falsely arrested and jailed. I yelled, "When was the last time you heard of someone being arrested for failing to dim their lights?" I continued my ruckus for another 30 minutes or so, to no avail. I finally settled in for the night.

The next thing I knew, it was morning and a tray of pancakes and sausage magically appeared through the opening at the bottom of the cell door. Actually, they didn't look too bad, but of course, I pushed them away—just like on television or in the movies.

Fortunately, a little after 8:00 a.m., Ronnie arrived and bailed me out of jail. As I was getting my watch, wallet, and other personal items, I heard a couple of the inmates talking about that youngster who was in "The Hole" last night. One said to the other, "I'm not sure what he was in for, but he was a real hell raiser."

33 BACK-BREAKING WORK

As I ENTERED our home one muggy hot summer evening in 1967, after working from 8:00 a.m. to 6:30 p.m. at a construction site, I saw my father sitting in the living room with a faint smile on his face. I realized he'd been watching me through our front picture window as I walked up the steps. He had a real knack for watching and observing—without anyone noticing. My father, over time, honed this skill quite well before my brother and I arrived on the scene.

Judging from the smile on his face, he was getting the biggest kick out of watching me walk up the front steps, in slow motion. I was almost out on my feet, barely able to make it to the top of the steps. Fortunately, we had white iron railings that supported me as I climbed up the red painted cement steps, one by one.

Walking past my father as he sat in his favorite chair was like the student, me, walking past the instructor, my father. I'd finally gained a first-hand appreciation and respect for the work my father had routinely done most of his life. Nothing needed to be said. My drooping shoulders, tired baby steps while hanging onto the railing for dear life, and slow walk up the steps with a sunburned face, said it all. However, he couldn't let it go without saying, "Construction work kind of hard, huh?" The only comment I managed to muster was, "Yeah." The face he saw that evening, totally exhausted, drained physically and emotionally, was one that he'd never seen before. He enjoyed every moment of it.

Kind of hard, however, was an understatement. It was backbreaking awful work, especially for me at 130 pounds. Throughout the workday, I had to push a wheelbarrow loaded with wet cement weighing about 75 pounds. This Herculean feat was made more difficult by having to push the loaded wheelbarrow on elevated wooden planks to the designated spot about 30 feet away. Each time I performed this task, it seemed as though the distance became longer and more excruciating.

If I'd been honest with my father, I would have said, "How do you manage to do this, day after day?" After three days, I was ready to quit. I didn't need this kind of backbreaking work.

I realized his "construction work kind of hard, huh" comment had several meanings.

He wanted me to know the type of work he endured to support his family because of his lack of education and training.

He was willing to take almost any job to make sure my brother and I could attend college and not follow his path.

My father had gained a sense of satisfaction knowing that I had an up close and personal view into his world. Unlike me, his construction job wasn't one to make some extra money for the summer. For him, it was a way of life to support his family.

The physical aspect of the construction job was something I expected; however, the emotional toll of the job was something I didn't have a clue about. Each day before going to the job site for work, all of the Black laborers met at a pick-up point around 7:45 a.m. We were loaded onto the back of the truck like cattle, and then transported to the job site. The few White workers always sat in the cab of the truck.

I expected the job would end around 5:00 or 5:30 p.m. However, the workday ended when the White supervisors decided to call it a day. This was the reason we were driven to the construction site and loaded onto trucks. We were captives, with no way of leaving; and no one dared to question this arrangement for fear of losing the job.

If rain was in the forecast for the next day, the workday lasted until 7:00 p.m., or longer.

The good news was we were paid on an hourly basis, and we were paid at least the minimum wage. Being paid minimum wage was like winning the lottery for me, because this was a gigantic increase over the Marilee's Flower Shop top wage of $13 per week for 6 days of work from 8:00 a.m. to 6:00 p.m. However, the bad news was that, because there was no set workday schedule, overtime pay or extra compensation was a non-issue.

I understood why my father said, "If you have no choice of your comings and goings to and from work and if you couldn't miss a day of work when you were sick or had an emergency because you couldn't miss a paycheck, then you didn't have a job, the job had you."

Working for about two months in the construction field was an eye-opening experience. I gained an increased respect for my father's work ethic, and admiration for the work he did without complaint, all while working under intolerable work conditions. Little did I know when he left home what a courageous man he was. Both of my parents were courageous because they had to sometimes sacrifice their dignity for their children.

34 CHOICE WORDS FROM POP

My FATHER SELDOM, if ever, commented on matters of race and race relations. However, I remember vividly one time when he did. It was the summer of 1967, and I'd come home for the summer from my junior year at Morehouse College.

It must have been 90-plus degrees as my mother was driving down what was then called the Bessemer Superhighway. My mother had recently purchased a spanking, brand-new Buick Skylark. The Skylark was dark blue, with a matching blue vinyl top, blue fender skirts, and white wall tires with silver rims. The Skylark was the first car our family had owned. In the past, when transportation was needed to go to the grocery store, doctor's office, or school, or to visit a relative or friend, we either walked, took a taxi or bus, or caught a ride from a friend. Most of our friends and neighbors were in similar situations.

On this summer day, my father rode shotgun, the front passenger seat on the right side of the car, and he rode it like only he could. He was probably wearing one of his vintage caps with its many creases and folds that had been crafted over many life experiences and Father Time.

If he'd been traveling on a Saturday, he would have been wearing one of his Dobbs hats that were carefully and neatly stacked in the closet he and my mother shared. They were always just above his suits and shirts in the closet. If it was Saturday evening, he'd be dressed to the nines to meet up with some of the fellas at Morris Mayfield's Filling Station to swap stories and have a little taste of whiskey.

As the air conditioner gently and softly hummed away, providing a cool breeze with calming white noise, riding on the Superhighway that day felt like we were experiencing a magic carpet ride. The buildings, houses, and trees floated by in what seemed like slow motion. Inside the car there was no music or conversation, just the AC doing its thing and doing it quite well.

Suddenly, my father noticed a White hitchhiker on the right side of the road with his right fist and curved thumb uplifted to the sky. To Ken's and my shock, surprise, and delight, my father matter-of-factly stated, "You have been free all your life, you should have a car."

The Skylark had been quiet earlier and now with my father's out-of-the-blue as well as out-of-character comment, for a few seconds, it was deafeningly quiet. After my brother and I recovered from our surprise, we looked at one other in disbelief. Did we just hear our father, Will Mack Long, make such a comment? Previously, I'd heard him comment on racial injustice and segregation by saying things like, "That peckerwood may not have much, but he always thinks he's better than you," or "The construction boss has Blacks do jobs that take more heavy lifting and bending than Whites."

Also, he'd sometimes comment on how some White men who were TV sportscasters could hardly read but were given the opportunity to learn on the job, but Black people couldn't get in the door. He also noticed that, given how they dressed, they didn't have a pot to piss in. However, he emphasized that over time their reading and wardrobe would improve. One of his comments that is my all-time favorite is, "Money will bring you out of the crack."

My father, in just these few words, "You have been free all your life, you should have a car," said so much about the inequities and discrimination he'd faced throughout his life.

Pop was ahead of time in 1967 when he talked about White privilege and all the inherent advantages that go with it.

35 UNLIKELY TEACHER

My four years at Morehouse College went fast. It was hard to believe I was three weeks from graduation.

As I sat in the college cafeteria, there were many different thoughts swirling around in my head concerning graduation, friends and family coming to town, job interviews, and relocation possibilities. As this mental exercise was occurring, I gained an incredible lesson from an unlikely source.

The source of this learning experience was made possible by a total stranger who was about ten years old. The experience probably consisted of ten minutes of actual time but has had a lasting effect on my thinking and how I view the world. I haven't seen my muse since and by chance, if I ever had the opportunity, I wouldn't recognize him. Prior to meeting my new best friend, I was about to feast on one of the specialty treats at the cafeteria, a hot dog split. It was prepared like a hamburger with all or some of the fixings, including lettuce, tomato, pickle, cheese, and the customary mustard and ketchup. Instead of a hamburger patty, the cook would take a hot dog, split it in half, place it on the grill, and cook it until it was seared a nice brown on one side. Then the cook would place it on a soft buttered bun that had been grilled alongside the split hotdog; the bun and split dog then became one.

After I took my first delicious bite from the split, I quickly realized I needed something to drink. A bag of potato chips was at the ready and a nice cold orange drink would make this afternoon treat a wonderful trifecta.

While walking to the soda vending machine, out of the corner of my left eye I noticed a young kid who seemed to be no more than ten years old. He was watching each step I made toward the vending machine. After I deposited a quarter in the machine, the young man left his seat and in a matter of seconds he was standing right next to me. I looked down, as we exchanged hellos, and proceeded to try to purchase an orange drink. I could hear the quarter slowing making its way down the vending machine, and as it traveled, I pushed the plastic button designated for orange drinks. Suddenly, I heard a plop sound at the bottom of the machine, but instead of a drink rolling out, my quarter had made its way from the top of the vending machine to the bottom. Well, I thought, this happens sometimes on the first try, no problem. I reinserted the quarter, but unfortunately, I had the same results.

Now I had my quarter in hand and I didn't feel like the third time would be the charm. At this point, I was thinking my yummy hotdog split was getting cold, and I sensed that, if the orange drink didn't escape from the vending machine and fall into my clutches, my quarter could get locked up as well. Then I would forever be known as the three-time vending machine loser.

My new best friend still stood next to me. He got my attention by gently tugging on the white, button-down collared shirt I wore. He looked up at me and earnestly asked, "Do you still want a drink from the machine?" Surely, he had witnessed my acts of futility and frustration and was coming to my rescue. I think he knew before I inserted my first quarter what the outcome would be. I hesitated slightly before easing the quarter from my hand to his, hoping no one would see me—soon-to-be college graduate—being bailed out by a ten-year old. After the kid inserted the quarter, he signaled me to make my choice of drink, and I immediately pushed the plastic button for the orange soda I still wanted.

The young stranger spun around and bravely faced my tormentor—the vending machine—not in the least intimidated. Suddenly, with his left hand placed on the edge of the machine, he kicked the mid-section of the machine with his left foot and as soon as he finished the kick, he repeated the same herculean feat but with his right foot. When both kicks were accomplished, he bumped the front of the vending machine with his right shoulder.

After he'd kicked and bumped the machine, he looked at me with his arms folded, waiting for the melodious sound of the orange soda being paroled, although for a short life.

I waited and waited and waited for it, then bam, there it was. The kid had delivered. He was my orange drink savior. He picked up the drink from the vending machine, gleefully gave it to me, and slowly strutted away, never to be seen again.

As I looked at him leaving, I muttered under my breath, "Who was that kid?"

Regardless of age or a person's station in life, they can teach you something if you are receptive and listen.

PART V
MY PROFESSIONAL LIFE
1968-2006

36 SEATTLE AND CORRECTIONS

ON OCTOBER 21, 1968, I started my career in Washington State government as a Parole and Probation Officer Trainee. A little less than five months before that, in June 1968, I'd graduated from Morehouse College in Atlanta, Georgia, with a Bachelor of Arts degree, majoring in political science and minoring in history.

I'd also graduated from sleeping on the floor to the couch at Ken and Jacque's apartment in Seattle. I will always be grateful to my kind and thoughtful brother, Ken, and sister-in-law, Jacque, for their hospitality. I was earning about $531 before taxes, netting around $375 and had room and board expenses of $50 per month. With my uptick in income, I could afford to buy a single sofa bed thereby leaving the floor accommodations. I felt the sky was the limit and Seattle was indeed a place of opportunity as my brother had stated.

LaTonja Long (now Hunter), my brother's first born and my niece, was about eight months old when I moved in with Ken and Jacque in the summer of 1968. She was a happy little girl, always glad to see me, her uncle. We kind of grew up together, with her being eight months old and me being 21. An added bonus was, as she got older and we hung out together, she was a chick magnet. Wherever we went, beautiful young ladies would "ooh" and "ah" over her. When they learned I was her uncle and not her father, pay dirt. They thought, what a wonderful guy he must be to have such a close and loving relationship with his niece. I'm not that smart; I didn't plan it that way, but I loved it.

The first time I babysat LaTonja alone, she went into the kitchen and lay down on the floor, face up, with her eyes closed. It really scared me. I wondered what the heck was the matter. Something bad is happening. After I rushed over to her, she turned her head toward me and gave me a huge smile. "Gotcha," her smile said. Since that incident and big smile, she's had me ever since.

. . .

I remember vividly my first day as a Parole and Probation Officer Trainee. When I arrived at work at the Seattle Smith Tower—once the tallest building west of the Mississippi—I was awestruck. I'd never seen a building this tall before with such an unusual shape. It reminded me of the first black and white *King Kong* movie I'd watched at the Black-only Lincoln movie theater in Bessemer, Alabama. Kong was hanging onto the top edge of the Empire State Building with one hand, while using the other hand to swat at the planes trying to kill him with machine gun fire. The most memorable scene was when King Kong swatted a plane like it was a gnat and it crashed to the ground.

Once I stepped inside the Smith Tower and entered one of the elevators, things got even more interesting as I attempted to go to my office located on the 28th floor. Instead of pushing a button to go to my floor, a real live operator opened the elevator door. He was nattily attired in his attendant uniform: a light gray jacket, matching gray pants, white shirt, slim black tie, and black shoes.

The passengers indicated their office floor to the elevator operator and our ride began. The magic and skill of the operator would be demonstrated when you arrived at each floor. Stopping the elevator was totally manual and the elevator operator would start slowing down as he got close to each floor because his goal was to stop the elevator even with the floor to ensure a smooth exit. If this didn't occur, the elevator operator would continue adjusting the height until the elevator floor was even with the main floor.

In addition to the usual morning challenges of getting to work on time, including navigating traffic, finding a place to park, and having the necessary change to feed the parking meter, I faced another unique challenge. When I started working at the Seattle Smith Tower Building in 1968, the Seattle Urban League was located on the 16th floor. The elevator operator often stopped at the 16th floor, expecting me to get off even when I'd instructed him to stop on the 28th floor where the Parole and Probation Office was located. The Urban League staff was primarily African American and for a couple of years I was the only African American working at the Parole and Probation Office or in any of the other offices in the entire building.

The elevator operator's logic probably went something like this: Most African American men dressed in a suit and tie are usually going to the Urban League Office. Since he's wearing a suit and tie, surely he's going to the Urban League on the 16th floor even if he asked for the 28th floor. I must admit I probably made things worse on a couple of occasions by not paying attention to the floor I was on and exiting the elevator on the dreaded 16th floor of the Seattle Urban League. I'm sure some of the elevator operators were quietly thinking, I knew he belonged on the 16th floor whether he knows it or not.

. . .

I was asked and accepted the responsibility of traveling to Reno, Nevada, to transport a Washington State parole violator from Reno back to Seattle. The good news is that my plane departed on a Friday at the end of the month, which meant it was a state payday, and returned on the following Monday. So, on Friday and Saturday night I was in Nevada on state business and had just gotten paid. Good news, bad news. Good news, on state expense; bad news, I wasn't good at all playing slot machines.

Fortunately, I kept most of my wits about me and didn't lose my entire paycheck, but I came close.

Being asked to travel to Reno was a real feather in my cap. It signaled I was doing a good job, because I was being rewarded with this challenge and opportunity. There was no lack of fellow colleagues who would have loved to take this exciting and somewhat dangerous trip of bringing a fugitive back to face justice.

After arriving in Reno, I had been instructed to check in with Nevada's Washoe County Sheriff's Office to alert them of my arrival. I was to advise them that I would be transporting one of their prisoners back to Seattle. He had committed parole violations of attempted burglary and leaving the state without the permission of his parole officer.

This was pretty straight forward. I thought once my plane arrived in Reno, I would go directly from the airport to the Washoe County Sheriff's Office by taxi to check in as instructed. As I walked into the sheriff's office, I saw the reception area where a uniformed sheriff was sitting, looking down at documents. He had a receding hairline, and his short-sleeved uniform revealed arms that were once muscular but were now soft. As he heard me approach, he slowly looked up. There was no smile, no frown, just a blank stare on his face. His expression reminded me of the Alabama bus driver from my first bus ride.

I was flying high, excited about my mission and responsibility. After all, I was here representing the state of Washington. I was the official designee to transport the parolee back home to answer to the Washington State Criminal Justice System. Surely, I would be welcomed and respected with open arms by my fellow corrections colleague. Although not a sheriff, I was an officer of the court, which meant the sheriff and I were law enforcement brethren.

Before I could say one word to the deputy seated at the reception desk, I couldn't help but notice his uniform. Why? The closer I came to him, his shirt looked tighter and tighter to the point where it might explode with any sudden movement. The buttons on his shirt seemed to be crying out for help. The strained configuration of buttons seemed to be pleading, "save us from this cruel existence of buttoning down a too-small shirt."

When the deputy saw me, his expressionless face became contorted and he looked at me as if I was from the moon. Without missing a beat, in a stern, loud, and sarcastic voice he uttered, "Boy, what do you want?"

For a moment, I went into suspended animation. I started flashing back on my journey from a child growing up in Bessemer, Alabama, and hearing White men call Black men, whether 21 or 91, "boy." White males in Alabama seemed to enjoy calling grown Black men "boys," even when they knew they were men. Sometimes, when Whites came to our neighborhood selling insurance, watermelons, and other fruits, they still had the nerve to call grown Black men, "boy." The message was the same. "It doesn't matter, Black man, whether you're rich or poor, in my eyes, you're a "boy", less than a man. The one something I'll always have over you is my White skin color. That's right, Mr. Black Man, regardless of your educational attainment, professional achievement, civic commitment, and/ or charitable work, nothing will wash your Blackness away or your innate inferiority. That's just the way it is. Get used to it. A nigger is a nigger!

So here I was in Reno, Nevada, an officer of the court. A recent graduate of Morehouse College. I was a duly sworn Parole and Probation Officer, who had traveled from Seattle to Reno to be called "boy." Quite frankly, no different than when I was a sophomore in high school and Mr. Wright of Marilee's Flower Shop wanted to know if "that 'boy'" sweeping the street in Bessemer, Alabama, was crazy. My experience in hearing people use the word "boy," was that it came from ignorance, hate, disdain, or just putting some uppity nigger in their place.

What was my response to the first out-of-state slight and insult in my personal life and professional career as a Parole and Probation Officer in 1970 in Reno, Nevada? I looked the deputy directly in his eyes and slowly said, "I'm not sure where you come from, but boys, even from Texas, don't come in my size." If his eyes could have killed, I would have been dead and buried by now. The deputy, my fellow brother, was seething.

Now that I knew the iron was hot, I showed him my official Parole and Probation Officer badge and asked to see his boss. I informed him I was there on official Washington State business to transport a convicted felon and parole violator from Nevada to Seattle, Washington. I ended by pointing to one of the chairs nearby, stating I was taking a seat. I told him when his supervisor, with emphasis on the word "supervisor," arrived, to please let me know.

The big bad wolf, aka, deputy, was quiet and seemed to be at a loss for words. Seconds later he picked up the telephone and over the intercom I heard him ask for his supervisor because there was a Parole and Probation Officer from Washington State that needed to speak to him. Maybe he realized by now, the "boy" he thought he saw earlier somehow had grown up before his very own eyes.

I was progressing in my corrections career, when an event occurred that made me reassess my career goals. Did I want to continue in corrections and be a one-trick pony, someone who could only excel in one area?

I remember vividly where it happened. It was on a Saturday in the spring of 1973, in Seattle, Washington, at a former night club, The Heritage House. The night club had closed due to bankruptcy and the building then housed an employment and training program called Operation Improvement. This program provided funds for vocational training, retraining, direct job placement services, and supportive services for people unemployed and underemployed. It was geared toward persons of color, inner city youth, veterans, and the disabled. In addition, Operation Improvement rented out space to public and private agencies and organizations to use as a staff development and training facility.

On a spring Saturday, the facility was being used by state agencies and community-based organizations. They provided employment counseling and vocational and supportive services to ex-offenders reentering the community, as well as people on parole and probation who already lived in the community. Ex-offenders relocating or returning to Seattle after five years of incarceration faced enormous challenges.

At this time, I had worked in the field of adult corrections for about five years. My job titles had ranged from Parole and Probation Officer, Volunteer Coordinator, and Statewide Volunteer Coordinator, to my most recent position as director of the Corrections Clearinghouse. These positions had one consistent theme: providing employment counseling, job placement services, vocational training and retraining, career counseling, and an array of supportive services for adult ex-offenders to help them successfully live crime free.

I performed well in the regulatory environment of being a Parole and Probation Officer with specific "do's" and "don'ts" for parolees. These included finding a job, locating suitable housing, attending Alcoholics Anonymous or drug counseling if required, and reporting monthly to their parole officer. My job was to assist the parolee in achieving these required objectives. I remember once saying to a parolee, "Thanks for coming by to see me." He responded by looking at me and probably saying to himself, "You must be kidding me," and then saying, "Thanks," in an annoyed tone. This was followed by, "I had no choice but to come to see you."

He was correct. This wasn't a social or nice-to-do visit. It was required that he meet with me at least once a month to provide an update on his status in the community.

Where I really flourished in adult corrections employment and training was where there was no template or rule book to follow. The bigger the challenge, the more motivated I became, especially when I was told it couldn't be done. As the first paid Volunteer Coordinator in King County for Adult Corrections, my task was to use citizen volunteers as sounding boards to assist adult offenders in the areas of housing and long-term employment. I soon realized the challenge of ex-offenders successfully re-entering society and not re-offending was more complex and layered than what I'd originally been led to believe. I learned working full time and having a decent place to stay wasn't the alpha and omega for ex-offender nirvana. After years and so many instances of ex-offenders being told what they couldn't do, what rights they didn't have, and how limited their chances of succeeding in the outside world were, offenders were being programmed to fail.

Given this history, my thoughts and actions led me to believe that training workshops for offenders aimed at reversing this thinking of what you can't do to what you can do was critical. Two examples of seminars I initiated and coordinated to chip away at this negativity: The Washington State Board Against Discrimination provided workshops on the rights and responsibilities of ex-offenders and the Washington State Employees Credit Union (WSECU) in Seattle provided advice on budgeting, re-establishing credit, and successfully managing finances.

In addition, I also leveraged my business and professional relationships for the benefit of my correctional clients. My optometrist at the time agreed to provide free eye exams and eyeglasses at cost to ex-offenders who needed these services. The Washington Air National Guard and the military were exploring ways to improve their images given the negative blowback from the unpopular Vietnam War. As a Parole and Probation Officer and member of the National Guard, I thought of a win/win opportunity for the Guard and family members/loved ones of offenders assigned to the Washington State Penitentiary in Walla Walla, Washington, a distance of over 260 miles one way.

Pilots in the Air National Guard needed to have a certain number of flying hours to maintain their certification as active pilots. From working with families and other loved ones of ex-offenders, I learned how time-consuming and expensive it was to travel from Seattle to Walla Walla for a visit. It sounded like a match made in heaven to me. Fortunately, everyone agreed, and we were able to have the National Guard, for two weekends, fly families and other loved ones from Seattle to Walla Walla and back. It was a very successful effort with everyone involved feeling good about this unique opportunity.

The big boss of Adult Corrections at the time, Ellis Stout, sent me a memo that I'll never forget, because it started out with a word that I wasn't familiar with, "Kudos." This acknowledgement was a big deal and caught me by surprise.

What happened during the training conference in Seattle? A question arose that was specifically geared to the field of adult corrections. When this happened, one of the attendees immediately responded by saying, "Merritt is the correctional expert, let's ask him." My immediate mental response and reaction surprised me. I actually resented being viewed as a correctional expert. Although the correctional arena was my world, I didn't see myself as a correctional expert, nor did I want to be viewed as one. I saw myself as an innovator, problem solver, and skilled program manager. I realized why the person called me a correctional expert, but from that moment on I knew I wanted to work and excel in multiple disciplines, not just one. This clarity was important to me as I considered and started to pursue different career options.

37 WASHINGTON NATIONAL GUARD

GROWING UP IN Bessemer, Alabama, I would pass by a building that was named Air National Guard. I was familiar with the Army, Navy, Marines, and Air Force, but the National Guard had no meaning for me at all. Throughout middle school and eventually college, I'd never seen anyone that looked like me or even close to me who was a member of the National Guard. I didn't know the National Guard was a means of meeting one's military obligation. To me, it didn't exist.

That changed. Through my brother's connections with Alfred Cowles, the director of the Washington State Board Against Discrimination (now the Washington State Human Rights Commission), I was hired as a temporary community worker by Mr. Cowles. During August 1968, he had been pressuring the National Guard's Adjunct General, Robert King, to recruit and admit African Americans into the Guard. When my draft status was changed to 1-A and I was on the verge of being drafted into the military, I talked with Mr. Cowles about the change in my military status. He immediately called Adjunct General King and presto, I was in the Guard. Timing is everything. I was in the right place at the right time.

Before going to Lackland, Texas, for military basic training, I decided to get all my hair cut off and deprive the military of that pleasure. I felt that if I made the decision, I was still in charge of my life for a little while longer. After arriving in Texas for the next six weeks of basic training, my world, as I formerly knew it, was turned upside down.

On my third day of basic training, I was walking around the base after dinner with my new friend, Howard Blum, from New York City. As we leisurely walked around our barracks, out of nowhere we heard this voice say, "I cannot believe my eyes, a nigger and a Jew walking together."

His voice wasn't aggressive or challenging, but a voice of curious certainty. He knew what he was seeing and was in a state of disbelief. It was like he had seen one of the seven wonders of the world. Why would he make such a statement? I can only speculate. In his world, this type of self-expression was the norm, perhaps even encouraged by family or friends.

By stating his feelings, he was expressing the lesser of two evils. Instead of physical confrontation, he chose a verbal insult. Maybe he wanted to be known as a badass who didn't like African Americans and persons of the Jewish faith.

As the man walked past Howard and me, we looked at each other in disbelief, shook our heads in amazement, and continued our walk and conversation as though nothing had happened. Neither one of us looked back to see who he was, nor did we ever speak of the incident.

I think that in our respective worlds, the incidence of racist and anti-Semitism comments wasn't unusual. Over time, we both learned to shrug them off and keep stepping. If not, one would be forced to react often to some form of insult or slight. Howard had a certain Zen-like quality about him, an aura of serenity and inner peace. He was comfortable in his own skin, especially for someone in his early 20s. Being around Howard, everything seemed to slow down a bit. Everyone else was on 75 RPM; Howard maxed out at 45 RPM. He was about five-feet, four-inches tall. He had a roundish face, short coarse black hair, and a big smile. His face was framed with black-rimmed glasses, and his eyes seemed to always have a mischievous twinkle.

My memory of Howard Blum contrasts markedly with some of my other memories of six weeks of basic training for the Air National Guard in Lackland, Texas. The star of the show, or actually the executive producer and director of the show, was Sergeant Jose Colon. He was top dog of our particular training flight of about 50 young men from across the country. He was the drill sergeant and drill he did, way beyond military drills of marching, physical exercise, and firing a weapon for the first time. Sergeant Colon seemed to have a chip on his shoulder toward the entire training flight. But, for lucky me, he carried a boulder on his shoulder. While my basic training movie was a miniseries that lasted only six weeks, at times it seemed like a movie marathon. I was the reluctant but dutiful star of Sergeant Colon's production.

Sergeant Colon seemed to always have a scowl on his face, as if he were mad at the world. He was about five-feet, five-inches tall, weighing about 155 pounds. His military fatigues were always fresh and crisp with creases in his pants that said, "I know I look good, and you can count on me in every way." These green starched fatigues were inserted into his boots perfectly, which allowed them to balloon out just so. Sergeant Colon's black high-top military boots, with black tightly tied shoelaces, were second to none. The very tips of his boots were like small mirrors that had been shined to the point where if you looked close enough, you could see your face.

Sergeant Colon's military hat obviously had been placed on his head with great care. It had a little tilt to the right and was meticulously placed that way each and every day. Meticulous to the nth degree.

I had no knowledge or idea of our drill sergeant's career path, but he seemed like someone who had been in the military since his early 20s or late teens. It appeared he was now in his mid-30s, and after doing 10 years or so, maybe he felt he had peaked at the rank of staff sergeant.

I remember quite clearly during basic training when his venom began to flow in my direction. I was afforded the special status of being disrespected and humiliated in front of my peers when he learned I was a college boy. I believe, with the exception of a couple of other individuals in our training flight, no one had gone to college. I had not only attended college, but I had graduated.

During the second day of basic training, each person was asked to give a little background information on what they had been doing prior to coming to basic training in January 1969. Almost half of the 50 members of our training flight had recently graduated from high school. With the exception of a few others, everyone but me had been working in manufacturing or blue-collar jobs. I also reported I'd been hired as a Parole and Probation Officer Trainee located in the downtown Seattle Smith Tower.

One evening while watching the evening news, in what was called the common area, after the completion of the first week of basic training, I had another special title added to my training plan. Sergeant Colon came by our barracks with his glossy boots. I soon found out that his boots weren't glossy enough and he wanted the lone African American in our training flight, aka college boy, to shine his boots. Of course, wanting me to shine his boots wasn't a request, but an order. Top Sergeant wanted me to know that, although I may have had a college degree and he didn't, he was in charge and he wasn't about to let me forget it.

Ironically, I loved shining my shoes and took great pride in keeping them in mint condition. I picked this trait up from my father, who took excellent care in the maintenance and the shining gloss of his shoes. When I was in middle school and walked to school on dusty roads, I used a cloth to dust my shoes off when I arrived at school. I placed a worn, but clean sock in my back pocket. When I arrived at school, I pulled out my sock at some discreet location and voila, I was Joe Cool again. My shoe motto: love and take care of your shoes and they will love and take care of you.

Just because I enjoyed shining shoes didn't mean I was thrilled and honored to be the shoeshine boy for Sergeant Colon. However, I said, "Yes, sir," and shined his shoes that evening, giving them the care and love I would give my own shoes. It wasn't the shoes' fault that the ego needs, insecurities, power trip, and maybe racism of the owner had placed them temporarily with me. While shining the Sergeant's shoes, I zoned out, as I usually do, taking my time, losing myself with every brush stroke. When not hurried, I find shining my shoes and all that goes with the cleaning, polishing, and adding special protectant against the elements, very therapeutic.

Another evening when I was busy shining Sergeant Colon's shoes, I had my head down and I could feel someone walking towards me. Suddenly, this person was towering over me and I looked up and was about to say, "What the hell are you doing standing over me like that?"

Fortunately, I didn't say anything right away. This was good because when I looked up, Sergeant Colon stood over me. I caught those few intended words and kept them in my mouth. He looked at me as if to say, "What the hell were you about to say to me?" He couldn't accuse me of saying anything, because I hadn't. He reached for his shined shoes, slowly turned around, and not one word was spoken. However, I think Sergeant Colon felt my message of disdain, but it probably meant nothing to him.

One day as I walked toward a table for lunch, Sergeant Colon stopped me. He took a close look at my lunch selections and noticed I had chocolate milk to drink. He said that was unacceptable and requested I return to the milk station and pour a glass of white milk as well. I turned around, filled a glass with white milk and sat down and ate my lunch followed by two glasses of milk, one chocolate, one white. It was no big deal for me since I liked milk.

While at basic training, a considerable amount of time was devoted to learning and exercising various military drills and formation. I was chosen by Sergeant Colon to be the "guide flag carrier." I was responsible for carrying the unit's flag while marching out front and setting the pace and rhythm for the unit. Because of my long legs, and being a little over six-feet tall, I struck gold again, kind of.

One day, while on what was called the drill pad, we were going over several different drill exercises. Sergeant Colon became enraged because of what he perceived as me not listening to him and royally screwing up the drill. His voice became louder and louder, and you could see veins popping in his neck. His face got redder and redder by the minute. Spit started coming out of his mouth. No matter what I did, it was wrong. The Sergeant could not stand me for some reason.

Out of nowhere appeared a colonel, who had heard the ranting and raving of Sergeant Colon as he passed by. He came over, got nose to nose with Sergeant Colon, and told him to stop this treatment of screaming and belittling me. He told him he was an embarrassment to the military and his behavior was totally unacceptable and he never wanted to witness anything like that by him again. My first thought, there is a God! This was the last time the Top Sergeant screamed at me. During the remaining two weeks at Lackland, my experience was totally different. It was normal, like everyone else's.

38 COMMISSION FOR VOCATIONAL EDUCATION

I REMEMBER VIVIDLY the first time I interviewed for the Executive Director position at the Commission for Vocational Education (CVE). The special assistant to the director at that time was Linda Broderick. I talked with her about my interest and asked what steps I needed to take to be considered for the position. I'd been working at the agency for more than a decade and had held senior-level management positions of increasing responsibility, the current position being administrator of the Planning and Research Division. The responsibilities of this division comprised the majority of work for the six-member policy commission.

Linda tried to discourage me from applying because she thought it would be a waste of time and effort. She said a senior-level administrator in the Vocational Education Division at the Office of the Superintendent of Public Instruction (SPI) had the votes necessary to secure the position. Essentially, the decision had been made. I was persistent in my request, regardless of what seemed to be the planned outcome. I wanted the opportunity to go through the process and experience an interview where the agency directorship was at stake. Career opportunities of this type didn't occur often, especially for African Americans and people of color working in state government.

Finally, Linda relented and asked me to provide her an updated copy of my resume. She said she'd add my name to the interview schedule. Linda knew my work history and educational background, which easily qualified me to be a candidate. I did my homework and developed and practiced answers to possible questions.

Finally, my big interview day arrived. I felt prepared and was calm and relaxed during my interview. The Commission members took a break following my interview and, by chance, I happened to be in the men's restroom with Commission member and Superintendent of Public Instruction, Frank "Buster" Brouillet. He surprised me by saying, "You know, Merritt, if I didn't already have my guy, based on that interview, you'd be my guy."

I thanked him for his comment, and we went our separate ways. I appreciated the superintendent's honesty of letting me know straight up how he'd already given his word to someone else. I knew once a commitment was made at his level, there would be no going back. I respected, appreciated, and got a big smile out of his candid comment.

I wasn't upset, angry, or disappointed that Linda was right on the mark, as usual, especially in the political arena. From my experiences over the past several decades, whether in the public sector or private, the idea of securing and buttoning down votes in advance for a position, referendum, or legislation was commonplace, especially if you wanted to help shape the results. I have learned to understand, accept, and live by these informal rules, win or lose. Actually, I enjoyed the challenges and rewards of the process. Regardless of the outcome, I was better prepared the next time around.

Two years later, the directorship opened again. I had been doing my homework in those two years by working closely with commission members so they could get to know me. My division's responsibilities included the primary areas the commissioners were most interested in.

Also, in the meantime, two key Commission members had been appointed by Governor Booth Gardner: The Reverend Samuel B. McKinney of the Mt. Zion Baptist Church in Seattle, and Ike Ikeda, Director of the Atlantic Street Center, also in Seattle. Reverend McKinney played a pivotal role in establishing the Seattle Opportunities Industrialization Center, a private, non-profit vocational training center. Through his organization, Mr. Ikeda advocated for immigrant and migrant rights and opportunities, social justice, and social services. Both added diversity to the commission. When I made my interest in being the director known to Reverend McKinney and Mr. Ikeda, both indicated their support, and I knew they would be strong advocates for my appointment.

When I was appointed Executive Director of the Commission for Vocational Education in 1985, I received my first and last call from Superintendent Brouillet. It began with him saying I had overwhelmed him this time around and he was calling to congratulate me on being appointed as the Executive Director of the Commission for Vocational Education. I heard a little smile in his voice when he mentioned this time around, because I am certain he was thinking about when I had previously applied for the director's position and he informed me that if he didn't already have his guy, I would be his guy. Also, he was sending me a message that the soft touch phone calls I had orchestrated from the business community and labor organizations resulted in his being overwhelmed this time in my favor.

I thanked him for the call but most importantly, in retrospect, I thanked him for the lessons I learned in the process. Once you reach a certain level in the public or private sector, there are always influencers who can determine your career path by one or more phone calls.

Being appointed the executive director didn't always mean being recognized as such. In 1988, Scott 'Rob' Fieldman, a Vocational Education Program Specialist at the Commission for Vocational Education, suggested that we travel to Tacoma, Washington, about 30 minutes north of Olympia, to meet with the President of Western Washington University (WWU). The Commission had just awarded the University a $500,000 contract to develop and provide statewide teacher training for existing and new teachers.

This curriculum model and teaching philosophy would be based on the projected demographic changes that would occur in the Year 2000 classroom. The forecast was that school districts across the state would become increasingly diverse, with unique challenges and opportunities.

Rob suggested we set up a photo opportunity with the WWU President. Normally, we would have had to travel to the Western Washington University campus in Bellingham, Washington, about 150 miles away. However, since the president would be in Tacoma on other business Rob thought we should take advantage of his proximity and take a photo of the two leaders for an article in our agency newsletter. Excellent idea, I thought, let's do it. The meeting and photo shoot were scheduled for the next day.

Rob and I arrived at the Tacoma Sheraton Hotel at the appointed time. We had agreed to meet the WWU President in the lobby of the hotel. Rob and I stood side-by-side as we stepped onto the escalator and made our way up to the lobby. We immediately spotted him at the top of the stairs, awaiting our arrival. I noticed he had zeroed in on Rob and had started to smile at him. Not once did he look in my direction. It was as if I was not even there.

Suddenly I saw and felt Rob's body language shift. Like me, he knew what was about to happen and there was no way to stop it. As we both stepped off the escalator, the WWU President, with two outstretched arms, reached out to Rob. "Mr. Long, what a pleasure it is to meet you."

Rob quickly pivoted to me. "No, I am not Mr. Long. Here is Mr. Long." Awkward and telling.

The WWU President momentarily just stood there, speechless, frozen in time with a stunned look on his face. Judging from his facial expression, he looked like a man struggling to wake up from a bad dream. Surely, this wasn't happening to him, the president of one of the state's most progressive higher education institutions. An institution that had recently won a statewide competitive bid request, winning out over some of the state's longer-standing universities.

My thoughts and emotions ranged from surprise, embarrassment for Rob Fieldman at being caught in the middle of an awkward situation—ironically because he was White—and finally the realization on my part of "what's new?"

This was not the first time, and I knew it wouldn't be the last time, when a White person would make assumptions about my place, where I should fit or not fit, or ignore me altogether because of my skin color.

I don't remember much about the rest of the meeting. I was processing what had just happened, which reminded me of working in Seattle as a Probation and Parole Officer Trainee in 1968. At that time, there existed a state-funded initiative called the New Careers Program. In the adult correctional arena, this program was aimed at assisting ex-offenders gain employment and attend and graduate from college with a four-year degree. While attending college, the ex-offenders worked as assistants to parole officers with the goal of becoming full-fledged Parole and Probation Officers. Several Blacks participated in the New Careers Program.

During my first three months on the job I would sometimes be asked by my White colleagues whether or not I was in the New Careers Program. Viola!! I am Black and probably an ex-offender, so I must surely be in the New Careers Program. After being quizzed this way on several occasions about my legitimacy, I flipped the script and started asking my White colleagues, "Are you in the New Careers Program and if so, how are things working out for you?" You would have thought I asked them when was the last time they were arrested for failing to pay child support. Some were incredulous that I would ask them such a question, especially the White supervisors. However, shortly thereafter, the word got out and everybody was peaches and cream.

My parents, relatives, and other Black friends cautioned me that, as a Black person—regardless of my income status, number of degrees, community and philanthropic efforts—I should always remember that some White folks will never get past my skin color or more bluntly stated by some, "a nigger is a nigger."

. . .

As I walked toward the head table arranged at the Convention Center in Yakima, Washington, I was amazed at its sheer size. It looked like there were over 30 people assembled at the head table. While searching for my designated seat, a staff person for the hosting organization, the Yakima Opportunities Industrialization Center (YOIC), recognized me and fortunately directed me to my seat at the head table. That evening, I was there to represent Washington State Governor Booth Gardner. As the Director of the Commission for Vocational Education, the Governor's Office thought my organization would be the appropriate agency to represent the Governor.

YOIC at that time provided employment, training, retraining, and supportive services to assist individuals in securing and keeping a family-wage earning job. These individuals from the greater Yakima area included unemployed, underemployed, and low-income persons of color, as well as Caucasians. Specific training programs included welding, carpentry, office skills, and other occupational skills requested and needed by local employers.

As I got closer to my seat, I spotted a face that looked very familiar. However, I couldn't fathom the idea that Rosa Parks, who sometimes is referred to as the "Mother of the Civil Rights Movement," was in Yakima, Washington, with me—Merritt...Merritt Long.

Suddenly, a series of images flashed before me of Mrs. Parks' iconic face on small and large screen TVs in vivid technicolor and in newspaper articles, magazines, and books. You name the media outlet, and her recognizable face looked right back at you.

Mrs. Parks' actions on December 1, 1955, in Montgomery, Alabama, just 93 miles from my hometown Bessemer, and her refusal to give up her seat to a White passenger when requested by the bus driver eventually led to a successful bus boycott in Montgomery. This bus boycott then contributed to changes in the social, political, and economic systems nationwide.

I slowly and carefully took my seat next to Mrs. Parks. I was awestruck, but in a matter of seconds I was very much at ease. The aura surrounding her, and her calm and collected presence, relaxed me. It felt like I was sitting between my mother and grandmother and for a while nothing needed to be said. It was as though I was sitting on my grandmother's porch again where joy, peace, and serenity abounded.

After about five minutes, I leaned over to Mrs. Parks and introduced myself. I couldn't wait to tell her that I was from Bessemer. Like me, I am sure the furthest thing on her mind that evening was that she would be meeting someone from Alabama. When I informed Mrs. Parks that I was from Bessemer, her stoic face lit up with a big smile, dimples, and all. She paused for a moment, looked into my face and quietly, with a faint southern accent, inquired, "Merritt, what are you doing way out here?" Mrs. Parks asked me this question like we were at a family reunion, and I was someone she hadn't seen in a very long time.

While traveling back to Olympia, I reflected on the evening and my time with Mrs. Parks. I also thought about my first bus ride with my family, but this time Sister Rosa's spirit was on the bus with us as we rode in the back. She sat there, serene and stoic, looking very determined with her hands resting on the black purse in her lap. The look on her face seemed to signify that someday soon the back of the bus madness would cease to exist. A new day was coming.

39 TWO ROLE MODELS

For a moment, he was Muhammed Ali and I was Angelo Dundee. I had no idea when I met The Reverend Samuel B. McKinney shortly after I arrived in Seattle in June 1968, the impact and influence he would have on my professional career and personal life. He was the pastor of the Mount Zion Baptist Church, arguably the largest predominantly African American church in the greater Seattle area. I soon learned that his ministry extended beyond his church parishioners to the civic and political movers and shakers at the city and state levels. During the election season he was known for not telling his congregation who to vote for; rather, he told them who he was going to vote for, thus keeping the separation between church and state. Current and aspiring elected officials sought his informal endorsement and support because of his political clout.

Rev. McKinney was a graduate of Morehouse College and a classmate of Martin Luther King, Jr. In the mid-1960s he convinced Dr. King to come to Seattle to address civil rights issues ranging from housing discrimination, voting rights, and unequal and unfair employment practices concerning people of color, particularly African Americans. Dr. King's visit was welcomed with enthusiastic crowds and heightened the city's awareness of civil rights injustices prevalent in both public and private sectors.

Somehow, Rev. McKinney learned I was a recent graduate of Morehouse, and he reached out to meet me. Rev. McKinney had an eternal bond with the college and any graduate of Morehouse in the Seattle area was someone he wanted to know. Rev. McKinney co-founded the Seattle Morehouse College Club made up of alumni who had settled in the area.

When we met in his office at Mt. Zion Baptist Church, Rev. McKinney was very gracious and welcoming. Even though we had just met, I felt as though I had known him for years. He was very attentive, listening to each and every word. He encouraged me to join the Seattle Morehouse College Club and, within several years and with his support, I became the president of the club. Rev. McKinney wasn't a leader and power broker who wanted to hang on to power for power's sake; he believed in getting younger people involved in the economic and political affairs of the city and state. After our initial meeting, our relationship blossomed and spanned over 50 years.

When our daughter, Merisa, was born, I asked Rev. McKinney if he would christen her. I can still visualize three-month old Merisa in her lovely white satin dress with small ruffles around her collar, sleeves, and hem. Marsha had used a small piece of Scotch tape to attach a petite white bow to her head because her hair was sparse.

Marsha carefully handed Merisa over to Rev. McKinney as she literally slept like a baby. Rev. McKinney looked at Merisa, began to smile, and blessed her in his deep booming voice, which resonated throughout the sanctuary. Marsha and I savored this special moment because we realized how fortunate we were to have a person of Rev. McKinney's stature and heart bless our daughter as she started her life's journey.

Rev. McKinney served on a number of boards and commissions at the local, state, and national levels. Fortunately for me, he served on the Washington State Commission for Vocational Education when I was a candidate for the agency director position. With his stellar support and others' concurrence, I was selected. However, the future and fate of the agency was uncertain. Legislation had been drafted and debated in the Washington State Senate and House to sunset (eliminate) the

Commission. Ironically, two statutory members on the Commission (Superintendent of Public Instruction and Director of the State Board for Community and Technical Colleges) were the primary proponents of this death knell. These two entities were the 500-pound elephants in the arena, and the Commission's power and influence paled drastically in comparison.

One particular Commission meeting stands out during these battles and skirmishes around the issue of sunsetting the agency. Incidentally, although the arguments for elimination always portrayed what would be "best" for the students, the true debate was about power, control, and money. This Commission meeting was held at Seattle Central Community College on an especially wet, windy, and dreary Fall day. We knew the meeting would be well attended by observers because of the parties involved and what was at stake.

Coincidentally, when I arrived and entered the lobby just outside the meeting room, I saw Rev. McKinney shaking his umbrella. We greeted each other and began to walk toward the front of the meeting room to our designated seats. As Rev. McKinney confidently led the way, I proudly followed him. I could feel his personal power and, by his demeanor, sense that he had been in meetings like this before. That is, you know before taking your seat you don't have the votes of your colleagues to achieve what you believe is fair, just, and for the common good versus the insatiable wants of the institutions. All eyes focused on Rev. McKinney and out of nowhere I flashed on Rev. McKinney as Muhammed Ali about to enter the boxing ring for a championship fight, and I was his trusty trainer, friend, and number one fan, Angelo Dundee. I knew that Rev. McKinney, like Ali, when facing a stacked deck against us, would use his smarts, astuteness, and ring generalship to mitigate the odds. After serious debate from all sides, Rev. McKinney was able to extend the decision about the future of the Commission to another meeting later in the year.

As I looked around the room as the meeting was about to conclude, I realized this was the first meeting in my 20 years in state government where the chair of the Commission and the agency director were both

African American. This reality contributed greatly to making the day unforgettable.

Rev. McKinney also played a pivotal role in the establishment of the non-profit organization, the Seattle Opportunities Industrialization Center (SOIC). The Seattle Center was one of many locations across the country. SOIC provided job readiness skills training, vocational training, counseling, supportive services, and employment placement services for persons of color who were unemployed or underemployed. Rev. McKinney served for many years as chairman of the SOIC Board, and during his tenure hired James L. Williams as the director of SOIC. Jim had been the director of the Phoenix OIC.

Jim Williams was a charismatic leader, and he exuded self-confidence with a zeal and fire I had never witnessed up close and personal. Jim used his booming voice to get and keep your attention. He often took full advantage of his six foot, two inch height to underscore his larger-than-life presence. Jim would purposefully cross the invisible line of one's personal space to drive home a particular point. During one-on-one conversations with him, I remember he would literally grab my hand or arm and pull me close to accentuate his meaning. Sometimes we were almost nose to nose.

That was Jim, all in, all the time, no in betweens. Jim was generous with his time and advice, and he shared what he had learned dealing with the "big boys," primarily corporate CEO's and government agency heads. He opened my eyes to the importance of one's external political environment and the folly of leaving this arena to chance. Paramount in his thinking was establishing and maintaining good relationships with funding sources. He often emphasized the value and benefit of exceeding one's contractual obligations while foregoing any additional compensation because goodwill between you and your funder is something you cannot put a price on.

Another core principle that Jim shared with me over the years was the value and benefit of a chief executive officer seeking advice and counsel when facing a major issue, challenge, or opportunity. He staunchly believed that you should seek the advice of the best, brightest, and most trusted subject matter expert. This advice will help you sort and sift the options prior to decision making. You only know what you know.

Jim was the first African American executive I'd developed a relationship with who ran a multi-million dollar operation. SOIC consisted of three separate training facilities in Seattle, and after many years, a brand-new building was constructed to consolidate all sites into one. Regardless of whether you had visited the earlier, modest facilities, or you walked into the new high rise, you couldn't tell the difference in terms of the professional demeanor and dress of SOIC employees. All staff carried themselves with pride and a commitment to their mission. Jim set the standard: he would always button his top suit button whenever he stood up. Like IBM employees of yesteryear, Jim usually wore a white shirt with a dark suit and conservative tie.

Similar to Rev. McKinney, Jim recognized the benefit of integrating the political arena with your business interests. Public policy and the influence of elected officials could help or hurt your cause. Always pragmatic, I recall Jim stressing that if you had backed a certain candidate and they did not win the election, you needed to congratulate the winner and offer your support. A phrase he often used was "You have to make the peace."

Both Rev. McKinney and Jim embodied values of fairness, justice, and integrity and acted on those values as they advocated for "the last, the least, and the lost" in our society. I am so fortunate to have known them, to have studied them, and to have benefitted from their affection for me.

40 THANK YOU, GOVERNORS

I WAS APPOINTED Director of the Human Rights Commission after serving seven years as the Executive Director of the Washington State Board for Vocational Education (formerly the Commission on Vocational Education), and I served for four years. Both of these positions were part of the Governor's Small Agency Cabinet. Small Agency Cabinet meetings were chaired by the governor's deputy chief of staff. The governor seldom attended these meetings.

Both of these positions had missions and purposes that were meaningful and significant, but I thought I was ready to contribute in a bigger way to serve the people of Washington State. I felt ready and capable of stepping up to more responsibility by being appointed to the Governor's Executive Cabinet, which included 24 of the largest agencies in state government. Being in the Governor's Executive Cabinet would be the capstone of my career in state government.

The Governor's Executive Cabinet meetings were usually chaired by his chief of staff and occasionally by the governor. Retreats with the governor were usually held twice a year. The purpose of the governor's retreats with all large agency directors and all of his senior advisors was to discuss, in an informal and relaxed setting, the future challenges and opportunities facing the state. The goal of these retreats was to craft a flexible strategy to respond to issues whether they be in early childhood education, transportation, adult corrections, social and health services, the environment, or higher education, to name a few.

. . .

In 1996, a long-time friend and colleague, as well as our daughter's godmother, Phyllis Gutierrez Kenney, Democrat, ran for Secretary of State against incumbent Ralph Munro, Republican. Although not elected, Phyllis went on to serve with distinction in the Washington State House of Representatives from the 46th District in Seattle from 1997 to 2013.

Phyllis held her Secretary of State campaign kickoff at the King Street Station in Seattle. My wife Marsha and I decided to attend and drove from Olympia to Seattle to support her. As we traveled north on Interstate 5, Marsha reminded me that Norm Rice, the current mayor of Seattle, was a candidate for governor, and Gary Locke, King County Executive, also a candidate for governor, would probably attend this major campaign kickoff. She asked me what my answer would be if both aspiring governors asked for my support and endorsement. Both Democrats, Norm Rice was African American and Gary Locke was Asian American.

I appreciated Marsha asking me the question and getting me queued up for the possibilities. The decision was easy and automatic for me. I'd known Gary since 1982 when he was a freshman legislator in the Washington State Legislature, having defeated incumbent Peggy Maxie, an African American woman, in the 37th District of Seattle. Representative Locke had had a meteoric rise in the Legislature as a policy wonk and budget whiz. Eventually, he became chair of the House Appropriations Committee, one of the most powerful positions in the Legislature.

We had a number of mutual friends in common. One person in particular was Ruth Woo, Gary's political mentor, advisor, confidante, and one of his best friends. Throughout my career in state government, Ruth proved to be an invaluable sage and fun confidante. Ruth was smart and politically savvy, a real gem whose spirit and ideas live on in the many people she mentored and nurtured.

Professionally, I'd worked with Representative Locke on funding issues for workforce training projects when I was the director of the State Board for Vocational Education. I remember one instance when I had to testify before the House Education Committee about how funds were being used to assist businesses in training and retraining their employees through the community and technical college system. Some concerns had been raised about how public state funds were being utilized to benefit private businesses. The issue made the Seattle newspapers and had the possibility of going sideways on my agency and me.

Fortunately, during the oversight hearing, everything went exceedingly well. After being grilled by Chair Locke and other committee members, they seemed satisfied and the hearing was adjourned. Chair Locke came up to me and said with his boyish smile, "Now, that wasn't so bad, was it?" I smiled with relief while thinking, easy for you—you weren't sitting in front of your committee, with the media covering every word.

The one thing I think about when I think of Representative Locke, King County Executive Locke, Governor Locke, United States Commerce Secretary Locke, and Ambassador to China Locke is that he was always prepared, did his homework, and knew your subject area better than you if you failed to prepare. Because of my respect and admiration for his work ethic, he brought the best out of me. He pushed me without pushing me, which is the best push of all.

When I wasn't reappointed as director of the Workforce Training Board (formerly the State Board for Vocational Education and formerly the Commission for Vocational Education), I received a call at home one evening from Representative Locke. He asked me to join his staff to work on welfare reform issues, which at that time loomed large at the federal and state level. I was surprised and honored to receive the unexpected call. I let him know that two days earlier I'd accepted the position of Executive Director of the Washington State Human Rights Commission. I thanked Representative Locke for thinking about me and told him how much I appreciated the call. Following our conversation, I told Marsha how, in some ways, I was sorry I couldn't take Gary up on his employment offer, because I felt I'd missed my golden opportunity to work for and attach myself to a superstar whose future was extremely bright.

But most importantly, I never forgot, and never will, the thoughtful and timely phone call from Representative Locke when I was between jobs. Those are the times that make permanent impressions when someone you respect and admire reaches out when they don't have to.

Mayor Norm Rice and I had known each other for several years, but our relationship was more as acquaintances, not colleagues. We'd never worked on any specific projects together, as his activities were generally Seattle-focused and mine were statewide in scope. I've always been a fan of Norm's and admired his ability to bring together folks from the business, labor, and community-based organizations to rally around and support issues such as education and school levies. Transportation and affordable housing were also important issues during his administration. At Phyllis' kickoff, I saw Norm and we exchanged pleasantries, but did not have a conversation.

Gary, on the other hand, approached me. Looking directly at me, he extended his right hand and asked me if he could count on my support as he ran for governor. Previously, I've heard pundits talk about how candidates for elected office must have the "fire in the belly" to have a chance of being elected. After shaking Gary's hand and observing him that day, I could feel his "fire in the belly." His energy level, enthusiasm, and fierce competitive drive were evident, and he had elevated his game to another level.

I said, "Yes, count me in." I was so proud of Gary, because I knew that whatever the election results, he was all in and would always give it his all—nothing more, nothing less.

Gary Locke defeated Norm Rice and won the Democratic primary election on September 17, 1996. He then went on to soundly defeat his conservative Republican challenger, Ellen Craswell, in the November general election by a margin of 58 to 42 percent.

At the governor-elect's celebration in Seattle's downtown Westin Hotel, Gary and his wife, Mona, were surrounded by a huge throng of people offering their congratulations and best wishes. Without any warning, a herd of reporters including the foreign press, engulfed the governor-elect and first lady. They were momentarily thrown off balance by the unexpected surge of reporters. I leaned down and whispered into Marsha's ear, "You know what? We've just witnessed Gary and Mona's lives changing forever." It was special to be part of this remarkable moment in history, the election of the first Chinese American Governor in the United States. Like me, I was sure many people in that ballroom, around the state, indeed around the world, felt a connection to Governor-Elect Locke's victory. It was a proud moment, especially for people of color.

. . .

The election behind us, I met with Tom Fitzsimmons, Chair of the Governor's Transition Team, and point-person for recommendations for cabinet appointments. Tom was the Thurston County Executive and a colleague of then-King County Executive Gary Locke.

Several of us, including Tom, served on the Olympia Steering Committee for the campaign. He and I clicked, and I believe he enjoyed working with me as much as I enjoyed working with him.

My meeting with Tom was informal and relaxed. I was glad to see he was the same down-to-earth Tom, trying to do his best to recommend individuals who would carry out the Governor's agenda, and efficiently and effectively run their agencies.

My interview with Tom, although informal, was strictly business, which was as it should be. Tom, familiar with my employment background, indicated that he thought, given the diversity and richness of my experiences, I might possibly be interested in serving the governor-elect in a number of capacities, including, but not limited to: Commissioner of the Employment Security Department or Director of the Department of Labor and Industries.

After talking generally about these agencies Tom stated, "Merritt, the Lottery Commission could be a possibility as well." I didn't go into my meeting with Tom with a wish list for particular agencies. I was clear that I wanted to be a part of the Governor's Team once he took office and beyond that, I wasn't particular.

As Tom and I started to wrap up our conversation, I remembered an interview that I'd seen on a black-and-white television set in 1968 at a neighbor's home in Bessemer. A news reporter was interviewing Jake Gaither, former head football coach of the Florida A&M Rattlers, about being considered to be named a head coach in the National Football League. This was before Art Shell was named the first African American head coach in the NFL by Al Davis, owner and general manager of the Oakland Raiders. The reporter asked Jake, "How does it feel to possibly be the first Negro head coach in the NFL?" Jake's response was something like this, "In order for me to become the first Negro coach in the NFL, I first must be in the race to win the race. I am glad to be in the race." In some ways, that was how I felt when I left Tom's office. I was glad to be in the race. Tom indicated he'd be speaking with the governor-elect over the next several days and would get back to me.

The waiting game began. The question was, would I receive a call about a cabinet appointment? Marsha and I had both worked on the campaign together, and she was an extremely accomplished leader and administrator in state government. Marsha had held a series of positions of increasing responsibility. At the time, she was working for Jennifer Belcher, Public Lands Commissioner. Marsha was one of five deputy supervisors and was responsible for administrative services at the Department of Natural Resources. Commissioner Belcher and Governor-Elect Locke were very close friends, stemming from their days as colleagues serving in the House of Representatives. Marsha was happy with her current position and wasn't looking or expecting to be considered for a cabinet position.

However, because of Marsha's obvious skills and talents, the rumors were that we both were being considered for cabinet appointments. In fact, one rumor had Marsha being talked about as an excellent choice as the governor's chief of staff. This was Olympia inside political baseball at its best, people trying to figure out who was on first and who may have been tagged out before the game started.

As we do every year, Marsha, Merisa, and I traveled to sunny Phoenix, Arizona to celebrate New Year's with Marsha's family. New Year is a big holiday in the Japanese culture. It was in the high 60s and low 70s, a change from the gray winter gloom of Seattle and Olympia. Marsha and I were staying at her older brother's home, Dr. William Tadano, for the holidays. One morning we decided to go for a walk in the hilly neighborhood to get some exercise. After walking for about ten minutes, I mentioned to Marsha that I'd been thinking about my meeting with Tom Fitzsimmons, and the more I thought about the Lottery Commission as an option, the more I liked the possibility. Marsha admitted that she hadn't thought about the Lottery Commission as a possibility for me, but she thought it could be a fun job with opportunities to utilize my entrepreneurial skills.

We later drove over to Marsha's mother's home in Glendale. I needed to gas up the car so I went down the block to a gas station to fill up. When I went inside the convenience store to pay, the clerk asked whether I wanted to buy a lottery ticket. I purchased a couple of lottery tickets and couldn't wait to tell Marsha what had just happened.

I rushed back to Michiko's home and told Marsha that of all the times I'd purchased gas at a convenience or grocery store, never before had anyone ever asked me to purchase a lottery ticket. I told her this was the sign that I'd be offered the position of Lottery Director. I was pretty jacked up; I couldn't believe that the hand of fate and destiny had intervened on my behalf.

We spent most of the following day in Glendale, visiting with Marsha's mother, Michiko Tadano, and sisters Betty Takesuye and Reiko Tadano. It had been a leisurely day, one of those days that illustrated why so many people from Washington State liked to winter in Arizona. I decided to go for a long walk and buy a *New York Times*, my favorite newspaper. The weather conditions were perfect, sunny, but not hot, low 70s with a light breeze. About the midpoint of my walk, I stopped at a local *Starbucks*, had a cappuccino, and read the newspaper.

When I returned to Marsha's mother's home, Marsha immediately announced, with a big smile on her face, that the governor-elect had left a message on the phone answering machine, saying he needed to talk to both of us. Now, Marsha's smile had turned to laughter, her two sisters laughing as well. First of all, I didn't think the joke they were playing was funny at all. I was expecting and hoping for this call, and now Marsha and her sisters were playing around. She could plainly see that I didn't believe her and realized that I was getting annoyed by the fun and games. Marsha got up from the kitchen table, walked over to where I was standing, looked at me quite seriously and said, "Merritt, seriously, he did call." This melodramatic move on her part caused me to start laughing to the point of my saying to her, "You know, Marsha, you almost got me that time. You're really good at pretending." I started to walk to the guest bedroom.

She followed me. We both sat on the bed. Once again, she stated that the governor-elect had called. Since I didn't believe her, she suggested we listen to the answering machine. We went back to the kitchen, and Marsha attempted to play back the governor-elect's recorded message. For some reason, the machine didn't work. I knew it. No call. No message. It was so unlike Marsha to go to this length about a phone call that meant so much to me. By now, she was almost hysterically laughing, but continued to stay on message regarding the supposed phone call. Finally, Marsha got the answering machine to work and retrieved the message from Governor-Elect Locke. He was trying to reach us and asked us to call him back at his King County Executive Office.

The moment had arrived, the suspense thickened. I called the governor-elect, and we exchanged hellos and happy holidays. Then he said he wanted to speak to Marsha. She and I both were a little surprised because Marsha hadn't talked to anyone about being interested in being a part of the new administration. The governor-elect quickly came to the point and indicated to Marsha he wanted her to be the director of the Department of General Administration.

Marsha's initial response was to thank Gary for the recognition and honor of possibly being a cabinet member, but she was reluctant to accept such a position with the possibility of having two cabinet directors from one household. She further stated, "Gary, you only have a limited number of these positions and you may want to spread them around more." The governor-elect told Marsha he wasn't taking "no" for an answer and wanted her to think on this some more before making a final decision.

After the governor-elect's conversation with Marsha, he asked her to put me back on the phone. The governor-elect said he definitely wanted me to be a member of his cabinet and there were a couple of areas he was thinking about. He indicated he needed to finish a little more homework and wanted to talk with me in a few days. I pushed back a little by asking, "Tell me what you are thinking about, give me an idea." He stated he wanted me to become the director of the Lottery but needed to talk with other personnel affected by this change before making an announcement.

Governor-Elect Locke concluded our conversation by letting me know he was serious about Marsha being a part of his team and was counting on me to make it happen. My response to him was: consider it done. This would be my first official act on behalf of the governor-elect.

Marsha was appointed director of the Department of General Administration. And about a week later, I received the appointment as director of the Lottery. The endless work hours and Saturdays away from family had paid off. I believed it was my time. I had done it the old-fashioned way: I'd earned it.

. . .

It was January 1997, and I was walking up the marble steps leading to the Governor's Office as the newly appointed state Lottery Director. I thought I'd stop by to see if there were any familiar faces starting to appear in the new administration. As I entered the Governor's office, I was surprised to see Governor Locke and his wife, Mona Lee Locke, standing quietly in the lobby. The Governor was nattily attired in a charcoal gray suit, crisp white shirt, red tie with a faint blue pattern, and shiny black shoes. He carried a large dark brown leather briefcase with two leather fasteners on the side. The First Lady stood at the Governor's side, exuding confidence, grace, style, and a regal bearing. Mona had previously worked as a television news reporter at one of the Seattle stations. On and off the air, she always looked like she had just stepped out of a bandbox. What struck me the most on this historic day was how two people standing side-by-side appeared as one. This oneness of spirit and dedication to the people of Washington State became one of the hallmarks of the Locke Administration.

When the clock struck noon, Governor Locke indicated to Mona and me that it was okay to enter the governor's private office. With quiet self-assurance, he stated almost as an aside that he didn't want to enter the private office of outgoing Governor Mike Lowry, until Lowry's time on the clock officially concluded and his time had begun.

This attention to detail spoke volumes about the state's new governor. He always did his homework, and he was a stickler for doing things the right way the first time. He wanted to begin his administration on sound administrative and legal footing. Once the governor gave the all-clear sign, I reached quickly to carry his briefcase and one other bag that Mona had into his new office. I placed the briefcase beside Mona's bag on top of the desk. I said goodbye, leaving Mona and Gary Locke, the new Governor and First Lady, to enjoy the moment.

It took less than ten minutes from the time I entered the governor's office until the time I left. However, when I think about the arc of my journey from Bessemer, Alabama, to the Washington State Governor's Office, I realize it's the culmination of my life experiences over some 40 years. It has been an amazing and satisfying journey.

. . .

After about a year on the job as the Lottery Director, I had the opportunity to attend the late fall meeting of the National Association of

Lottery Directors in Boston, Massachusetts. This meeting was somewhat of a coming out party for me because I hadn't met any Lottery directors from the 30-plus states that held lotteries. I quickly learned that Lottery directors were very open to sharing marketing and sales strategies to improve the sale of lottery tickets. They were also open to sharing the latest technological advancements to maintain the life blood of the lottery—the integrity of the game itself, lottery security.

Day one was jam-packed with meet and greets, presentations on how to work with state legislators, and ways in which to ensure the lottery was always designed as entertainment, not gambling. Techniques and incentives encouraging major grocery chains to place lottery products in their stores were also emphasized. In the lottery business we used to ask, what can we do to avoid lottery games being lost in the "noise" of the overall grocery retail business?

Finally, it was lunch time. What a morning, I thought, I am just loving this. My mind was absorbing and filtering this new information at a breakneck pace. I was pleasantly surprised that the considerable information I was acquiring made sense to me after only a year on the job. I began to envision game design and different price points to possibly increase sales in Washington State. Given the bottom-line experience of the states, what was the cost benefit? If we made investments in new games, what would the benefit be when factoring in major items such as staff cost, opportunity cost, cost of promotion, and anticipated revenue and profit?

I sat there for a moment, savoring this gathering. Most important, I enjoyed being at the table. I realized how fortunate and blessed I was to have been considered for, and then appointed to, the position of Washington State Lottery Director.

Lunch was buffet style and there were about 20 Lottery directors from across the country dining together. After placing an assortment of cheese, ham, turkey, lettuce, tomato, pickles, and other condiments on rye bread, I added potato salad and potato chips to my plate. As I started walking to my seat, I was seconds away from sitting down for lunch with my new colleagues when the Lottery Director from Texas, seated at another table as I walked by, stopped me by touching my arm. He asked for, or rather ordered, a cup of coffee, black coffee. I was immediately taken aback. I thought, who is this dude? Here I am in all my glory, the pinnacle of my career in state government. The first ever African American to be appointed by the governor to this position.

My mind raced. It took me back in space and time to the Governor's Inaugural Ball following Governor Locke's swearing in. Paul Isaki, one of the governor's confidantes and key policy advisers in the area of economic development, who later became his chief of staff, was there. My appointment had not been officially announced by Governor-Elect Locke, but the word on the street was I would be appointed to an Executive Cabinet position. Paul and I had known each other for decades, and he knew of my pending appointment. He indicated he was excited for me. He said it was good to see a brother being appointed to a cabinet agency that generated millions of dollars for the state. He teasingly, but seriously said, "Brothers don't usually get the money agencies." If appointed at all, it was usually to the social service arena. Paul made an accurate and astute observation, one that hadn't previously crossed my mind.

That day, all the Texas Lottery Director saw was a Black face in the usual sea of White faces. He automatically assumed that this Black person at a Lottery Directors meeting must be a part of the wait staff. Maybe the supervisor. But he didn't care. Bottom line, he needed and wanted a cup of coffee. Black person walking by, stop the Black person and get him to fetch me a cup of coffee. Make it post haste, Boy.

After processing his request for a second or two, I looked him square in his eyes like my mother taught me as a kid. By doing so, in her mind, it immediately sent a message to the White person that you aren't afraid and wouldn't be intimidated. Once I drew that line in the sand, I looked at him from head to toe ever so slowly demonstrating my dissatisfaction with his request. I bent down, while holding my plate of food, and simply stated, almost in a whisper, close to his right ear, "Hey, man, I'm here just like you." I continued to look at him as I walked to my seat and didn't stop looking at him until I was comfortably seated at my table.

Ironically, about two months later, I was reading a national lottery publication that reported lottery activities by each state. This publication reported the Texas Lottery Director had been fired because of improprieties in his working relationship with a national lottery vendor and contractor. My first thought, it couldn't have happened to a more deserving guy. Good riddance.

. . .

The experience with the Texas Lottery Director wasn't the rule or the exception. It happened frequently enough for me to realize that as I went about my business of work, whether as a Parole and Probation Officer, Vocational Education Administrator, or Executive Director of a state agency, my skin color was always front and center. There I was trying to conduct business, and the person I'm dealing with can't get past the color of my skin.

Regardless of others' perceptions and hang-ups, I usually focused on what I needed to do to get the job done. Skin color, race, or ethnicity and how that played out, wasn't a part of the equation. Yet, when I heard White folks say, "I don't see color," I knew then the fix was in. Unless you are blind, I don't understand how people cannot see "color."

During my first month as Lottery Director, the research director told me he'd never worked for a Black person before. He wasn't sure what to expect from me or what he should wear to work. I appreciated his candor, but I was surprised that in 1997, someone would be making a statement like that. He and I worked well together over the next four years. He even figured out what to wear to work. Clothes.

. . .

After a 33-year career in state government, starting as a Probation and Parole Trainee and ending as Director of the State Lottery, I decided it was time to retire. I looked forward to having time to do anything I wanted.

It was not meant to be. Several months after retiring, I received another fateful call from Governor Gary Locke's Office. He asked, "Would you fill in for a few months as chair of the Washington State Liquor Control Board (WSLCB)? The current chair is retiring, and the person I want to appoint will not be available for a few months."

Sure, I thought, piece of cake. Just filling in for a few months. How difficult could that be?

The "few months" turned into five years. The state-controlled liquor business (excluding beer and related products) at that time fit my entrepreneurial leanings perfectly. We were a business the state depended on to generate revenue. Each year, our revenue projections fed into the state's overall revenue forecast, which legislators used to make budget decisions. We operated a huge distribution center and distribution system, delivering liquor products to more than 200 state-owned and state-contracted stores across the state of Washington. The Liquor Control Board decided which liquor products would be carried in the state stores; we controlled the liquor marketplace.

I learned a lot.

. . .

As the powerful chair of the House Ways and Means Committee, then Representative Gary Locke for a number of years held a tongue-in-cheek 39th Annual Birthday Party. It was held in Seattle's International District at the popular Chinese restaurant, House of Hong. This event was always held in January prior to the yearly legislative session to avoid violating campaign finance restrictions. This fund-raising event had become quite popular and was attended by influential lobbyists representing some of the top tier businesses in the state, as well as grass roots community activists fueled and funded primarily by their issues and causes.

I attended as the director of the state's Human Rights Commission, primarily because my agency budget would be voted upon by the House Ways and Means Committee as part of the overall state budget. Essentially, I was there to shake Chairman Locke's hand and provide soft touch hellos with other members of the Committee who might be attending, as well as other legislators.

This particular evening, I noticed that Becky Bogard, a prominent independent lobbyist, was squiring around Christine Gregoire, the state Ecology Director, who would sometime in the near future announce her intention to run for and become Washington State's first female attorney general. Becky walked toward me, Chris at her side. She asked, "Do you know Chris?" Chris noticed my somewhat hesitant response, stepped in right away and asked me, "Did you know Chris O'Grady, instead of Chris Gregoire?" As soon as Chris became O'Grady, it was as if I was a Parole and Probation Officer Trainee again standing at the receptionist desk in Seattle's Broadway Parole and Probation Office, a stone's throw from the then Yesler Terrace Housing project.

As I traveled back in space and time to over two decades ago, I flashed back to the time when Chris O'Grady, Clerk Typist II, was seated at the receptionist desk looking directly up at me with probing piercing eyes. How ironic, I thought, because the intensity of those eyes still possessed the power to strip a man to his core.

Over the hour-long drive home from Seattle to Olympia that night, I had plenty of time to reflect upon reconnecting with a former colleague whose career had been turbo-charged since the last time I knew her identity.

Within the next few months, Chris and I enjoyed a fun-filled lunch, lots of laughs and reminiscing about the good ole days working in the correctional arena.

During this lunch, I learned that when Chris interviewed for a promotion from the position of Clerk Typist II to a Parole and Probation Officer Trainee, she had a life-changing moment. Chris, similar to yours truly, in the early 70s had recently graduated from college and was eligible and qualified to be a Parole and Probation Officer. However, during the interview, the regional administrator at the time informed Chris that he had his "token" female parole officer and didn't need another one. WOW!! Can you believe that…in front of God and everyone he proclaimed his truth.

In retrospect, as Chris changed careers and graduated from law school, her mind-bending experience with the regional administrator was one of the best career-altering moves of a lifetime. Chris indeed became the first female attorney general for the state of Washington, serving two four-year terms.

It gets better, we are still talking about the Clerk Typist II who for some reason was not adequate enough to be a Parole and Probation Officer Trainee. Wait for it. Wait for it. Chris O'Grady Gregoire became the 22nd Governor of the state of Washington, as well as only the second female governor. She served two four-year terms as Washington's governor.

Prior to Chris becoming governor, I had been appointed by Governor Locke as the first African American chair of the Washington State Liquor Control Board (WSLCB) in its 60-year history. However, my term on the Board would expire during the first year of the Gregoire Administration. I met with Governor Gregoire at her office, and we agreed that I would continue as chair of the Liquor Control Board for the next two years. The governor had specific areas of the Board where she wanted me to focus my time and attention.

As the governor spelled out her expectations and deliverables, I leaned in from my chair directly across from her and gently interrupted Governor Gregoire and asked, "Governor, can we just take a moment to enjoy the moment?"

As boxing promoter Don King would say, "Only in America…" where two people, one a Clerk Typist II and the other a Parole and Probation Officer Trainee, meet 30 years later in the Governor's Office. Blessings have been bountiful for both: the former clerk typist is now the governor of the state, and the parole and probation officer trainee is chair of one of the state's major revenue producers, the WSLCB.

During her successful tenure, Governor Chris Gregoire and First

Gentleman Mike Gregoire played a key pivotal role in the establishment of the Learning Seed Foundation, which Marsha and I founded to help students attend college. We will always be grateful for their commitment and support.

. . .

After becoming agency director of several state agencies during my career in state government, I would often be asked, "What does it take to be successful?" My response was to answer that question by asking this question first, "What price are you willing to pay for success, because success usually doesn't come without sacrifice?"

The sacrifice may be time away from family and friends, being preoccupied or distracted with work when you are with family and friends, and, of course, the toll over time the demands of your responsibility take on your body and mind. Also, as your career advances, you realize your previous best may pale in comparison to what is required in your new, higher level endeavor.

My 40-plus years in the public, private, and community sectors have taught me that, if I am doing something for the right reasons, with the right people at the right time, good things will happen. My instincts have never gotten me into trouble. But when I approach something solely focused on my end of the deal, just the opposite occurs. When I become too heady with the sound of my voice and the brilliance of my thinking, my Pinto Pony will take me on a journey to no man's land.

41 LEARNING SEED FOUNDATION

PRIOR TO MY first retirement from state government in 2001, my biggest concern and challenge was how I would spend my time and fill this new role without the demands, pressures, and rewards that had consumed me for the past two decades when I headed up various state agencies. As someone without any real hobbies who was not particularly fond of travelling and had no special projects at the ready, what in the hell was I going to do all day? What would be my new purpose in life where previously work and the pursuit of work had been my passion, always striving to grab the brass ring. After securing the brass ring, several in fact, now what? In so many ways my positional power chase had been the alpha and omega that defined me.

As I contemplated retirement from state government and specifically from the Washington State Lottery, I knew what I was leaving but not where I was going. I had mixed emotions ranging from a new sense of freedom and excitement to remorse and a sense of uncertainty. However, I slowly began to realize that retirement would afford me the freedom and choice to write the final chapters of my life.

With Marsha's assistance my future direction and purpose evolved rather quickly. She suggested that during my first week of retirement I spend some time alone relaxing on the beach at Ocean Shores,

Washington. In fact, as she often says to me, "Be nice to yourself." I thought this was an excellent idea, especially since she would join me on the third day and discuss my retirement plans. Marsha was still working as Governor Locke's Director of the General Administration Department.

I know what some of you may be thinking—was Marsha really looking out for me with her thoughtful assistance, or looking out for herself by making sure this newly unemployed person didn't drive her crazy with all this time on his hands? Well, knowing Marsha, her first thought would have been concern for me but I am sure it wasn't lost on her that my newly-found free time could be problematic for us both.

Over the years we had made individual contributions to many charities and good causes. However, at this stage in our lives we wanted to make a meaningful and lasting difference in the lives of others, especially the younger generation. Education was the obvious choice. Because of the sacrifices and hardships faced by our parents we wanted to "pay it forward" by helping young people go to college.

As we walked on the beach we decided to establish an educational foundation that would award scholarships to students with financial need. There were many scholarship programs, and we wondered what would make our scholarship different, and needed? We knew that many students of color did not have role models—a parent, older brother or sister, cousin, etc.—for going to college, so we decided to focus on students of color. Based on our life experiences, we were also keenly aware of the dynamics of exclusion and decided the scholarship would include all students, regardless of race or ethnicity.

We also knew that scholarships tended to go to students who we called "super achievers," e.g., 4.0 GPA, class president, star athlete, etc. What about the C+/B- student, the student who worked a part-time job to help their family financially, the student who helped care for a sibling with disabilities or a grandparent? We believed this student also had great potential, but because of their circumstances couldn't display it. It was clear we would aim to award scholarships to a range of students, not just the 4.0 student.

How do you start a scholarship foundation? The initial donation of $500 came from employees of the Washington State Lottery when I retired as the director in 2001. Many friends committed to "seed" the fund by donating $1,000 each. This group became the founding members and now includes 49 wonderful and generous supporters. (Please see list at the end of this chapter.) Marsha and I made a personal commitment of contributing $50,000 over the first three years and have continued our financial and organizational support over the years.

We chose to establish the Learning Seed Foundation fund at The Community Foundation of South Puget Sound, a 501(c)(3) organization. The Community Foundation manages and administers the fund for a fee of two percent. Because the Learning Seed Foundation is based on volunteers, 98 percent of contributions go to the fund.

The first scholarships were awarded in 2002 to four young women from the North Thurston School District in Lacey, Washington. Since 2002 and as of 2020, a total of $447,750 has been awarded in new and renewable scholarships to 109 students from Thurston and Pierce counties. Also, a $50,000 endowed Learning Seed Foundation scholarship has been established at The Evergreen State College through a matching grant from the Bill and Melinda Gates Foundation for students at risk of dropping out due to financial challenges. And, in 2019 a $30,000 endowed scholarship was established at South Puget Sound Community College for second-year students who are active in the Diversity and Equity Center and at risk of dropping out. We also continue to build an endowment fund that will sustain future scholarships.

We cannot take credit for the amazing success of the Learning Seed Foundation. Early support from the Lottery employees and our founding members helped us jumpstart the fund. Golf tournaments, dinner auctions, concerts, and art auctions helped gain more supporters, individuals, and companies, and to spread the word about the Learning Seed. Our tireless volunteers, including many Learning Seed Scholars, deserve the credit for the success of these events. Thanks are due, too, to the many volunteers who have served on our Scholarship Committee. The hours spent reviewing scholarship applications and making difficult recommendations were investments in our Learning Seed Scholars. (Please see partial lists of companies, organizations, and volunteers at the end of the chapter.)

Early backing from Governor Gary Locke and First Lady Mona Lee Locke when they signed on as Founding Members and participated in Learning Seed events was a key to others signing on. Support from the governor's office continued with Governor Chris Gregoire and First Gentleman Mike Gregoire when they became Founding Members and hosted many dinners in the Governor's Mansion to benefit the Learning Seed. Governor Gregoire always made sure she and Mike could attend. These dinners attracted a beautiful cross-section of society: political leaders, community representatives, corporate and business executives, tribal leaders, education officials, individual supporters. The Gregoires hosted seven dinners and helped to further establish the Learning Seed Foundation as a credible and effective organization.

Our current governor, Governor Jay Inslee, and First Lady Trudi Inslee have bolstered the Learning Seed by not only hosting dinners at the Governor's Mansion but also making personal contributions. We are so thankful for the Inslees, the Gregoires, and the Lockes for their wholehearted commitment to student success.

As we were growing up, our parents had aspirations for us to go to college, even though they never had the opportunity to do so. They instilled in us the value and importance of education beyond high school. The Learning Seed Foundation through the new and renewable scholarships it awards to high school seniors is a very fitting homage to them. Their educational wishes and dreams live on.

Equally important is the recognition that one does not have to be a millionaire or billionaire like Bill Gates, Warren Buffett, Oprah Winfrey, Jay Z and Beyonce, or Dr. Dre to make a difference in the lives of others. Most of us can, in some way even if not financially, make a difference. As the Black Panther emphasizes: Each one, teach on.

. . .

The mission of the Learning Seed Foundation is to help students achieve. Our sincere appreciation and thanks to the following individuals, companies, and organizations for their continuing support of Learning Seed Scholars.

Learning Seed Foundation Founding Members

AstraZeneca

Charlie Baum

Robert Branscomb

Linda Villegas Bremer

Sharon and David Cammarano

Sue and Craig Cole

The Community Foundation

Joe Dear

Donald Dybeck

Al Eckroth

Eli Lilly and Company

Kathy Baros Friedt and Paul Seabert

Fred Goldberg

Julie Grant and Lloyd Wright

Governor Christine Gregoire & Mike Gregoire

Paula and Denny Heck

Doug and Kathy Henken

Dan and Merisa Tamiko Heu-Weller

Dr. John D.and Lillian Ishii

Tore Johnson

Edmon and Sue Rivera-Lee

Governor Gary Locke & Mona Lee Locke

Merritt and Marsha Tadano Long

Marge Mohoric

Mike Murphy and Cheryl Duryea

Pfizer, Inc.

Dr. Thomas L. "Les" Purce & Dr. Jane C. Sherman

Lyle Quasim and Shelagh Taylor

Alan Sugiyama

Michiko Tadano

Virgil Adams Real Estate

Jim Walton

Dr. Ernest and Gail Yamane

Joan Yoshitomi

Major sponsors and contributors

Verizon

Comcast

Haughton Family Charitable Fund

Confederated Tribes of the Chehalis Reservation

Olympia Federal Savings

State Farm

Lexus of Tacoma

Safeway/Albertson's

Muckleshoot Indian Tribe

Washington REALTORS

Columbia Bank

Puget Sound Energy

Pfizer

AT&T

TwinStar Credit Union

UniBank

G-Tech

Cammarano Resort Properties

Washington Mutual Bank

Eli Lilly

Virgil Adams Real Estate

Our Education Partners

South Puget Sound Community College

The Evergreen State College

Saint Martin's University

Hands On Children's Museum

Individual contributors

Fred Goldberg/Saltchuk

Rhonda Weaver/Comcast

Congressman Denny Heck & Paula Heck

Linda Villegas Bremer

Lorraine Lee and John Felleisen

Chris Marr and Barb Bumann

Craig and Sue Cole

David and Dione Hayes

Alfie Alvarado-Ramos & San Juanita Flores

Stacie-Dee Motoyama

Jim Walton

Dr. Ernest Yamane and Gail Yamane

Lyle Quasim and Shelagh Taylor

Sukjoo and Changmook Sohn

Albert Shen

Dr. Thomas "Les" Purce and
Dr. Jane Sherman

Jennifer Belcher

Anyone who ever attended a Learning Seed event, from the 2002 golf tournament
and dinner auction to the 2020 Dolen Perkins-Valdez author presentation at SPSCC,

THANK YOU!

Volunteers

Susan Rivera-Lee and Edmon Lee

John McLain

Nancy Wicker

Mona and Dean Moberg

Kim Tanaka

Saul Arrington

Dr. Rachel Wood

Kimi Smith

Frances Munez Carter

Paula Heck

Linda Villegas Bremer

Steve Francks

Jim Walton

Javier Womeldorff

Sue Shoblom

Nancy Kelly

Deb McCurley

Chris Marr

Barb Bumann

PJ Driver

Bruce Tanaka

Yoshi Mayeda

Learning Seed Scholars Erin Aquino, Sothear Sam, Anne Taylor, Marisa Gonzales, Tali Smith

Long family

Tadano family

We realize this is a partial list of all who have participated in and volunteered at Learning Seed events over the past 19 years. To everyone, we salute you and thank you!

PART VI
MISTAKEN IDENTITY

42 WHO AM I?

THE QUESTIONING OF my identity first started one cold, blustery winter's evening in 1985. I had just arrived in Bessemer, Alabama, from an all-day, tiring trip from Seattle, Washington. As I walked up the steps to my childhood home, I heard someone call out to me, "Hey, Kenny, how long are you going to be home?"

Growing up and being raised in Bessemer with my older brother, Ken, it was understandable how someone, especially from a distance on a dark winter night, could mistake us for one another. Unlike me though, Ken did not have a full beard and was about five-feet-ten inches tall, while I was just a little over six feet.

As I continued to walk up the steps and got closer to the top step where the porch light illuminated the small front porch, the voice again rang out, "Hey Kenny, how long are you going to be home?" I turned to my left where the voice came from. "Sorry, I'm not Ken. I'm Merritt. I just arrived from Seattle, Washington, and will be in town for about a week."

At this point, the voice said, "Come on, Ken, I know that's you. Why are you pretending to be your little brother, Merritt?"

I could tell this guy was convinced I was Ken. I laughed and tried to reason with this person. "Don't you think I know who I am?" Then, the absurd became more insane when he started to laugh and said, "Ken, you're really good at pretending you are your brother, Merritt."

I gave up. I just shook my head, opened the front door, and went inside to see my parents. As I entered the house, to my amazement, Mom said, "Hi, Little Brother. I thought I heard your brother Ken outside."

I didn't realize then that this identity crisis in Alabama would be a prelude to a continuing saga of the misadventure of "Who Am I?"

. . .

I've had experiences during which someone assumed I was someone famous, including the president of a liberal arts college in Olympia, Washington, an Oscar-winning movie star, and an extremely successful and generous businessman.

On a trip to visit my parents in Bessemer, I had a layover in Dallas, Texas. As I scanned the waiting area, I spotted what looked like a cozy seat in the back row. This seat by the window, with a bonus vacant seat next to it, looked perfect. I settled in, thinking, now I can just sit here, close my eyes, space out, and peacefully let the time roll by.

But it was not to be. As I walked toward my seat, I noticed out of the corner of my eye a White female with salt and pepper hair and tortoise shell eyeglasses watching my every step. Before I could comfortably slouch down in my chair, close my eyes, and slowly drift off to Neverland, she was next to me—and I do mean next to me. She sat as close to me as possible, whispering, "I know you're someone famous, but who are you?"

I was blown away. I'd been approached in a number of ways, but nothing like this. I smiled, and just for fun, leaned toward her and whispered, "I am Merritt Long." She reacted as if she'd been rebuffed, because I was pretending to be this Merritt Long character. She looked at me carefully, shook her head, and said, "No, you're not. Tell me who you really are. I won't blow your cover, I promise. I just want to know, who are you?"

My smile turned to laughter because this woman was deadly serious. She thought she'd spotted a famous person and couldn't pinpoint exactly who he was, and he was playing hard to get. The more I professed to be me, the more she believed I was some famous Black guy, who was a little over six-feet tall, with salt and pepper hair and beard.

My new "best friend" reluctantly stood in exasperation and began to walk away. After about four or five steps, she whirled around and triumphantly proclaimed in a loud voice, "Give me a few minutes and I'll figure out who you are. I know you're someone famous."

I wondered then about the promised anonymity of a few minutes ago. After this intriguing exchange, I started to wonder about the identity of this famous person. Perhaps Ed Bradley, the African American correspondent on the Sunday evening TV program, *Sixty Minutes*. Ed's hair and beard were similar to mine, and he had inspired me to have my left ear pierced like him. I thought Ed Bradley was a super cool dude, so if by chance I was mistaken for him, that was okay with me.

I thought Bradley's interview with Lena Horne on *Sixty Minutes* was one of his best. They both seemed to be having such a good time and everyone watching could see and feel their on-air chemistry. If I was just mistaken for Ed Bradley, this means that Lena Horne and I just clicked on national television. What a moment for me to be Ed Bradley, an incredibly lucky guy indeed.

As I left the world of Ed Bradley and started to slouch in my seat, I thought that my previous interrogator might not be the only person in the Delta waiting area who assumed I was Ed Bradley. Maybe I should sit up straight and not blow Ed Bradley's cover by slouching in my chair.

. . .

I entered Top Foods, a supermarket in Olympia, Washington, one winter evening to pick up a few grocery items. As I walked toward the deli section, I heard a voice call out, "Mr. President, Mr. President, Mr. President." I knew immediately I was being mistaken, yet again, for the then president of The Evergreen State College, Dr. Les Purce. I have known Les for several decades. He is an outstanding person, a highly successful college president, and a true Renaissance man. In addition to his impeccable background in higher education, he played the guitar and had recorded a CD with the proceeds going directly to scholarships at the college. I'd also had the pleasure of working with President Purce as one of his trustees at the college for more than three years, an appointment by then Governor Gary Locke.

I thought if I ignored this person, he would eventually give up and walk away. However, I heard his footsteps getting closer and closer. The faster I walked, the faster he walked. I realized I needed to turn around and confront my determined pursuer.

Ironically, about six months earlier I had attended the funeral services of a legendary Republican state senator from Wenatchee, Senator George Sellars. His funeral was attended by Democratic and Republican leaders from across the state, including Governor Locke and various state agency directors like myself. During this time, I was the director of the State Lottery. Senator Sellars was a respected leader who always, in my experience, put issues before partisanship. As the former Senate Majority Leader, George was a powerful person. However, he was never too busy to meet with me, a long-standing Democrat. His sage advice and counsel served me well in the legislative arena. Equally important, he had a great sense of humor and we had some great laughs together.

While at the service, Senator Jerry Saling from Spokane, who chaired the Senate Education Committee, came up to me, put his arm around my shoulder, and proceeded to tell me what a wonderful job I was doing at that college in Olympia. His comments were made with such certainty around a couple of his White friends that I couldn't embarrass him by saying, "I'm not who you think I am."

When I was the director of the Commission for Vocational Education, I'd provided testimony before Senator Saling's committee on several occasions. My deputy director at that time, Linda Broderick, had introduced me to the senator because she and her husband, Dave, a lobbyist, were good friends of his. I accepted the senator's compliments by nodding my head, shaking his hand, and thanking him for his kind words.

The following day, my first call was to Les Purce. I told him that if he saw Senator Jerry Saling in the next week or so he needed to remember he had been in Wenatchee at Senator George Sellars' funeral and the senator from Spokane thought he was doing a wonderful job at the college. Les and I both cracked up. We teasingly reminded one another to stay out of trouble because if not, there would be adverse consequences for us both.

As for my Top Foods supermarket admirer, when I finally turned around, I recognized my pursuer. He was a likable, charming man, who'd retired several years ago from a senior level position within the Department of Social and Health Services. For a short period of time, we'd served together on the Board of Directors of the non-profit organization, Community Youth Services.

He and I had chatted a few times. With my work as a former Parole and Probation Officer in the adult correctional field and his years in juvenile rehabilitation, we'd sometimes shared war stories. He had a beautiful head of white wavy hair, which I admired. He also had an easy-going manner about him, and he usually seemed unhurried and relaxed.

But when we met at Top Foods, he indeed was in a hurry to get my attention. Why was he hailing, "Mr. President, Mr. President?" My inquiring friend's sister was visiting from Georgia and her daughter was a freshman at The Evergreen State College. He was delighted to have the opportunity to introduce his sister to the president of The Evergreen State College. His wife was standing there as well, admiringly looking at me as if I was the best thing since sliced bread. For a moment or two I traveled off to dreamland and thought, "You know, being Dr. Les Purce, President of The Evergreen State College, occasionally isn't a bad deal. I have all of the recognition, prestige, and adoration, with no headaches from faculty and staff, not to mention students and parents. This could be pretty cool."

I snapped back to reality when I looked down to the end of the aisle and saw a couple of people coming toward me, the presidential imposter. These were friends who knew me well, and I needed to move fast before they saw me and blew my cover. I turned my back to the people approaching me and allowed my friend to introduce his sister to me,

President Les Purce. She was quite pleased and told me her daughter's experience at Evergreen had been very positive. She raved about the college and how much her daughter had matured and grown during her freshman year.

I thanked her for entrusting her daughter to the college and, as diplomatically as possible, started to make my exit. Reversing direction, I indicated there was an item I'd forgotten to get from the produce section. Thankfully, I was able to escape the clutches of my Evergreen Fan Club before my friends came along.

After being repeatedly called "Mr. President, Mr. President" and then meeting his wife and his sister from Georgia, whose daughter was blossoming as a freshman at Evergreen, how could I destroy the moment with the truth? I felt more harm, embarrassment, and loss of face would occur if I told the truth. I thought about one of my mom's witticisms, "Sometimes you can be right and be wrong."

. . .

My next experience of mistaken identity elevated me to the status of motion picture star, Academy Award winner of *Driving Miss Daisy*, and God all rolled into one: Morgan Freeman.

While attending a Northwest Regional Training Conference sponsored by my employer at the time, Pfizer, in La Jolla, California, my perceived celebrity persona moved from the little screen, television, to the big screen, movies. Marsha and I had been "window shopping." I decided it was time to find a relaxing spot, a nice cappuccino, and the day's *New York Times*. It was a five-star day. There was a blue sky, with a few puffy white clouds tinted with faint shades of pink, indicating the sunset was just minutes away. It was one of those scenes you see on television or in the movies.

I claimed a seat at a small table in front of a sidewalk café, purchased my *New York Times*, and ordered my cappuccino. A few people walked by, there were friendly hellos, the weather was ideal, I had time to just relax:

everything was in balance and I was a happy camper. Seconds later my cappuccino arrived. Just from the weight of the cup, I knew it was perfect. Just the right amount of milk, heavy on the light foam, a real cappuccino not a milk-infused latte posing as a cappuccino.

Then a man walked by and glanced my way. He did a double-take and shouted from the top of his lungs, "My God, Morgan Freeman!" No whispering in my ear, "I know you're someone famous, but who are you? Please tell me. I won't blow your cover, I promise."

I thought, do I come clean by telling him I'm not Morgan Freeman? I remembered my poor track record of not convincing others that I wasn't my brother, a famous person at the airport in Dallas, or a college president. I wondered why people kept mistaking me for others. I'm an African American male, six-feet tall, with a salt-and-pepper beard and hair. My left ear is still pierced with a small diamond earring. I'm wearing a white, long-sleeved linen shirt, White linen pants, an off-white Panama hat with a blue-and-red band, blue leather slip-on Van sneakers, no socks, and dark brown sunglasses. Well, okay, maybe I could be a movie star type.

The exchange with the admiring man went something like this:

"Mr. Freeman, what a pleasure it is to meet you. How long will you be in town? I have been and continue to be a fan of your body of work."

I looked up from my newspaper, smiled, nodded, and extended my hand for a shake. I grasped his hand firmly with both hands, released it, and returned to my newspaper.

"Wow, what a pleasure to meet you, Mr. Freeman."

The man smiled happily at me while he walked away.

I thought the way I looked up from my newspaper, clasped his hand firmly, extending myself, but not too much, was classic Morgan. However, at no time did I tell this man I was Morgan Freeman. However, at the same time, I didn't tell him I wasn't.

. . .

It was more than 35 years ago when it first happened. In Tumwater, Washington, near Olympia, there used to be a hotel called the Tyee Motor Inn. It was popular, especially during Washington State legislative sessions when a number of legislators and prominent lobbyists stayed there. During the 1990s, a two-martini lunch wasn't a big deal. Liquor, the hard stuff, not Washington wines, was the drink of choice. Legislators and lobbyists weren't the only ones who frequented the Tyee Motor Inn. It was one of the favorite watering holes for state employees, legislative staff, local and out-of-town businesspeople, tourists, and others. The Tyee was the place to see and be seen.

At a party or banquet at the Tyee, you'd always find wannabes, used-to-bes, and never-will-bes. Given this mix of people and booze, someone was constantly jockeying for position, pretending to be important, spending lots of money they didn't have, and chasing women at a full gallop.

In this environment and atmosphere, as a 30-something on the rise, the Tyee was definitely part of my evening rotation of places to see and be seen. One evening as I sauntered into the bar with my 10-inch afro blazing skyward, I wore a custom-made steel-gray suit with extra deep-cut side vents in the jacket, cuffed trousers fully lined to accentuate fit, no back pockets to avoid bulkiness, one right front pocket just because, and covered buttons on the suit, as well as the vest. The back of the vest was made of a bright red Asian brocade. There was only one pocket on the right side of the vest for a pocket watch, but it was mostly for show.

I had just parked my pearly white, 1970 Mercedes-Benz with its unique black vinyl top directly in front of the Tyee. The Benz glistened like new money under the bright lights of the hotel. It looked good, adding a little class to the Tyee.

I continued my glide into the hotel, with my Sherlock Holmes-style pipe for accent. I was feeling okay after having had a couple of gin and tonics at another bar earlier in the evening. Soon after I sat down, I noticed a couple of White dudes at another table really checking me out. I heard them whispering something like, "I think that's him; don't you think so?" They both got up and slowly approached me, all the while looking to see if I was really who they thought I was. Finally, one of them said, "Freddie, what a great tan you have. Where have you been? To the desert?" The other guy chimed in. "How did you manage to get it so even?"

I was really taken aback. I realized these two guys thought I was Fred Goldberg. I know Freddie and over the years have gotten to know him quite well. Freddie, at the time, also smoked a pipe and had one similar to the one I had that evening. Also, he was driving a gray Mercedes-Benz, although it was a larger four-door model. Freddie was someone who wore extremely nice clothes and dressed with real flair. Freddie is an astute and highly successful businessman who built a business empire, and very generously donates to a wide range of philanthropic causes.

Freddie is Jewish, tans easily, and has salt-and-pepper curly hair. Depending on the number of drinks these guys had, maybe I could be Freddie's twin brother.

Laughing, I responded to the question of how I was able to get such a smooth and even tan. I said, "You wouldn't believe what I had to go through to get this special tan, and believe me, this is one tan that you don't want." These two inquiring men were trying to figure out what was going on. They looked confused, glancing at each other as they digested my response.

I laughed and laughed, and after about five minutes I left the Tyee with my smooth and even suntan and a great big smile on my face. Little did I know there would be many experiences in Olympia during which I would be mistaken for Fred Goldberg.

. . .

A few years ago, when I was leaving the Tumwater Valley Athletic Club, I stopped to talk with my friend, Jim, in the parking lot. Someone called out, "Freddie, when did you get back from the desert? You look great. What a tan you have!" I looked up and saw a man leaving the club.

When my friend Jim realized the man was talking to me, he started to get agitated because Jim thought maybe the man was being intentionally rude. I told Jim not to worry about it. It was simply a case of mistaken identity.

. . .

Several years ago, I was at Freddie's home leaving some items for him. As I was closing the front gate to leave, I noticed his executive assistant was on her way into his residence. She and I acknowledged each other. I noticed as we walked toward each other, based on her body language and engaging smile and demeanor, she thought I was Freddie. I smiled and asked, "Did you think I was Freddie?" She gave me a big smile. "Yes, I did."

I called Freddie and gave him a bad time because this was the woman that prepared and finalized the checks he approved for his considerable and far-reaching philanthropic efforts. When I talked to Freddie, I told him that I was starting to get close to the keys to the castle: the woman who writes the checks. We had a good laugh as we always did.

PART VII
MY FAMILY

43 MY WIFE MARSHA TADANO LONG

As a young 25-year old Parole and Probation Officer in the summer of 1972, my primary responsibility was helping offenders recently released from prison find employment and housing, as well as offering specialized counseling, depending on their needs. I also worked with individuals who had been granted probation for their crime instead of being sentenced to prison.

Occasionally, I traveled to the Monroe Correctional Complex in Monroe, Washington, about 30 miles north of Seattle, to advise and assist inmates as they prepared for re-entry into society. A young woman named Ginger Evans also worked with the inmates, and she and I often drove to Monroe together to help inmates with their pre-parole planning.

Ginger was employed by the Seattle Opportunities Industrialization Center (SOIC) whose mission was to provide career counseling, pre-vocational and vocational training, counseling services, and job development services. In addition, SOIC offered supportive services such as transportation, clothing, and work-related tools for low-income, disadvantaged individuals, primarily persons of color, who were unemployed or underemployed in the greater Seattle area.

One day, I arrived early to pick up Ginger, and went into the SOIC building because I'd never been inside. I knew a few people who worked there, but I was curious about this old, rundown looming building in the central area of Seattle where people seemed to be coming in and out, always in a hurry.

While standing in the lobby area and looking around, I saw this stunningly attractive young woman walking my way. In fact, I stood in her path. As I watched her, I realized she didn't see me or anything other than the mission she was on. Laser-focused, her body language said, "I'm all business and if you are entertaining the thought of stopping me with some idle conversation, please don't. You're wasting my time and yours." My response was to step back to make sure she had all the room she needed. I don't know if I've ever seen such a confident stride before or since.

SOIC wasn't an organization that hired only African American employees, but the number of African American staff was easily more than 80 percent. I wasn't sure of the specific ethnic background of the person I described earlier, other than Asian American. In addition to her appearance, I was also drawn to this young woman because of her presence and self-assuredness. Anytime you're in the minority, whether in an organization or society, it's usually not a smooth path. For me to see someone move with such confidence and calmness said this person was comfortable in her own skin.

As the young woman faded away, Ginger came into view. We left SOIC and headed for the prison. We hurried along, because when you have a scheduled appointment with an inmate whose primary cellmate is time, you better be on time because they're watching and listening as the seconds go by.

A series of events occurred so that I was able to see the attractive young woman I admired again. I received a call from my friend, Lucy Thomas, who worked at SOIC as a part-time evening counselor for the Office Skills Program. Lucy was also the director of the Upward Bound Program for Western Washington State College in Bellingham, Washington. The school, now Western Washington University, is located an hour-and-a-half drive north of Seattle.

The Upward Bound Program required Lucy to be on campus for the summer months. She called to ask if I'd be interested in filling in for her for three months as the Office Skills counselor. The evening program hours were from 6:00 p.m. to 10:00 p.m. It sounded fantastic, because I usually worked from 8:00 a.m. to 5:00 p.m. as a parole and probation officer. The Office Skills Program was about 15 minutes from my office. Plus, the office skills counseling position paid considerably more on an hourly basis than the Parole and Probation Position.

Lucy Thomas had discussed having me as her summer replacement with the Counseling Supervisor, Marsha Tadano, and everything seemed to be squared away. Except, there was one final step, which required me to interview with Marsha and another member of the Counseling Department. At this point, the job was mine to lose if I came across in a way that Marsha felt wasn't a good fit for this position.

When I walked into the office, I discovered that Marsha was the striking young woman who several months earlier had taken my breath away. During the interview process, Marsha hardly asked any questions, although I could tell she was really listening and checking me out. During the interview, I made a definite point of making eye contact with her on every question that was asked by her White associate. The questions were nothing out of the ordinary and ranged from why do you want the job, to would the position conflict with your full-time job, to did I realize the position was temporary and would end after three months?

I paid particular attention when Marsha wasn't asking questions for a couple of reasons. Number one, I knew she was the ultimate decision-maker, and I believed she was sizing me up by not asking questions for ninety percent of the interview. Reason number two was layered in several ways. Often an interviewee will assume the decision-maker is the White person and ignore the person of color, especially when the person of color is being relatively quiet, and no job titles are given at the beginning of the interview. My guess was that Marsha had been in previous interview situations with White colleagues when she was the most senior person but because of her skin color she wasn't given the respect and attention she deserved.

Marsha sat through the interview with two fingers under her chin and from time to time she'd nod her head as I spoke. I knew she was tuned in and suddenly out of the blue, she asked me, "How well do you relate to women?" I totally understood the reason she was asking the question because 100 percent of all trainees enrolled in the Office Skills Program were female. I paused a moment, but not too long, and responded by saying that I related well to women. Also, I said I realized my primary job was bolstering the trainees' education by providing counseling and other supportive services.

While responding to her question, in my head I was thinking she was going to find out first-hand how well I related to women. I knew she was someone I wanted to get to know better.

I didn't blow my job interview, and I was hired for the summer. At the beginning of my employment, Marsha came to the evening program to train me in my various responsibilities and to bring supplies such as bus tokens. Over time, her visits were less frequent, but we had developed a personal relationship and were dating. After numerous lunches, dinners, movies, and jazz concerts the lines between supervisor and employee were blurring.

When Lucy returned from her Upward Bound role, I had been promoted to the position of manager of the Evening Program, and Lucy worked for me. I was no longer in Marsha's chain of command, so we could be public about our relationship.

Marsha was completely different from any woman I'd ever dated. I marvelled at her confidence, wit, intellect, beauty (inside and out), and certainty of purpose. Also, she possesses the ability to focus exclusively on one subject or activity at a time. I remember 40-plus years ago the first time I stopped by her office unannounced. As I walked up to her desk, she was talking on the phone. I started to say something and without looking up Marsha put her hand up signaling me to be quiet. She didn't pause for a moment to say hello or say something like, "Hang tough, I'll be there shortly." I didn't expect her to hang up or end her conversation. I merely wanted an acknowledgement of my presence. I've learned, come to respect, but not always like, that that's how she operates. Always.

Following the initial phase of our relationship that summer, our biggest challenge was about power and control: who would get their way? We wondered how we would navigate this potential minefield without blowing each other up. It wasn't easy. It forced me to think about what was really important to discuss, and resolve, if there were differences. I soon realized that 90 percent of everyday living decisions occurred quite well without my input or involvement. I saw how effectively Marsha made decisions. Also, I learned the more I gave and the less I was concerned about my end of the deal, the more I received. This approach, over nearly five decades, continues to yield a multitude of dividends.

I wonder what my life would be like today if Lucy Thomas hadn't taken a leave of absence from her Office Skills job. I honestly don't think I would have pursued meeting Marsha, we wouldn't have married, and we wouldn't have the blessing of our beautiful family.

44 OUR DAUGHTER MERISA

MERISA WAS BORN on December 26, 1979. Because it was so close to Christmas Day, some people commented about how nice it would have been if she'd been a Christmas baby. However, my excitement about the timing of her birth was that she brought an immediate financial benefit to our family from a tax perspective. We had five days of child-related expenses but were able to get a full tax deduction for 365 days. I thought this was a good omen, which meant that financially she'd always be a benefit.

Merisa's life growing up in Olympia, Washington, was very different from mine. For her, there were no "Colored" water fountains and toilets, and there were no libraries or swimming pools she couldn't use. We live in Ken Lake, one of Olympia's nicer neighborhoods. Our home looks out over the small lake, and the ballpark, basketball court, and swimming areas are easily within walking distance.

Olympia is the State Capitol, and it's inhabited by mostly White residents. We've lived there for more than 40 years. Given the demographics of the Olympia area, we knew that expecting the school district to be diverse was unrealistic.

One time when I drove Merisa to her kindergarten class at McLane Elementary School, I was uncomfortable and annoyed. That day I drove slower than usual. I was in no big hurry to get to her school, because of the thoughts I'd been having since the night before.

As a father, this was a surreal day because I wondered if my daughter would be teased, ridiculed, or bullied because of my skin color. I was disappointed with myself, and society in general, for even having these thoughts in the first place. Annoyed because I knew that racial progress had been made but, unfortunately, not to the point where skin color doesn't matter. Life is challenging enough without adding stereotyping and racism to the mix.

I started to wonder if Marsha and I should have taken a different approach as we prepared her to go to school. Our approach was to point out the value, unique history, power, and strength that comes with her multi-racial background, and to emphasize how fortunate she was to be so special. Her high self-esteem would ward off any attacks based on her ethnicity. However, that day I wondered if we'd prepared enough.

Merisa has always been a keen observer and, at a young age, moved in and out of different situations very comfortably, whether enjoying a Japanese American Citizens League potluck in Olympia; celebrating New Year's at Mema and Pepa Tadano's home in Phoenix; worshipping at the African American First Baptist Church in Bessemer; or attending McLane Elementary School in almost totally White Olympia.

Marsha and I decided against making race a focal point of Merisa's upbringing, realizing that through living and experiencing life together, we would discuss racial situations as they occurred and take that natural opportunity to pivot to a "learning moment." We didn't want her bogged down, paralyzed, or paranoid about her ethnic makeup. It was, and is, an asset to be celebrated and touted.

Our bottom line was we felt the more comfortable Merisa was with herself and the more secure she felt in her own skin, she could and would be able to handle whatever came her way.

. . .

When Merisa was four years old, I was doing one of my favorite things: reading the newspaper. Merisa asked me what I was reading. I responded by telling her I was reading about politics and then asked her if she knew what politics meant. She placed the first two fingers of her right hand under her chin, hesitated for several moments before loudly blurting out, "Favors."

It was like a lightbulb had been turned on in her mind. She had, I thought, recognized the tie connecting politics with favors. While I was having this exchange with our daughter, what really jumped out at me wasn't what Merisa was saying, but how she was saying it. She spoke with confidence, excitement, and pride that she'd figured it out.

A few minutes later, I raced down the hallway to tell Marsha about Merisa figuring out what the term politics meant and how surely after accomplishing such a feat, she was destined to be a child prodigy.

That night, Merisa asked me to read her a story before going to bed and, if I did, she promised not to get out of bed later that night. One favor deserves another, she'd also figured out.

. . .

It was one of those typical Pacific Northwest winter days—gray skies, raining all day with varying degrees of intensity, wind blowing just hard enough to turn your umbrella inside out, and the temperature in the low 40s. This combination of wind, rain, and low temps caused a chill to one's bones.

While driving to work, the windshield wipers on my car would periodically stop working, making it almost impossible to see. After arriving at work, things didn't improve. The new staff person scheduled to start that day to manage a technology project already two months past due, decided to take another job. It was about 10:00 a.m. when he finally called to let me know his decision. Also, the wind and rain had reached a point where utility poles and wires were being affected, causing momentary power outages for most of the afternoon.

I'd had a very trying day at work and it was time to pick up Merisa from day care. I slowly drove down the freeway in the far-right lane to compensate for the erratic behavior of my wipers. By now, home was 15 minutes away and all I could think about was turning on the gas fireplace and kicking up my feet in my brown leather easy chair.

Merisa was almost always in a good mood as a child growing up. However, for some reason when I picked her up that day, she wasn't happy. I asked her a couple of times what was wrong, but her response was to cry. When she wasn't crying, she was whining. This behavior continued for another five minutes, so I said, "Merisa, if you keep crying and whining, I'm going to start counting each and every time you do it." She immediately stopped, looked at me in amazement and asked, "Daddy, why don't you count every time I'm happy?"

My five-year old daughter had effortlessly made a keen and accurate observation. This comment by Merisa has remained seared into my mind forever. What an important reminder to focus on the positive and not accentuate the few negatives. Fortunately, Merisa ended the counting game before it started, or better yet, before I was counted out.

. . .

For several years, Merisa was involved with the Creative Theater Experience, a local children's theatre group that performed plays during the summer months. She performed a variety of roles, from being in the background to starring in the play.

One play Merisa performed in, which had the greatest impact on me, was based on Mark Twain's *The Prince and the Pauper*. Merisa had been in previous plays, in various roles, and was excited by the possibility of getting a major lead role.

However, the casting of the play didn't go the way she wanted. Merisa didn't get the lead role. She was extremely disappointed, and the energy she'd built up earlier in the summer disappeared. Merisa went from a soaring balloon to one that had been popped and was spinning down to earth.

Merisa had been assigned the role of the character Grammer, the grandmother of Tom Canty, a poor boy who has accidentally traded places with the heir to the throne of England, Edward Tudor, son of Henry VIII. Marsha, after learning Merisa's tale of woe and disappointment, shared some ideas with her on how to turn perceived lemons into lemonade. Because Grammer was a grandmother, she needed to be portrayed as an old woman. Her personality, mannerisms, quirks, speech patterns, and demeanor could be defined by whoever played the character.

Over the next few days, Marsha and Merisa began the character development of Grammer. They found a very old looking shawl Grammer could drape over her shoulders and a shirt and blouse they "dirtied" with brown shoe polish. They decided on no shoes for Grammer; bare feet would add an air of being eccentric and unconventional, a person who doesn't need to please or appease. To crown off Grammer's ensemble, Merisa's hair would be a "bird nest," a total mess. I thought of the branch in the garage I'd been sanding to make into a cane. This was a perfect prop for Grammer to use while walking and her weapon of choice when things weren't going the way she wanted. Merisa absorbed the character of Grammer. On opening night, she took Grammer to another level. Her level.

When it was showtime for Merisa, she came on stage, walking slowly with the aid of the cane with a slight hobble. Her shawl was barely hanging on her shoulders, so lopsided it looked like it might fall off any minute. Merisa grumpily continued walking on stage in her bare feet before sitting with much attention-getting fanfare in a rocking chair. As the scene unfolded and she exchanged lines with other members of the play, Merisa was either picking her nose, picking at her feet then smelling her hands, or placing her hands in her armpits to check them out as well. As Merisa carried out these antics, she was hitting her lines with vigor and the other gestures were synchronized as part of Grammer's whole being.

Marsha and I were blown away; Merisa, Miss Prim and Proper, was all in, no hesitation or reluctance, she was totally in character; in fact, she was Grammer. We were so proud of our daughter. Merisa stole the show.

During her performance, she had the audience in the palm of her hand with every word and move. She transformed a minor almost throw-away character into the limelight. I'm sure she learned that just because the title doesn't say lead, it doesn't stop you from leading.

. . .

During late fall of 1997, I was wrapping up a meeting in Seattle and received a call from Merisa, who was amped to the nth degree. To say she was ecstatic would be a huge understatement. I felt her joy, excitement, and happiness of being accepted at the college of her choice—Stanford University. Marsha observed this was the most excited she'd seen Merisa since she had gotten her first pair of roller skates.

During our campus visit to Stanford, we were all impressed by the diversity of the student body and faculty, the attentiveness to detail of the scheduling of activities, and the ease and informal yet professional manner of everyone we met. Interestingly, the one intangible factor that sealed the deal for Merisa was it just felt right. Her four-year experience at Stanford was incredible and exceeded our outsized expectations for our daughter.

The capstone of her educational experience at Stanford was the Semester at Sea Program offered through the University of Pittsburgh. In this program, Merisa took the opportunity to travel around the world. Sailing out of Vancouver, British Columbia, Canada, her stops included Japan, Vietnam, Malaysia, India, Singapore, Kenya, South Africa, Brazil, and Cuba, before finally concluding in New Orleans, Louisiana. Highlights of the trip included an audience with Desmond Tutu in South Africa and a herculean seven-hour speech by Fidel Castro in Cuba.

It was an incredible experience where she met and saw people from all over the world and from all walks of life. This experience led her to want to pursue issues of social justice.

. . .

It began when Merisa was a middle schooler and it escalated from there through high school. Probably because our daughter is our only child, I started thinking early on about her graduating from high school, going off to college, getting married, and having a family of her own. You know, living the American Dream. Initially, this all felt like a logical natural sequence. Because of the amount of time that Marsha, Merisa, and I spent together, I started thinking about how it was going to feel with her not being part of our cozy little nest. At times, she'd go away for days, weeks, and even months, but she always returned, and I was her number one guy.

While Merisa was in high school, sometimes on those long drives from Olympia to Seattle, I'd think about her getting married. As these thoughts occurred more frequently, tears would roll down my cheeks. I couldn't control the tear faucet—before long the teardrops were coming at such a rate and force that I pulled over because I was unsafe driving on the freeway. Can you imagine trying to explain to a Washington State Trooper that I had been weaving in and out of traffic because I was crying, thinking about my young daughter getting married at some point in the future.

I was starting to grieve for a loss to come. I felt as though when Merisa married—it didn't matter to whom—I would lose an integral part of me. I realized over time I had failed to master a fundamental lesson in life: sharing. Fortunately, with her marriage to Dan Heu-Weller and the arrival of our grandkids, this sharing learning curve was happily expedited.

From her fortuitous birth date to today, Merisa has been a blessing in my life, and I will be forever grateful to have been her father.

45 OUR FAMILY GROWS

A TELEPHONE CALL that was made over 20 years ago still rings in my ear and often brings a smile to my face. Once the call was completed, I could hardly wait to tell Marsha about the caller. My initial comment to Marsha was, "I must admit the boy has a little game." This young man, Daniel Heu-Weller, the incoming Associated Student Body President of Olympia High School, was calling our daughter, incoming Senior Class President of Capital High School. He indicated he was calling Merisa because of their respective elected roles, and he wanted to meet with her to talk about ways to improve the relationship between the two schools.

Because of the rivalry between the two schools, relationships could be a little strained. Right away I knew that Mr. Heu-Weller wasn't concerned about the relationships of the two schools. Instead, he wanted to meet my daughter and had come up with a creative way to pursue her. I must admit I liked his approach even though I knew his game.

His rationale for calling Merisa told me several things about him. Number one, he was a leader and a scholar. Number two, he was a creative thinker. Number three, he was respectful and courteous to his elders.

I informed Dan that Merisa was going to be out of town for most of the summer attending a six-week summer program at Spelman College in Atlanta, Georgia. I took his telephone number and promised to pass it along to Merisa with his message. I told Dan that she'd probably call him when she returned home.

Shortly after Merisa came home she called Dan and they started their "dance" even before they had their first official dance. They were soon going out on "nondates," and before long, they started having long talks, and Merisa often dined with the Heu-Weller family.

Dan and Merisa share a number of commonalities. Both are biracial—Merisa, with a Japanese American mother and an African American father; Dan, with a Chinese American mother and a Caucasian father. Both self-sufficient and independent thinkers, extremely smart, focused, and goal oriented. At the same time, they concerned themselves with the welfare of others and gave generously of their time, talents, and resources.

Crosstown rivals Olympia High School and Capital High School reveled in their rivalry, and basketball was no exception. Merisa was a senior at Capital and on the cheerleading squad so, of course, we attended just about every home game and every away game.

For the first two quarters the basketball game was pretty even until the last five minutes of the second quarter. Capital went on a scoring streak and the half ended with them being ahead by ten points. At the beginning of the third quarter, the Olympia coach assigned a different player to defend Capital's quick playmaking point guard. Crouched over in a ready position and waving his arms to obscure the vision of Capital's point guard, this new defender matched up with Capital's point guard at mid-court, causing him to commit back-to-back turnovers. Olympia then capitalized on the turnovers and scored. At this point in the game, I leaned over to Marsha and asked, "Who is this guy from Olympia High School who plays defense like it was a game of life and death?" She calmly replied, "It's Dan Heu-Weller, a new friend of Merisa's."

I had never witnessed before or since a high school basketball player with such intensity, grit, and determination on defense. His in-your-face, take-no-prisoners defense was the flint that sparked his teammates on and off the basketball court. The turnaround by Olympia High School was underway, and Capital never recovered.

As I reflect on this basketball game of over two decades ago, I didn't realize that it provided a glimpse into the values and attributes of my future son-in-law, Daniel Heu-Weller. He is a fierce competitor, hates to lose regardless of what's at stake, is quite willing and able to do the work that may not be the most glamorous but is for the good of the team. Dan has an amazing intellect, and he is always seeking knowledge and understanding. These are some of the qualities that make him a remarkable husband, father, and son-in-law.

Dan was also accepted at Stanford but elected to attend the University of Washington, majoring in Economics and History. He is extremely well-suited for the world of finance because of his love of numbers, what they mean, and how they can be interpreted. Dan's focus on and love of numbers brings to mind an experience from many years ago, when the four of us were in Phoenix, Arizona. We had conversations that were wide-ranging as we were getting to know each other and somehow the subject of cremation came up. Marsha has consistently expressed her preference for cremation, the simpler the better. Over time I have wavered from the traditional burial to cremation. I am not 100 percent there yet, but close.

At this point, Marsha asked Dan if he had a preference. Without any hesitation he stated "cremation" very matter-of-factly. Marsha and I both wondered if being Chinese included some cultural significance to his decision, and we asked him, "Why cremation?" His quick response was, "It's cheaper." Marsha and I started to laugh, because of our misguided cultural assumption without considering one of Dan's core principles: What do the numbers say especially as it relates to cost benefit? Over the years I have grown to appreciate and respect how he almost always factors the metrics into his decision-making.

Following Dan's completion of his undergraduate studies at the University of Washington and Merisa's from Stanford, they took two years off to work and earn money in preparation for law school. They started law school at the University of Washington in 2004 as a married couple, and they both completed law school in three years. On time and on schedule. Dan continued his education for an additional year to earn his MBA.

. . .

Dan and Merisa's most significant contribution in Marsha's and my life has been our grandchildren, Marcus Merritt Heu-Weller, currently 15 years old, and Eden Tamiko Heu-Weller, 13 years old.

They have given me the chance to try to make up for some of the physical and mental absences, lack of patience, misplaced priorities, and regrets for not being present and as involved as I could have been during Merisa's childhood.

When Merisa was growing up, friends and acquaintances would ask whether or not Merisa was spoiled. Marsha would answer by saying that Merisa was "spoiled" but not "spoiled rotten." Fortunately, I think we've crossed the Rubicon and are no longer teetering on the edge of spoiling the grandkids. To give you an essence of our grandkids, here are a couple of stories you may enjoy.

When Marcus was about five years old, we were riding around in downtown Olympia, with no specific destination, just out and about. Marcus was anchored in his car seat in the back seat, which he hated. He wanted to be in the front seat where there was more action and activity. I'm sure he was interested in playing with the dials on the radio, the lever for the windshield wipers, and the color-coded switch for hot and cold. After 15 minutes of just cruising around, I said to Marcus that one day he'd be driving Papa around. Marcus answered without missing a beat. "Yeah, and you are going to be in the back seat." His tone and quick reaction to exiling me to the back seat was his retribution for the miserable and unacceptable years he was spending in the back seat.

My granddaughter, Eden Tamiko, also showed her spunk when we visited Merisa and Dan one weekend when she was only four. During our visit, Eden was sitting on my lap in their upstairs living room while I read a variety of handpicked stories from books that she wanted Papa to read to her. Sometimes right in the middle of a book, she'd abruptly decide she was done with that one and we needed to move to her next selection. Under her magical spell, I was delighted to carry out any and all of her wishes.

After about 30 minutes, I needed to go downstairs to help set up a table. As I started to gently move Eden from my lap and told her I had to go downstairs, she looked around in complete surprise. "Papa, you can't go, you are holding me." I wasn't allowed to leave until she released me. My response: I remained seated until I was released. Eden was and continues to be quite clear about what she wants, and your defined role is to help make it happen.

I have been blessed with many opportunities and wonderful people in my life, but by far the greatest blessing is my family: Marsha, Merisa, Dan, Marcus, and Eden. I learn from them, I am inspired by them, and I am loved by them.

FINAL THOUGHTS

My journey is a journey of perseverance against the odds in a small southern town where college dreams for young African Americans like my brother and I were the exception, not the rule. We were fortunate to have parental and family support, as well as the village of teachers, friends, and neighbors who projected hopes and dreams for our future. The desire and aspirations of our parents were especially unique and compelling, because they had no role models to follow. However, they decided that education beyond high school wasn't an option but a mandate if we were to have viable paths for success in the work and business world.

Even today, I can hear my father saying, usually after working weeks and weeks of overtime at the Pullman Plant, "I don't want you to be like me, using your back to make a living and not your head."

I am certain my life would be quite different if they hadn't had a vision of success for me, probably before I could walk or talk. It was as if I had a destiny, a bigger purpose, before I was even born.

The drumbeat of education was one of the pillars of my upbringing: **education is the great equalizer, and once you receive it, no one can take it away.** The other pillars focused on basics such as:

- Always treat others the way you want to be treated.

- Your word is your bond, and it is your most important asset.

- Never underestimate a person's value based on their station in life.

I am so thankful for my parents' guidance and sacrifices. They may not have spoken the words "I love you" very often, but it was unmistakably expressed through their actions.

ACKNOWLEDGMENTS

THIS MEMOIR WOULD not have happened without the expertise, advice, and encouragement of my family and friends.

My deepest gratitude goes to:

PJ Driver and Barbara Glass, two of the best administrative assistants I was blessed to work with, who patiently converted my hieroglyphic handwriting into manuscript form. Equally important was their passion and commitment to bringing my story to life.

Rita Robison provided early positive support and direction to my writing journey.

Laura Taylor's expert storytelling advice shaped my story and her extraordinary editing added polish to my writing.

Dolen Perkins-Valdez, whose feedback as an accomplished author and literary professor, buoyed me beyond words.

Congressman Denny Heck, when I first began writing 15 years ago, pushed me to tell my stories. His confidence boosted my confidence and determination.

Pamela Anderson, my second writing instructor, not only taught me practical aspects of writing but also spurred me to keep going with her positive feedback.

Jill Severn's wizardry with words greatly enhanced the book description on the back cover.

Special thanks to Merisa Heu-Weller for her thoughtful editing which sharpened the meaning and tone.

Nate Naismith, photographer extraordinaire, quite simply, made me look good. Thank you, Nate!

Sherilynn Casey and Nancy Wicker proofread the book and improved its readability.

My family has been my cheerleaders as they embraced my book, listened to my readings and celebrated my progress: my daughter Merisa, son Dan, grandkiddos Marcus and Eden; sister-in-law Jacque; niece La-Tonja, nephew David, grandnieces Masai, Kennedi, and Riyan; nephew Ny'Ika, grandnieces Si'Erra, and Kam'Ryn; niece Cassandra; nephew Brandon, niece Camille, cousin Ronnie.

Friends and relatives who would ask, "How's your book coming along?" kept me going because I knew I had to produce something! Vince and Jo Ortiz, Dave and Sharon Cammarano, Linda Villegas Bremer, Frances Munez Carter, Edmon Lee and Susan Rivera-Lee, Milt Doumit, Steve Francks, Lorraine Lee, Beth Morrison, Geoff Crooks, Al and Kathy Sugiyama, Roy Long, Barbara Catlin Owens, Shirley Lewis Norwood, David Ronnie Hood, Jan and Ham Kumasaka, Stacie-Dee Motoyama, Edy Heu and Dr. Glen Weller, Al Grace, Jr., Craig and Sue Cole, Marybeth Berney, Josie Preston, Fred Yancey and Ellen Goodman, Jennifer Belcher, Phyllis Gutierrez Kenney, Bettye Pressley, Betty Tadano Takesuye, Reiko Tadano, and Chris Tadano.

. . .

My life has been blessed with a wonderful family and wonderful friends. Some are mentioned in the book but many are not. I would like to acknowledge their importance to me.

My golfing buddies: Saul Arrington, Bill Moore, Nat Jackson, and David Hunter.

My Black Collective allies: Lyle Quasim, Jim Walton, Harold Moss, Thomas Dixon, and many others too numerous to list here.

My Morehouse fellow alumni: Omega Psi Phi brothers Thomas Sampson,

Jr., Labat Yancey, Michael Holmes, Howard Gary, Robert Boyd, Ernest Savoy, Zack Brown, and Alpha Psi Alpha brother Clayton Wade.

As always, my love for and gratitude to my parents, Will Mack and Katie Long, who showed their love by enduring many hardships to provide for me and my brothers, and who did their very best to guide us in a sometimes hostile world.

Thanks to my older brother, Kenneth Barry Long, for looking out for me as we grew up and for being someone I always looked up to. I will always remember the happy times as kids playing with Ken and my cousin, Gean White. Gean's beautiful family: daughter LaTosha and her husband Brian, son Claymon, Jr., granddaughter LaToya and her husband Mister, grandson Dylan, and great-granddaughter Madisyn.

My appreciation for my oldest brother, Mack Long, Jr., who I didn't grow up with but got to know as an adult. We've gotten to be good friends, and I feel blessed that he's in my life. He and Iris raised a beautiful family: daughters Cynthia, Phyllis and her husband Hiram, Jackie, and Crystal; granddaughters Karla, Tamiko, LynToy and Michelle; grandsons David, Daniel, Steven Paul, Timothy, and Solomon; and great-granddaugher Kaari.

It was my great fortune to marry into the Tadano clan, beginning with Tadashi and Michiko Tadano, including siblings Ben and Maggie, Betty and Jack, Reiko, Will and Margie, Ken and Pat, Terry and Lori, and Alan and Liz; nieces and nephews Ty and Juliana, Diane, Ed and Kinuyo, Brian, Rob and Ginny, Chris and Kellen, Corrie and Michael, Tiffany and Tyson, Tory and Chantal, and Traci and Aaron; and ending (to date) with grandnieces and grandnephews Tristan, Connor, Jackson, Jacob, Ashley, Kelsea, Logan, Raiden, Takeo, Preston, Payton, and Ariana.

Last but never least, my best friend and girlfriend who also happens to be my wife, Marsha Tadano Long, who has supported me through thick and thin, happiness and loss, and who has always expressed unconditional love.

ABOUT THE AUTHOR

MERRITT DOUGLAS LONG grew up in Bessemer, Alabama; attended More-house College in Atlanta, Georgia; moved to Seattle, Washington, in 1968; and to Olympia, Washington, in 1973. After an illustrious career in Washington State government, having headed four state agencies, Merritt retired and worked as a consultant for several private sector companies. He has served on a number of non-profit boards as well as two bank boards.

He and his wife, Marsha Tadano Long, founded the Learning Seed Foundation to help students go to college by awarding new and renewable scholarships. As of 2020, 109 students have been awarded $450,000 in scholarships. You can learn more at the Learning Seed Foundation Facebook page: www.facebook.com/learningseedfoundation.